TO
MARC HAPPY B-DAY
HAPPY

MAKING IT
BIG
IN THE MOVIES

Rw
Kwl

" JAWS "

MAKING IT BIG IN THE MOVIES

RICHARD KIEL

Reynolds & Hearn Ltd
London

First published in 2002 by
Reynolds & Hearn Ltd
61a Priory Road
Kew Gardens
Richmond
Surrey TW9 3DH

A CIP catalogue record for this book is available from the British Library.

ISBN 1 903111 31 5

Designed by Kate Pankhurst.

Printed and bound in Malta by Interprint Ltd.

CONTENTS

ACKNOWLEDGEMENTS

I would like to thank my wife Diane for letting me take the time to write this and for all her helpful suggestions.

To my mother, who taught me the value of persistence and the reality to face life as it was, not how I wished it could be.

To my father, who taught me early in life that selling the product was just as important as the product itself.

To my children, who gave me so many good stories to share, and especially to my oldest son RG, whose constructive criticism helped make this a better book.

To my good friend Bob Armstrong, who years ago encouraged me to start writing down notes about my life and who helped me so much with the construction of the book.

To my friends at Eon Productions, who so graciously approved the use of all their James Bond pictures in this book.

To writer and friend Gareth Owen, who introduced me to his publisher.

To Roger Moore, for being my friend and for writing the foreword with such flattering words.

Finally, to all my fans who made my career so gratifying and for their continued support, even though I am now handicapped and unable to chase James Bond like I used to.

FOREWORD

BY ROGER MOORE CBE

first met **Richard Kiel** in 1976 when we were about to make *The Spy Who Loved Me* and subsequently we worked together again on *Moonraker*.

I remember at the time of our first meeting that he had a charm about him that was even larger than his frame. He also had great wit. He told me when we were doing our round of interview shows for the launch of the first of our Bond films together that the question that really drove him mad was 'How big were you when you were small?'

Richard was never small – at least not in heart and intelligence. I am sure his story will make fascinating reading for all.

Roger Moore,
January 2002

THE WHITE HOUSE

WASHINGTON

March 17, 1983

Dear Mr. Kiel:

Thank you for writing. As President I am grateful for your support, and as a "fellow actor,"
I must compliment your performances. In playing
"Jawwws" you have managed to create a villain
with a large amount of audience appeal!

Also, as a fellow outdoorsman, I can understand
your environmental concerns. It is a very difficult task to handle the delicate balance which
must exist between man and nature. God gave man
dominion over the earth and its creatures, but
with that dominion went a tremendous responsibility which we are only just beginning to understand. I have witnessed extremism on both sides
of the environmental issue and have found that
not all of the emotion vented on these questions
is entirely generated by concern for the environment. There is, in my opinion, a responsible
approach one can take in preserving our natural
heritage without at the same time infringing on
the constitutionally guaranteed rights of our
people. This is the difficult task which I have
before me.

I have asked that your problem be brought to the
attention of officials at EPA and I am sure you
will hear from them soon.

Nancy joins me in sending our warm regards to
you and your family.

Sincerely,

Ronald Reagan

Mr. Richard Kiel
P.O. Box 2208 Rural Branch
Coarsegold, California   93614

Letter from
President Ronald
Reagan to
Richard Keil
(see page 149)

PROLOGUE

I was excited, really excited. I had been invited at the last minute to a special screening of *The Spy Who Loved Me* at MGM Studios. This was long before the Royal premiere in London, and those in Los Angeles and New York, where movie stars, the press and film critics had all been invited. This special screening was for blue collar studio employees and their families. Gate guards, prop men, grips, secretaries, telephone operators, people who worked in the commissary were all invited to the screening, which was held in one of the studio's biggest screening rooms.

The studio moguls used this kind of screening to test their films before a more 'normal' audience. By screening it for the MGM employees who were not in the film and hadn't worked on it, they were assured of an unbiased audience. The executives can tell from this kind of audience whether the film causes people to laugh, cry or be scared at the right times. They don't invite the press, as the producers may make changes in the film if it's obvious that certain scenes just don't work or the audience just doesn't react to certain scenes as they should. After a preliminary screening of this type, the studio might take an edited version out to a small town for another sneak preview screening – this time to see if the *changes* worked.

I knew that they had shot two versions of the ending, and in one of them my character died, like all the villains before me, and in another I lived to possibly go on to do another Bond film. I had no idea of whether I would live or die or how the audience would take to the 'Jaws' character. Director Lewis Gilbert had allowed more ad-lib humour from Roger and I than usual, and I wasn't sure how much of that would remain in the finished film.

The production staff waited until the audience was seated and the lights were turned off before sneaking me into the theatre. The movie started with the spectacular ski scene where Bond skis off the cliff and it looks like he's going to die until we see the Union flag parachute open and Carly Simon begins to sing 'Nobody Does It Better'. I was transfixed, listening to every murmur of the audience as I waited for Jaws to appear.

When Jaws first appears, it's all pretty serious, and I began to doubt that Lewis was able to get away with leaving all the humour that Roger and I had concocted to please him. Well, all of the humour stayed in and the audience loved it just as much as Lewis had when we did it before the camera. They laughed at all the right times and they were scared when they were supposed to be scared. The Jaws character even scared me when Barbara Bach opened up the closet in her compartment on the train and I was in there. They threw in a loud train-whistle blast at the same moment they shock-cut to Jaws' mouth filled with those ghastly teeth, and I jumped out of my seat like everyone else.

The first hint of humour involving Jaws comes when Bond and the Russian spy, Anya, encounter him at the pyramids and Jaws slaps Anya to the ground and goes after the microfilm. Bond slowly approaches him and Jaws picks up a two-by-four and waits for 007 with a looney grin on his face that makes Jaws almost likeable. Bond tricks him into swinging the club so that it knocks away one of the supports of the structure they're under, and the whole thing falls on Jaws – which elicits the line from Roger, 'Egyptian builders...' The audience laughed at that, but the laughter died down when they saw a huge hand come out of the rubble and Jaws get back on his feet again.

Then came the scene where Bond and Anya get away from me in the telephone van and I pick up a huge two-ton block to throw at them, but let it drop when I realise they're too far away. From the look on my face, it was obvious that it landed on my foot, and the audience absolutely roared with laughter.

I waited expectantly for the big scene when Roger and I had the fight on the train and he breaks the lamp and puts the electric wires in my teeth, then pushes me out the train window. We had rehearsed that scene in a mock-up train set with the stuntmen for weeks, and I hoped it would be as good as I thought it might be. When I rolled down the hillside, only to get up and straighten my tie and brush the dirt off my blazer, the audience roared with laughter again. They'd bought into Jaws' persistence and everything worked exactly as I had hoped it would.

When the villain's car crashes into the old Italian couple's little house and I walk out the door, again brushing off my coat and straightening my tie, and the little Italian man says 'Mama mia', they died laughing, and so did I. It was really fun for me to see the audience react so much and to be a part of it.

Roger's many ad-libs brought forth big laughs, and there were a lot of them. One of my favourites happened when Anya (Barbara Bach) was shooting her close-ups inside the van. She was actually driving, and the

English Ford van required double-clutching to change from forward to reverse, and Barbara didn't know how to do that. Roger was standing on the running board of the van giving Barbara someone to look at and react to. When he heard the gears grinding, he shot Barbara an ad-lib line: 'You want me to drive?' This was not in the script, and between the gears grinding and Roger's unexpected line, Barbara did a typical reaction of total frustration and surprise and the camera was right on her face.

Lewis Gilbert saw this when we were filming and got a close-up of Roger Moore saying this line and another one he ad-libbed. To me, these are the things that make this film really work, as they give relief between all the tense action scenes. In fact, while all this is happening, I'm ripping the top off the van and peering in at them with my horrific teeth glistening in the sun.

Another great ad-lib by Roger in *The Spy Who Loved Me* was when I was chasing him in Stromberg's undersea chamber, and he smiles at me while I'm standing under a huge electromagnet. I smile back. He looks up and I look up to see what he is looking at, only to get sucked up by the teeth with the electromagnet as Roger says, 'How does that grab you?'

The audience enjoyed that one as well. All this created a sort of Roadrunner and Coyote effect with Jaws always getting blown up, electrocuted, thrown off of trains, crashing into a house, yet always coming back with unstoppable determination. This was what I was hoping for, and it worked.

Finally came the scene where Roger releases me from the electromagnet into the waters below containing the shark. The audience has already seen the shark gobble up someone, and everyone expects it to do the same to Jaws. I waited with bated breath to see what would happen next. Jaws struggles underwater with the shark and takes a big bite out of the killer fish, then the scene cuts away to Bond and Anya escaping, leaving me and the audience wondering what happened to Jaws.

Do I live to fight in another film or do I die? It seemed like forever while I waited to find out. The camera is still on Bond and Anya as they're making their way out of the supertanker, which is exploding and coming apart, and it looks like that's the end of Jaws.

Suddenly, they cut to the surface of the ocean, and Jaws pops out of the water and starts swimming to shore. The audience cheers and applauds, and I was absolutely dumbstruck by the reaction of the crowd in the screening room. Wow! After 17 years of struggling as a working actor, I was suddenly an overnight success. I knew at that moment that I had finally made it big in the movies.

The lights came up and the public relations and production people were looking in my direction with big smiles on their faces. They had already seen the movie and pretty much knew how the audience would react, and that's why they had invited me.

As I stood up to leave, I found myself being congratulated and slapped on the back by everyone that knew me. Soon my family and I would find ourselves doing a whirlwind promotional tour that would take us to lots of exciting places all over the world. My career would be catapulted to new levels as producers would cast me in many exciting roles in films and commercials because of my success as Jaws in the Bond films.

How did I get started as an actor? How did I break into the movies? How did I get cast as Jaws? What happened after Bond? Have I always been this big? That's what this book is all about. It's a fun, exciting, and intriguing story filled with twists and turns. I hope you'll enjoy reading it as much as I did writing it.

IN THE BEGINNING

One of the most commonly asked questions that I get from journalists and TV and radio interviewers is, 'How big were you when you were little?'

Born in Detroit, Michigan, in 1939 at the Detroit Women's Hospital and growing up in rural Redford Township, my life as a little boy was just that: I was little.

In all seriousness, I was small for my age. Looking back at old family pictures of my sister and I when I was eight and she was only one, it seems like she was almost as tall as me, and I wore these really nerdy glasses.

I knew that I was different or at least going to be different from the very beginning. I have memories of being about a year old and standing in a doorway chewing on the paint of the door frame as I listened to my mother and father talking late one night. I can remember wondering why I was me inside this body looking out at them through my eyes. Perhaps this made me more sensitive.

Family life at the Kiels was simple and full of love. My father was a car salesman selling new Ford cars, and we always had a new Ford or Mercury. Dad also raised chickens; we literally had 'chicken every Sunday' and our relatives would visit and join in.

My fondest childhood memories are of having my dad teach me how to fly a kite and going fishing up at K P Lake or Twin Lakes. We had an extra lot next to the house that had several maple trees, and Dad would rake the multicoloured leaves into piles that I loved to jump and roll around in. I remember the beautiful red, brown and gold colours and the crunchy sound and smell of those maple leaves.

Dad made a natural but shallow impression in that extra lot even deeper, and he would fill it with water every winter so I could invite other neighbourhood kids over to ice-skate on our private outdoor rink. My first set of skates was double-bladed, which made it easier to stand and balance yourself. We played tin-can hockey and it was a blast.

We used to walk to school taking a short cut through the woods, and many times we would come upon wild raspberries and blackberries to eat. School was a two-storey brick building and the fire escape consisted of a metal tube that allowed you to slide down to the ground. Needless to say, I loved fire drills.

Mom had some great sayings that helped us get through life, like 'Two wrongs don't make a right,' 'If wishes were horses beggars would ride' and 'It's a dog eat dog world out there.' She was artistic and not only painted but also did ceramics as a hobby. She also put on puppet shows for the neighbourhood kids, which I participated in. From this she graduated to marionettes and finally to making me a ventriloquist's dummy, which I enjoyed using to entertain myself, my little sister and my dog Tina. I guess I was a bit of a ham, although a bashful one, as I enjoyed collecting magic tricks and entertaining my little sister and her friends with them.

Dad enjoyed going to all-black baseball games, and his favourite team was the 'Brown Bombers'. He felt that these teams were more fun to watch and that they were underrated. Dad had played catcher on an AAA team for the Kelly Coal Company, and he could really appreciate talented baseball players. I remember going with him and eating my first corn dog at one of these games. This experience helped me to be more comfortable around black people for the rest of my life.

Dad was very comfortable with them, as he sold lots of new Ford and Mercury cars to them. I remember going with him to make deals on cars in black neighbourhoods. He would often get invited for dinner, and I would tag along. One time in particular he took me with him and left me in the car. It was a brand new Mercury Demonstrator and it had plush fabric seats. It only took me a minute or so to find the cigarette lighter and discover that, when you pushed it in, it would pop out after a while and then, when you looked at it, the bottom was cherry red.

I was about five years old at the time and didn't know that the black circles I was burning into the fabric seats with the cherry red cigarette lighter were permanent and that Dad would have to pay much more to replace the seats than the commission on the car he was selling inside. Dad, of course, was shocked when he came out and found what I had done. Later on at home my mother told him that he shouldn't have left me in the car by myself and what did he expect of a five-year-old? In any event, I didn't get spanked or repri- manded. It was simply explained to me that this was not what the cigarette lighter was for and that I was never to do such a thing again. Little boys are curious, however, so I found other things to do like taking shotgun shells apart and trying to make the percussion cap explode by banging the centre with a hammer.

SCHOOL DAYS

They discovered in the first or second grade that I wasn't using my right eye, which was causing me to develop what eye doctors call 'lazy eye.' It hadn't gotten to the point where I was cross-eyed, but things were heading in that direction. My mother took me to an eye specialist in Ann Arbor, who showed my Mom how to get me to do eye exercises with her help, in a dark room and with a pen light. He also prescribed some glasses for me.

To my thinking, the glasses did not help me, at all, and as soon as I was out of Mom's sight, I would immediately put them in my pocket, which inadvertently caused them to be broken and replaced many, many times by my concerned parents. The eye exercises did work, however, and after months and months of my mother making me follow the pen light in a dark room, my eyes began to line up. I never did recover the sight in my right eye, but I must say that this gave me a distinct look later on in the movies as I move my head more than other actors in order to survey a scene.

My best friends were Louis Guida, Donny Brown, Brook Tilley and my Uncle Art, who taught us all how to make rubber-band and match guns when he came to live with us.

I grew up right at the end of World War II, so we played kill the Germans instead of cowboys and Indians. They sold War Stamps at school and you put them in a book, which when full could be traded in for a War Bond. There were Air Raid Wardens in the neighbourhood, and we would have Air Raid Drills where you turned all your lights off and searchlights would come on and light up the sky. Anti-aircraft guns were in place next to the searchlights and were manned by volunteers who would fire if we were attacked.

This was a time when 'Uncle Sam Needs You!' recruiting posters were up everywhere, and the 'Shhhh! The person you are talking to may be the enemy' posters were put up in plants making military equipment, Jeeps, tanks and aircraft. CrackerJack boxes had prizes that were war-oriented, such as a picture of the Axis leaders, Hitler, Mussolini and Togo, which when turned a certain way would put them behind bars.

I remember going with my parents to see a war movie called *The Seventh Cross*, which was about seven paratroopers who were caught when they dropped into a German town and were all hung on crosses to die in the town square. One rips himself off his cross and makes it to a farmhouse where he steals some civilian clothes and spends the rest of the movie eluding the Nazis, who are looking for him on motorcycles and on foot with Doberman dogs. It terrified me and made me fear and hate Germans.

One day Brook Tilley said, 'I'm English, what are you guys?' Louis Guida said, 'I'm Italian.' Donny Brown said he was 'An American.' And I said, 'I don't know.'

That evening I asked Dad at the dinner table, 'Dad, Brook Tilley is English and Louis Guida is Italian. What am I?' Dad said, 'Let's see, you're English,

Scotch, Irish and German.' I was devastated and said, 'You're kidding me, aren't you, Dad?' Dad said, 'No, I'm not kidding you. You're German.'

I didn't understand. I wasn't like those Nazis in the movies and neither was my dad, so how could I be German? I think this made me realise that one man's madness does not make a whole group of people bad. Just like Frankenstein's monster or Lenny in *Of Mice and Men* don't make all big guys bad.

Prejudice takes many forms and it isn't limited to Germans, Jews, blacks or very tall people. My wife is from Georgia, yet her hero in high school was Abraham Lincoln and she did her term paper on him. These things taught me that you have to judge each person as an individual and not as a race or as a group. Hitler wasn't very tall or black, nor was Napoleon. Yet blacks, and very big and tall people, were for years always cast as the bad guys.

My parents sold their home in Michigan the same day they listed it, and my sister Georgann and I soon found ourselves making our way to California in a brand new Nash four-door car. Some friends gave my father a small nickel-plated revolver to take with us on the trip (for security). I remember my mother making him throw it away in the desert one piece at a time. Dad never knew that I had got into his top dresser drawer before we left and clicked off a few shots. Fortunately, the six chambers were all empty. I was about eight years old and still curious. Later on, I would try again with one of his rifles and not be so lucky, shooting a hole through the wooden garage of our next-door neighbour, almost hitting her and her grown son.

About four years later I repeated the incident in another neighbourhood, shooting a hole through our garage and hitting our neighbour's fence. About that same time I bought a pellet pistol and shot myself in the thumb with it and, after digging the pellet out, I managed to live with the throbbing pain without telling anyone, as I did not want to give up my new pistol. Needless to say, my children grew up without guns in our home.

Another important lesson that I learned in 1947 was that you shouldn't throw comic books away. I had been very fortunate to become the owner of a huge number of comic books that my Aunt Anne discovered at her apartment incinerator; they were about to be destroyed. We were visiting her at the time, and I was asked if I would like to have them. These were classic *Superman*, *Green Hornet*, *Plastic Man* etc, and I enjoyed reading every one of them over and over. When it came time to leave for California, however, my parents made me give most of them away. I managed to stash a big stack of them in the car, which they made me throw away on the trip, because they considered them just litter. Today, as I attend comic book and celebrity autograph conventions, I wonder just how much those old comic books would be worth.

I was an avid reader and I could read the *Reader's Digest* when I was six years old. I had a cousin, Gloria, who came to live with us for a while; she was a few years older than me and taught me everything that she learned each day in school. She was a great teacher and I was an apt pupil, making school pretty boring for me when I started because I thought I already knew it all.

Our first home in California was one of those little green trailers that was about half as big as many motor homes today. Dad bought it cheap, and we stayed in the trailer park until he could sort out what he was going to do and where we were going to live. Mom didn't want to leave her home, friends and relatives in Michigan, and looking at the photo of that little trailer, I can imagine how she must have felt. Dad bought a secondhand business and he found a little mobile home park up the road and across the street from an oil refinery that shook the ground when it was in operation. After giving the lady the money for the business and inventory, he found out that she had lost her lease and we had to move everything immediately.

Mom and Dad found a house on a main road where they could have their secondhand and antique store in front while we lived in the back. I don't recommend this kind of arrangement, but it was better than the little trailer, which ended up parked in the side yard. Business was good, and we stayed there for about a year. I found a new friend who had a donkey that we rode together, and it was a lot of fun living there. There was a train track about a half block away, and the noise kept us from missing the noisy refinery.

Our next move was to a larger two-storey building on Garvey Avenue in South San Gabriel. It didn't have any yard, and we lived upstairs over the business. I got to have a dog and I named her Tina Longears Kiel. Tina went with me everywhere and, whenever I bought a popsicle or ice cream, I got the same for her. The San Gabriel River was nearby and the river bed, with all of its trees and cattails, had all those things that make little boys happy.

Mom approached the new school with a letter she had from my school in Michigan, which suggested that, because I was so far ahead of the other students, I should be moved forward a grade. The principal said 'Let's wait and see,' and I suppose it didn't help that I got into a fight with her son who attended there also. It wasn't until the fourth grade in California when we were studying California history, something that Gloria hadn't taught me, that I began to be severely challenged. The principal then knew that she was right and the teacher in Michigan was wrong.

Dad got a job selling appliances in South Arcadia, and we moved again, this time to North El Monte. I liked the house we rented there because it had a big yard and over the back fence was the Rio Hondo River and river bed. The house was on at least an acre or more, and it had peach, plum, orange, lime, and grapefruit trees. In fact, there were three or four different kinds of plums. My chums and I would climb over the back fence and hike in the river bed, which contained a river and lake-like ponds with ducks and everything. If my friends and I wanted to go to the movies, we would pick some tree-ripened fruit, polish it up, and put it in baskets, which we would sell on Peck Road, the main road out front.

Dad did real well selling appliances, and he got another job in downtown El Monte where he was a top salesman. He followed up leads furnished by the gas company for people who were interested in a new gas range or gas (or electric) refrigerator. Dad was doing so well that he and Mom bought a new home in North El Monte across the street from a judge, no less.

Mom was happy again, as this was a real nice home with a big lot in a nice neighbourhood. Dad added a guest house to the garage and put a roof over the patio so we could eat in the shade when he barbecued. The lot was big enough to have a garden behind the guest house where Dad grew tomatoes and dahlias.

As I grew older, I was still short for my age until about age 12. All of a sudden, I started growing so fast that I developed stretch marks on my shoulders, like a pregnant woman gets, because my skin couldn't keep up with my bones.

Through the eighth grade, you would have expected me to possibly end up a professional athlete, as I was extremely good at sports. I was the pitcher on our local softball team, the Driftwood Dairy Bulldogs, and not only was I an excellent pitcher and hitter, I could catch the softball in my gloveless hand without a problem, even line drives. Football was the same. I would play with the older boys at the park and could throw and catch long passes with the best of them. Looking back, those were some pretty happy days.

The appliance business was booming and Dad decided that we should own and operate our own store. My parents opened an appliance and television store in Baldwin Park, California and, of course, the whole family moved there. We had to use the money from selling our nice home in North El Monte to put us in the appliance business and we rented a small, plain, stucco house in Baldwin Park. Over the back fence was Little John Dairy, and although the house itself was livable, the cows attracted flies that used to decorate the walls of the house, and there was no chance of barbecuing or living outdoors.

We had a new Mercury car, and Dad bought Mom one of those 'upside-down bathtub' Nash cars so she could learn how to drive and help in the appliance store by chasing down gas company leads. Dad had tried to teach Mom to drive once before, having bought an old Hudson Terraplane, but quit trying to teach her before it caused a divorce. This time he hired an instructor company, and Mom was driving and selling in no time.

During the time that Mom was still taking lessons, the car would be sitting there when I got home from school. One day I decided to try backing it up and running it forward a couple of times. This worked okay until I got it in second instead of reverse. When it kept stalling, I gave it more gas and the car lurched forward and halfway into the garage, even though the aluminum door was closed. Dad took a lot of ribbing about coming home drunk and crashing through the garage door, which didn't help me any. He simply made me pay for a new garage door and the installation out of my earnings, which at the time were $12 a week. This was going to take too long, so I found another job at a nearby bakery where I could make $25 a week. Before I started, though, Dad decided to match the higher pay, as I was quite big and good at helping to deliver the gas ranges and refrigerators he and Mom were selling.

I remember moving to this small town of Baldwin Park, California from the nearby town of El Monte and how everyone wanted to challenge me and pick on me when I started my last year of junior high in a new town. In fact, that's how Arthur Oaks and I got to be friends. He took me on during the first day in PE class, and I ended up wrestling him to the ground and making him say 'uncle' before I would let go of him and let him get up. Later that same day, another kid named Wesley McCoy walked by and threw a big Sunday punch straight at my jaw. I went unconscious for just a split second and I literally saw stars flash in my head, as he had hit me right on the 'button', or dead centre on the chin. I remember Wesley's face as I recovered and came back to reality. Without blinking, I looked him straight in the eye and asked, 'Is that the best you can do?' He was not only astonished that he didn't knock me out, he was also impressed by my apparent unconcern over his 'knockout' punch. Unless he reads this book, he will have had no idea how close he came to knocking me off my feet.

My first day at Baldwin Park High School should have been a disaster. For some twisted reason, the freshmen were required to come to school a day earlier than the upper classmen. This meant that every freshman student was a target for the seniors who were lying in wait to take them up into the San Gabriel mountains and haze them. Hazing was really a polite term for a group of bullies taking off some pimple-faced kid's clothes, putting gobs of lipstick on him and leaving him naked alongside the road in a desolate mountain area where people were reluctant to pick up strangers, let alone naked young men wearing lipstick.

I had no idea of what was in store for me when a carload of seniors pulled up alongside me as I walked from the high school to our family business. I must have sensed something in the attitude of the all-male group as they stopped to challenge me. As they looked at my 6'8" 275-pound frame, it was obvious from the looks on their faces that they felt they had made a mistake, and I sensed somehow that they were up to no good. 'Are you a freshman?' one of them asked in a hesitant tone. I do not know why I answered him like I did except to say that something inside of me caused me to reply, 'Do I look like a freshman?' I responded in such a derisive tone that they immediately left without further ado. Today, as a father of three sons and a daughter, I wonder about the commonsense and wisdom of a school board that would not only allow these kinds of things to happen but, by having a special 'Freshman Orientation Day,' unwittingly helped to *make* it happen.

School started and it was a hot day in late September as I sat watching the second hand of the clock on the classroom wall, advancing so very slowly one second at a time. Mr Greely's fifth period Freshman English class was a total bore to me, as I had no idea what a dangling participle was, let alone how to diagram a sentence. The only thing I remembered from eighth grade English was that a preposition was anything a mouse could do to a jar. I thought, 'So what?'

As everyone sat at their desks doing their assignments in class so they wouldn't have to do them at home, I watched Arthur Oaks crawl out the back door and move down the grassy area between classrooms. In spite of the muffled giggles and whispers, I soon followed him and we were both moving off towards town together. I was now about 6'9" and well over 280 pounds and growing fast. Arthur was about 6'4" and nearly the same weight. Looking back on this, I now realise that Mr Greely, who was about 5'2" tall (or at least that's how I remember him) couldn't possibly have not noticed us sneaking out the back door of his classroom. Now I realise that he chose not to notice and that he also took steps to help me cope with my lack of expertise in English in spite of myself.

If anyone deserves credit for getting me started as an actor, it would be John Greely, my freshman English teacher, who recognised my lack of interest and, instead of causing me to be expelled, found a way to encourage me to express my talents in other areas. It was Mr Greely who introduced me to speech class and suggested that it could replace the required sophomore English class, which he knew that I would hate. In fact, Mr Greely told me how I could take Speech II in my junior year and journalism in my senior year and get out of any more English classes altogether.

He introduced speech (public speaking) to us through a fun-filled week where we all were given a topic as we came to the front of the class and were asked to give a five-minute speech about it. Sort of like what the Miss America candidates go through except longer. I was terrified but, from my experience with Wesley McCoy, I had learned not to ever show fear because it made you vulnerable.

As I made my way to the front of the class, stopping by Mr Greely's desk to pick up my topic and begin my five-minute extemporaneous talk on whatever subject he handed me, I made up my mind that I would not show the fear that was in my heart at the time, as I was scared to death to be up there in front of everyone. You have to keep in mind that I grew up during the early years of television, and shows were live because videotape hadn't been invented yet. Soupy Sales was the rage, and so were shows like *Time for*

Beany, that was written by a couple of comedy geniuses named Bob Clampett and Stan Freeburg. I remember Stan Freeburg being featured on a New Year's Day Parade show where he explained things about something he obviously knew nothing about. As he stammered and bluffed his way, he was hilarious and he ended up making a fortune working for advertising agencies, coming up with ad campaigns for companies like Chun King, whose executives allowed him to humble their company with one zany and memorable commercial after another.

With my role models and heroes being people like Soupy Sales and Stan Freeburg, it was my choice to make my five-minute talk a laugh, or even five or six laughs, a minute. I do not remember today what my subject was or what I said in my panic that day, except that I remember the entire classroom was in stitches. Mr Greely was not only laughing, but impressed with my ability to capture this small audience and have them eating out of the palm of my hand. It was at the end of that day that he suggested I take Speech I and Speech II along with Journalism later, thus avoiding any more years of high school English.

Some purists may say that Mr Greely did me a great disservice by making such a suggestion, but on the contrary, I am thankful that he gave me the knowledge that out of fear can come great comedy and hidden talent. I am glad that many years later I was able to meet Mr Greely again and thank him for getting me started in what people call 'showbusiness.'

I wasn't always able to be humourous in my speech-making and I even competed in a contest put on by the Optimist Club, where they awarded scholarship money to the person in a region that made the best speech. I wasn't as good at the serious stuff and I remember coming in second to another student, Glen Fine, who started his speech with a poetic line about how 'Man started out as a cold dark being shivering in the storm.' I am sure that I am not doing him justice, as he was quite good at phrasing things in such a way as to make them interesting. My serious talk at the Optimist Club regional finals was about how the town of Baldwin Park was named after an infamous gambler named 'Lucky Baldwin', who happened to get into the real estate business by winning some land in a poker game, which he promptly named 'Baldwin Park'. Although it was of some interest to the local community to find out that their little town was named after a guy who settled in the area after taking up with a Mexican woman whose husband he had killed, it didn't go over too big in the regional finals.

I worked in our family's business all the way through high school. I may have ended up as a professional football player instead of an actor if it hadn't been for a few strokes of fate that just didn't let that happen. Our high school football team was on a winning streak when I joined them as a freshman. The varsity football team was in contention for the CIF championship my freshman year, so it really didn't matter to the coaches whether I learned the plays or not, because as a freshman on a championship team, I wasn't going to get to play anyway.

My father only managed to get through the eighth grade before he had to begin working for a living so he was unable to pass on to me those bits of wisdom about high school sports that one can only learn from experience. Because of this, I had no idea that you had to 'pay your dues' on the 'frosh' team or freshman team going on to JV before you normally joined the varsity players. I was so huge that the coaches must have felt that I should be on the varsity team, even if it meant sitting on the bench and watching the upperclassmen play.

I wasn't used to watching, as I had always enjoyed playing football and never had any qualms about scrimmaging with the older players. I could pass the ball as good as any quarterback in high school and I had tremendously long arms that could pull in the ball and huge hands that would engulf and trap the ball even if I could only get one hand on it. The part that I was not good at was running. The coaches decided, after hearing about my natural talents from some of the other players, that I should be an offensive end or what they call a 'wide receiver' today.

During practice, the first and second-string quarterbacks would throw passes to patterns that we were supposed to run. Unfortunately, I could not get out and over to the place that I was supposed to be in time to catch the pass. I couldn't even get the playbooks long enough to *learn* where I was supposed to be.

Not only did I spend the entire time sitting on the bench, I also had to go through the humiliation every game of running from the gymnasium where we suited up onto the field. And, like I said, I was not very good at running. And when you piled all those shoulder pads and other things on me and put me into those football shoes that just didn't fit right, I was clumsier than ever. I'll never forget how those football shoes felt. The big cleats made me feel like a sailor in high heels, and my size 10 helmet felt like it weighed a ton. When everyone ran out to the stadium, I found myself ending up about three blocks behind the rest of the team when we got to our position on the field. The drills would begin, and I was always ten yards behind where the quarterbacks threw the ball.

If I'd had some advice to 'hang in there' for a couple of years, I probably would have developed into a good football player, as I would have matured into my body and equipment. I am sure that during a real game, the quarterback would have accommodated my slowness and would have taken advantage of my reach and hands, as you can make first downs very easily five yards at a time. Later on in my life, when I did *The Longest Yard*, playing on the convict's team with Burt Reynolds, I learned that I probably could have been a successful football player. Perhaps not as a receiver, but as a defensive tackle.

I thought that I should be good at baseball, having done so well at softball, but not seeing out of both eyes made hardball literally a whole new ball game. I couldn't see the ball well enough to hit or field it, and after striking out time after time and getting hit in the head or knees trying to field that little ball that I really couldn't see, I finally called it quits.

But becoming a sports figure wasn't about to happen anyway, as my father really needed my help in the family business, and earning money and driving a new car sounded a lot better to me in my junior year than spending my time on the bench and always being the last guy to run onto the field.

I worked for my father and with his appliance service and delivery men the rest of high school, both after school and on weekends. We sold the heaviest refrigerators and gas ranges available, so I was tailor-made for the work. When I wasn't delivering refrigerators Dad would send me out into the neighbourhoods in Baldwin Park, giving away yardsticks, pot holders and fly swatters, all with the company name on them. I would knock on doors, introduce myself and give the family their choice of a present from our appliance and TV store.

I became a member of a car club called the 'Loafers' and we had black jackets with white leather sleeves, with a logo on the back of a guy in a penny loafer shoe with wheels like a car. We also had the traditional aluminum plaques in the back windows of our cars. There were about a dozen of us in the club, and even though it was against school policy to let us wear these jackets, none of the teachers had the nerve to try and stop us.

One night when my good friend, Mike Ross, and I were coming home late from the drive-in movies, we were run off Irwindale Road by a car load of Hispanics who probably saw our 'Loafers' plaque in the back window of my car and considered us a rival gang. I was ticked off and got out of my car to face four of them and they all had knives. Fortunately, that area was known for its rock quarries and I looked down and spotted a couple of large boulders, which I quickly picked up. With a big rock in each hand I took the initiative and advanced towards them, asking them, 'Who wants to be the first to get their head crushed by a rock?' They got back in their car and drove away before I could get my rocks off. No pun intended.

A friend of mine named Paul Crezee and I were always looking for ways to make a quick buck, and we found a place in downtown Los Angeles where you could buy imported products real cheap. We found these kits of 100 gold eye sewing needles that came with a threader and a thimble. We could get a gross (144) of these kits for $10 total, which made the kits only seven cents each.

Our favourite thing to do was for two or three or four of us to go door to door with these 100-needle kits and, wearing our 'Loafers' jackets, ask for donations for our car club so we could build a dragster and not have to race on the streets 'endangering your children'. Every mother was happy to donate a dollar to our cause and keep their children safe while getting one of our 100-needle sewing kits at the same time. Later on, when I started to get acting work, this kind of selling background helped me to survive between acting jobs, which could be few and far between.

It also helped me to get up the nerve to ask a girl out on a date. My friend Mike lived with his grandmother, and the Delmonico family lived next door. I noticed that Linda Delmonico, who was very pretty, was always at home and didn't seem to go out on any dates. I inquired of Mike's grandmother as to the situation, and she verified that this blue-eyed Italian girl never seemed to date. I reasoned that, because she was so pretty, the guys were afraid to ask her out as they feared she might turn them down. I had learned selling sewing needles that, if you asked, some would say no but others would buy. And I figured, what did I have to lose? I asked Linda out on a double date with Mike and another girl, and we went to the Egyptian Theatre to see the musical *Oklahoma*. It was just as friends, and I was too shy to even hold her hand.

I joke about my love life in high school, saying, 'The only thing I knew about girls then was that they danced backwards,' referring to how you slow-danced at that time and when you stepped forward the girl stepped backwards. I did go to the Senior Prom with a girl named Linda Ragus, who didn't have a date either. Her mother and my mother were good friends, and she would come over occasionally and we would shoot my target pistol together or make photos together in my darkroom. Unfortunately, I was so shy that making photos was all we did in the dark – although I think our mothers thought more was going on.

After graduating from high school, I decided to strike out on my own in another field and got a job as a salesman for *Parents* magazine, selling subscriptions. The families who signed up got a children's encyclopedia set. I had sold vacuum cleaners one summer at my father's suggestion and had done moderately well at it, so it seemed to me that this was a field I could succeed in without the back-breaking work that delivering appliances entailed. My father had also taught me how to sell refrigerators, televisions, and washing machines at his appliance company, and it was his belief that, as long as you could sell things, you would never be out of a job.

One day I came home from selling magazine subscriptions (the managers preferred that we thought of it as providing families with nurturing materials) and I was met at my car by my younger sister Georgann, who was crying as she blurted out, 'Daddy's dead,' and fell into my arms sobbing.

Things really changed for our family from that moment on, as Dad had been a great father and a successful salesman and businessman, but had not been a very good planner in terms of wills and life insurance. My Mom was suddenly in charge of a business that was struggling during a major recession

(1958) and a home, car, and family and all the payments and responsibilities that go with it.

Besides the recession, the road in front of our store was torn up for nearly a year while they put a big gas line alongside the railroad track that went through the middle of the street. We had diagonal parking for our store alongside the track, which made parking very convenient. While the construction of the pipeline was going on this parking area was covered with a huge mound of dirt, as was half of the road in front of our store. During that time, if you wanted to shop at Kiel's Appliances, you had to park a block away and walk in. I believe that frustrated my father terribly and may have even helped to cause his heart attack.

After Dad died, I helped Mom again with the store. My Uncle Art had a donut and sandwich shop down the street and hired a new waitress named Jeri, who, in spite of her name, was definitely a girl. In fact, she was the talk of the town since she was built like Jayne Mansfield. Soon, I was not only helping Mom but also helping my uncle at his donut shop where I could ogle Jeri (along with the rest of the men in town, who liked looking at her, too). Encouraged by my success in taking Linda Delmonico out, I started driving Jeri home since she didn't have a car. We would pick up her little boy on the way to her mother's house where she lived, and I got to be quite taken with her. We went out on a couple of dates, first to a drive-in-movie and then to the beach. I bought a whole chicken from the deli, along with some prepared salad and a bottle of sparkling burgundy. I tried my best to be a stud, but I think that I was so bashful I acted like a nerd.

One of the distributors we bought products from was having a big bash at a country club in Riverside and I decided to ask Jeri to go with me to the event. She said that she had nothing to wear, so I made arrangements to buy her an evening dress from the shop across the street from the donut shop and our store. The tailor fitted this dress to her more-than-ample body and she was the hit of the evening. In spite of my size, I had to fend off every salesman in the state, it seemed, as they all wanted to meet this busty beauty. Unfortunately, my Mom got wind of my plans and attended the event with one of our salesmen. Jeri and I decided not to stay and left the party early to get away from all the salesmen and Mom.

I was much too shy and inexperienced, however, to know quite what do with a girl like Jeri. This was for my own good as it turned out, as she had a little baby girl in addition to a little son, and I wasn't ready for the responsibilities of a ready-made family. Besides, she had other suitors who were better able to take care of her, such as an optometrist with a new Jaguar and a more mature boyfriend who managed a men's store, so I was soon out of the picture.

Mom and I managed to keep the store open for over a year, but the recession, coupled with the road construction, had put us so far behind that it was impossible to catch up. In addition, the trend had turned to discount houses in rural areas with names like White Front, More and Discount City. I marvel at how my Mom survived those years. I tried to continue to help with the appliance and television business, but Mom, in her Godly wisdom, knew that we both needed to do something else. Over the years, she had a number of sales and management positions, some with the very discount chains that put us out of business. Somehow she paid the house and car payments until she was able to retire in the desert with her own pond that has an island on it.

Mom's very first job after dad died and she closed the family business was selling families pre-need cemetery plots at a local cemetery. I was only 19 years old when I joined my Mom in working for Oakdale Memorial Park. Sounds morbid or weird, but I got some of my best acting experience in that job. Oakdale's sales manager was a smooth-talking southern gentleman named Bill Hayes. Mr Hayes was from someplace like Arkansas and had the ability to turn off the television and take over the house long enough to convince the man of the house that he'd taken on the responsibility of providing for his own demise 'when you walked down the aisle with the little lady.' He was so smooth that I think he could melt butter with his voice and, of course, he could sure charm the ladies with his silvery grey hair.

Mr Hayes gave me a sales manual that was written by the best in the pre-need cemetery plot business. I was only 19 years old when I was delivering lines from the cemetery sales script like 'When they pull that sheet over you, Mr Baker, it's too late to take care of these things. It's too late for your wife to ask you those important questions... Now is the time that you need to take care of this... Tonight, while I am here to help you with it.' Of course, my father's untimely death at age 53 and his lack of foresight – and insurance – had prepared us like no other preparation could for this rather ghastly business.

Mom and I were both very sincere about what we were doing, as our own life experience had taught us that these things needed to be talked about and taken care of before you die and it's too late. I think that we both got burned out, however, as spending your evenings talking about death and its inevitability gets to be a little depressing after a while, especially when you're only 19 or 20 years old.

I tried going back into the appliance business, doing contract deliveries and repairs for a large company. This was not for me as I had grown to 7'1¾" and 330 pounds, and getting my hands into the back of a washing machine in order to change a motor would usually result in cuts and electric shocks – and there was always some small child who was fascinated with this giant who was breaking mamma's washing machine. 'What are you doing, man?' 'What are you going to do to my Mommy's washing machine?' 'Why are you so big?' 'Why are your hands so big?' Years later I would capitalise on children's fascination with my size when I did *The Paul Bunyan Show*.

TWO

SHOW-BIZ... AND MARRIAGE

Thank God that the appliance repair and delivery company closed and I found myself looking for another job. I was at the neighbourhood corner gas station when I noticed that there was a guy there fixing the Pepsi vending machine. I thought this would be a perfect job for me, as I could handle a machine that size if it needed to be replaced or brought into the shop. I introduced myself to the man doing the repairs and asked him if he thought there were any openings at Pepsi for someone like me. He was really nice and arranged to meet me and take me to his supervisor on his day off. No jobs at that time were available, however, and as we returned to his house he had another idea.

'I have a brother who owns a nightclub in Hollywood,' he said, 'and a lot of directors and producers and actors go in there. Elvis even goes to the club every once in a while. He uses big guys as bouncers and ID checkers. Clint Walker from *Cheyenne* was discovered there! My brother might have a spot for you, if you're interested.'

We got together that weekend and drove out to his brother's nightclub. It was called the Crossbow and it wasn't in Hollywood. It was in Van Nuys and right across the street from a big General Motors assembly plant. I was hired that night on the spot by his brother, Tony Farah. It seemed that the previous bouncer had allegedly been a little rough on some customer and Tony's insurance carrier wanted him replaced. The guy that I replaced was Red West, close friend and sometime bodyguard for Elvis Presley.

MOVING TO HOLLYWOOD

I moved to the San Fernando Valley in an attempt to break into showbusiness. I remember packing my inadequate queen-size bed that my folks had bought me (it was 6'8" long and I was almost 7'2") on top of my old Ford car and sewing my Knapp size-15 'postman shoes' back together with a needle and thread and heading to North Hollywood in hopes of becoming an actor.

Being so big poses its own unique set of problems. At that time they didn't have all the 'Big Men's' stores that you see today, and I used to buy the biggest shirts I could find and I could only wear them a few times because they would shrink from washing and become too small. Suits were out of the question because they had to be custom-made and a custom-made sport coat cost about as much as a cheap used car. I could never find shoes to fit and I would find myself buying the biggest ones I could find and making do with them. King-size beds were something pretty new and commanded such big prices that you almost had to be a king to afford one.

I wasn't dreaming of being a 'movie star'. I just wanted to find a way to have a bed that was long enough, shoes that fit and to be able to afford to buy a custom-made suit or sport coat that would fit my giant body.

While most people heading to Hollywood had dreams of becoming the new John Wayne or Marilyn Monroe, my fantasy was being able to walk into a men's clothing store and find that they had a section for giants where I could take a reasonably priced suit off the rack and actually try it on before buying it. Something everybody else takes for granted.

Although the nightclub was not in Hollywood, everything else that the Pepsi guy said about it was true. Producers, directors and actors (most of them out of work) did frequent the establishment and, yes, Elvis did come in occasionally to see his Memphis buddy, Lance Legault, who was the headline entertainment.

I ended up in Van Nuys sharing an apartment for a while with one of the LA Rams football players. He owned a taco take-out type restaurant next door to the Crossbow and I ate a lot of tacos and beans during those months. Needless to say, I didn't have to use my car as much as I was practically jet-propelled!

Tony, the owner of the Crossbow, loved having me work at the club because, with me there, there were almost no fights. Unlike some bouncers, I really didn't enjoy fighting, so I did everything I could to keep things under control. When you're 7'2" and 330 pounds, you do not have to do a lot of bouncing. You simply have to look mean, talk very serious and people just do what you ask them to. As a bouncer, I got lots of practice being a tough guy (when I really was actually a pussycat) and it prepared me well to play the many stone-faced killers and villains that are the parts available to guys my size. People are very surprised when they meet me and find out that I am really a nice, soft-spoken guy and not at all like the characters I play on the big screen.

Besides, I made many friends among the numerous martial arts people and weight-lifters, so any time it even looked like there was going to be trouble, they were right there to help me out. A guy can be pretty drunk and antagonistic, but when he's faced with a giant, a group of the giant's martial arts buddies, and his body-builder friends, he tends to sober up quick.

Tony liked making me hang around while he counted the money and placed it in his safe, so I would still be there when he locked the front door and could walk with him to his car in the parking lot. He was pretty short and a good-looking Italian guy, somewhat like Napoleon in that he liked to wash up and primp a little before leaving. This meant waiting sometimes until 2:30

or 3:00 in the morning before he would be ready to go, and he never gave me my night's pay until he was getting into his car. Most of the time he would forget on Friday night to keep out my pay and would tell me he would give it to me on Saturday. This was 1960 and I was getting $20 a night, so if he didn't pay me on Friday, it meant eating tacos for lunch and dinner on Saturday at my friend's taco stand.

When his forgetting my pay on Friday night extended to Saturday nights, I started getting tired of working for Tony. It seemed he knew that if I came back to get my $40 on Sunday that I would probably spend some of it right there at his place. They made pretty good cheeseburgers at the Crossbow, but they were fairly expensive and, of course, the drinks that went with them were nightclub-priced.

I did actually meet a few producers at the Crossbow. One was working as a bartender there, as he was out of work due to the writer's strike. This strike had been going on for nearly a year, and most of the television shows were reruns. My timing was perfect. I also met some stuntmen and wranglers. The wranglers are cowboy-type guys who handle the horses at the studio and on location. One of the wranglers was Pinto Spahn, whose father owned the famous Spahn Ranch where the Manson family hung out.

After a while I got tired of nightclubs and eating tacos. Although I told everyone I met about my aspirations to becoming an actor, it sure didn't seem that anything was ever going to happen in that area so I began to look through the newspapers for a real job.

I found what looked like the perfect job for me. A classy company that sold Steinway grand pianos and Fisher-Ampex stereo equipment also sold Hammond organs. They were looking for someone to demonstrate Hammond's new reverberation (echo) unit that could be installed in existing Hammond organs. They wanted a guy who would go out and hook up a portable demo unit using alligator clips, and when the owner of the Hammond organ discovered that he couldn't live without one of these 'echo' units, I would go back and permanently install this electronic device into the equipment.

My background in sales and repair made me the perfect candidate, and my new employer furnished me with all the leads (Hammond organ owners) that I could use and a new Ford station wagon to drive. I was doing pretty well at this new job and was starting to get really used to driving a new car. One day, my boss and a couple of salesmen and I were sitting around telling Hammond organ war stories when a call came in for me.

I picked up the phone and said 'Hello' to an unknown person on the other end. 'Is this the big guy?' the voice on the other end said. 'Yeah.,' I said. 'How tall are you?' asked the voice. 'Seven one and three quarters,' I answered. (I later learned to round it off to seven two as it was easier to say.) 'That's what Pinto said,' said the voice. 'Pinto?' I asked. 'Yeah, Pinto Spahn, the wrangler. Said you were pretty husky, too. How much do you weigh?' 'Over three hundred,' I replied. 'How would you like to work in a TV show?' asked the voice.

I thought for a minute. 'How much does it pay?' I asked. 'A hundred bucks a day!' said the voice. Now, this was in 1960 and $100 a week was a living wage, so I almost didn't know what to say but 'Sure! When do I start?'

The voice identified himself as Bob Gilbert and told me how to get to his office, and we made an appointment to get together the next day.

My boss and the two salesmen wanted to know all about it and, to my surprise, everyone, even my boss, was excited for me. Of course, we all thought that I would be making $100 a day, every day, every week, and not for just one day!

I met with Mr Gilbert at his office on Fairfax Avenue, close to downtown Hollywood and just a few blocks from where Lana Turner was discovered in a soda fountain at Schwab's drugstore. Gilbert started to tell me about this exciting opportunity, which would turn out to be the most work that I would ever do for $100 in the whole of my life. But I was excited, really excited.

Bob Gilbert explained the potential job to me. They were making a television pilot for a show based upon The Phantom, the legendary comic strip character who wore a purple suit and mask. The network and potential sponsors wanted them to test three actors for the role. Mr Gilbert went on to explain that, because the role required someone that could do a lot of his own stunts, all three of these actors would be involved in stunt fights in their tests and that I was to be their opponent in each case.

The pilot that was about to be shot had a character named Big Mike, who tries to escape from a prison chain-gang doing road work in Africa. The episode was to be called *The Escape* and, if things went well and the network and sponsors liked me, then I would be cast in the role of Big Mike and make a hundred dollars a day.

Mr Gilbert made it sound like such a great opportunity that I had no idea just how much I was going to be used as a punching bag. 'When it's all over, I'll give you a copy of the tests,' he said. He went on to explain that the $100 a day didn't start until we actually filmed the pilot. So, in the meantime, I would just get a copy of the tests. I hadn't been able to get an agent, let alone break into the entertainment business, so I readily agreed.

'There's only one other thing,' said Mr Gilbert. 'There is one particular actor who did a pilot for us before that is Bob Hope's stuntman in all his movies, and we would like you to work with him on the weekend prior, so that he comes off real well.'

I thought about this for a second and realised that if working on the stunts with their favourite guy was going to make him look better, it would no doubt make me look better too. And with some good film on myself, maybe I would be able to get an agent. I said, 'Yes, I'll work with him on the weekend, just give me his telephone number and I'll call and make arrangements.'

Bob Gilbert stood and shook my hand and I made a deal that would change my life and occupation. I walked out the door with my first job (unpaid as it was) in movies and television and I couldn't wait to tell someone about my good fortune.

'POINKETY, POINKETY,' SAID THE NETWORK CENSOR
I stopped at a little sound stage on the famous Sunset Boulevard in Hollywood called 'Sunset Stages.' Bob Coulter, the former bartender at the Crossbow, was the stage manager there (not the producer that he claimed to be). I had run into him and knew that, after the Writers Guild Strike was over, he left bartending to resume his job.

It was after 5.00 pm when I opened the front door and walked inside. He was not in the stage manager's office, but I could hear voices coming from upstairs. I walked up the stairs and into an open office door where several men, including my friend, were working hard at consuming the last of a quart of scotch. Bob Coulter introduced me to the group, one at a time, ending by introducing me to his good friend and executive at NBC, Bob Wood.

'Poinkety, poinkety,' blurted out the executive, and in a slurred voice he began to convey something to me that seemed even more exciting than what I had to share with them. As bombed out of his mind as he was, Mr Wood clearly knew what he was talking about. 'Therzzz a parrrt thattt you woulddd be purfect forrr,' he slurred. 'Commm tuh my offficcce on Munnnday,' he continued as he handed me his card. Bob Coulter, who was equally inebriated, took me aside and tried to explain how important this guy was. 'Heeez thuuu headdd censorrr for NNNN BBBB CCCC,' slurred Coulter. 'Ya wanna drinkkk?'

I explained that I had to get back to Van Nuys and wondered if this guy would even remember meeting me when I showed up on Monday. 'No matter,' I thought. 'In any event, it's been a good day.'

The following Monday I showed up at NBC Studios in Burbank. A uniformed guard was stationed at a small desk in front of the elevator that took you up to the offices. I handed him the card that Mr Wood had given me and held my breath as he called to verify that I had an appointment. Would this head censor for NBC remember speaking to me last Friday? The guard hung up the phone, handed me back the card and said: 'Take the elevator to the penthouse and when you get off you'll be in Mr Wood's offices.'

I exhaled and quickly moved into the elevator before the guard could change his mind, and punched the 'P' button.

KLONDIKE WITH JAMES COBURN
As the elevator quickly climbed to the top floor, I thought about what might happen when I saw Mr Wood again. My thoughts were quickly interrupted

as the elevator stopped on the top floor and the door opened. In front of me I saw an outer office where the doors were open. As I walked in, I saw several other offices on each side and people busily working. I handed one of them Mr Wood's card and was immediately ushered to an office directly ahead. I proceeded in to find Mr Wood seated behind his desk and on the phone.

Bob Wood, as I would grow to know him, directed me to sit down and I complied. Looking around the room, I listened to one side of his conversation. 'Bill,' he said. 'I've got Duff Branigan sitting in my office right now. How tall is he?' Mr Wood motioned to me to provide him with that information. I used my fingers to make first a seven and then a two. 'Seven and a half feet tall,' he said to the party on the other end of the line.

I looked on the wall behind Bob Wood and couldn't help but notice a dart board, and I wondered what that was doing on the wall of an executive occupying a penthouse office. My thoughts were interrupted by Wood's voice. 'How much does he weigh?' Again, the executive looked through his horn-rimmed glasses at me for the answer. Again, I used my fingers to make a three, then flashed all my fingers twice to indicate twenty. 'Three hundred and fifty pounds,' said Bob Wood into the telephone. Then the magic words, 'I'll send him right over.'

Mr Wood told me how to get to ZIV-UA studios and who to see. As I was driving over there, I had no idea that William Conrad, the man I was going to meet, was the radio voice of Matt Dillon in *Gunsmoke*, or that he was already a successful movie character actor destined to become the detective Cannon and to later on star in *Jake and the Fatman* as another overweight detective.

I pulled up to the traditional guardhouse of ZIV-UA studios and told the guard that I was there to see William Conrad, the producer, and that he was expecting me. The guard made his obligatory call and then directed me to a parking area near Mr Conrad's office and told me how to find it. I walked into Mr Conrad's office, and after giving his secretary my name, I was immediately ushered in to meet the very large producer. His immediate reaction seemed favourable, and after shaking hands he motioned for me to sit down and handed me a script.

'Read Duff Branigan's lines where I have them marked,' he said. 'I'll read the other characters,' he continued. 'Take a few minutes to read it over, if you like,' he said in a kindly voice, having been an actor himself for many years.

I did take a minute or so to read the lines over a couple of times. Duff Branigan was obviously a bareknuckle fighter who was barnstorming around the country taking on all comers who were willing to put up their money in a winner-take-all fist fight. My lines in this particular scene were a retort to a challenge by actor J Patrick O'Malley, who played a hopeful's manager. The O'Malley character was putting up quite a bit of money and daring my character, Duff Branigan, to take the bait.

'You tell this Halliday that I'll meet him any time… any place!' I bellowed out in my most confident and authoritative voice. My voice, even at that time, was pretty distinctive, and I believe it impressed Mr Conrad, who made a fortune with his own distinctive voice doing commercials for companies like Zenith, where he said 'Zenith – where the quality goes in before the name goes on' in a voice that was as commanding as James Earl Jones' as Darth Vader.

I was elated when Bill Conrad announced, 'You'll do just fine. Go down the hall and see Bill Montgomery, he'll fix you up with a contract. Are you a member of SAG?' he asked. 'No,' I said, wondering if this was going to ruin everything. 'He'll give you a letter to take to them so you can join,' he said. 'That is if you want to?' 'Yes,' I replied, 'that would be great!' 'I'll tell Montgomery to throw in a little extra to help cover your initiation fee,' said Bill Conrad, and I walked out the door to get my contract and my letter.

My boss at the Hammond organ company was elated for me when he heard the news and said that he would loan me the money to join the Screen Actors Guild. The folks at SAG weren't as optimistic, however, and practically insisted that I didn't have to join under the Taft Hartley Law, which allowed non-union people to work for up to 30 days in a union job without joining. 'You don't have to join,' they said. 'This is probably a once-in-a-lifetime fluke, and you may never work again. Take advantage of the Taft Hartley Law, and if you continue to work you can always join.'

I thought carefully on this. The first question that every agent had asked me when I made the rounds looking for an agent was, 'Are you a member of SAG?' I figured that if I didn't join, I still would have a hard time getting an agent and probably these people's prediction that I would never work again would come true. So I handed the lady $300 (the equivalent of three week's salary today) and told her, 'It's okay. I'll join.' She shook her head, letting me know that she had tried to tell me, and that she thought I was crazy.

I was on top of the world. The part that I had was what they called a 'lead heavy' in the business, and an important one. I was naïve at the time and did not know that ZIV-UA's reputation was mediocre; their staple of shows consisted of *Highway Patrol*, *Rip Cord*, *Sea Hunt* and *Bat Masterson*. The show that I was cast in was *Klondike*, which took place in Alaska. To show how seriously these people *didn't* take their show, one only has to know that when the ratings started to sag they changed the setting and the name of *Klondike* to *Acapulco*.

Klondike starred James Coburn, who went on to enjoy great success making some 80 films and eventually winning an Academy Award for Best Supporting Actor in *Affliction* at age 70, and Ralph Taeger, who played a featured role in *The Carpetbaggers* and starred in *Hondo*, but eventually disappeared from the Hollywood scene without a trace.

One of the things that I remember about making Klondike was a scene where I'm supposed to backhand Ralph Taeger's character, causing him to fall backwards onto his butt in the mud. We shot the scene unsuccessfully several times, as Ralph would always look back before falling. The special effects and stunt people had dug a pit for Mr Taeger to fall into that was filled with water, with mattresses, mud and sawdust. There was no way that he could hurt himself, and the producers were getting very frustrated with him.

The director approached me and said, 'Look, we need to get this done. Next time, just smack him backwards into the mud.' I understood what they wanted but could not dream of *really* backhanding anyone, so I devised my own way of getting the job done. This time, while I was pretending to back-hand him with my left hand, I gave him a quick push in the solar plexus with my right hand, and the heel of my huge paw ended up pushing him right in the big belt buckle that he was wearing, sending him backwards into the mud before he could look back.

'Cut... Print!' yelled the happy director as a surprised Ralph Taeger pulled himself out of the mud. The director gave me a wink, not sure exactly how I had pulled it off, but letting me know that he appreciated whatever I had done. I thought that Ralph was going to come after me for knocking him in the mud, as he had a very upset look on his face, but an assistant director pulled him away and they walked off to do the next scene.

BIG BLOOPERS ON *THE PHANTOM* TV PILOT
The network and the sponsors loved the stunts that Roger Creed and I had rehearsed the weekend before when they saw them on film, and he was selected to play the lead in the new pilot for *The Phantom*. The best part, however, was that they liked me too and I got to play the lead heavy role of Big Mike. This time, though, they had to pay me, as it was a SAG production, with other major talents like Paulette Goddard, Lon Chaney Jr, Reginald Denny and Alan Nixon playing leading roles.

I couldn't believe it. Here I was, just 20 years old, with a part bigger than the famous Lon Chaney Jr, and about to be working with the beautiful and talented Paulette Goddard.

Miss Goddard was a friend of the producers and quite a bit older than the woman that I remembered on the big screen. She apparently had enjoyed a life of hard drinking, as her slightly crackling voice had turned into one that sounded more like a parrot than a human. How was I to know that the woman sitting in front of me on the 12-passenger stretch-out bus that was to take us to the location was Paulette Goddard herself? I said to the woman, who was wearing a scarf and no make-up, 'Hi! I'm Richard Kiel. What's your name?' 'Paulette Goddard,' she crackled in an indignant tone. 'Sure,' I said, as I chuckled.

A couple of hours later I found myself more than a little embarrassed, as I saw that the make-up and hair people had turned this seemingly old lady back into the sex goddess that I remembered on the big screen. I was lucky that she didn't have me thrown off the show.

Those weren't the only mistakes that happened on *The Phantom*. I had a scene with Alan Nixon, who played the prison camp doctor. In the scene I approached Alan and asked him if he has 'The file,' which I intend to use to escape. In return he asks me if I have 'The money.' The scene was being shot in Placerita Canyon late in the afternoon and the sun was going to be gone in about a half hour. The director, William Daniels, was worried and under a lot of pressure, as he was working on a limited budget.

At that time I was just 20 years old and not even capable of growing a beard, so they had to stipple on stubble using a bunch of rubber bands which the make-up man had cut off and dabbled into black stuff and then against my face and neck. The make-up man also accentuated my frown lines by shadowing them and, finally, he created wrinkles around my eyes and on my forehead, making me look like a dour-faced bad guy with a three-day growth of serious beard. All these things I used later to make myself look older and meaner than I really was.

With a half hour to go before the sun would no longer be picked up by the reflectors that were being used instead of lights, I approached Alan Nixon and threw him my line. 'You got the file?' 'Yeah,' said Nixon, 'You got the money?' I pulled out the money and he handed me the file. We both secreted our money and file and the director yelled 'Cut... Print.' Unfortunately, we learned that something had gone wrong with the camera and we had to do it over again. 'Let's go again quickly,' yelled the assistant director, and everyone jumped back in place and we ran the scene again.

'You got the file?' I demanded of Alan. Nixon fumbled in his pocket and blurted out, 'No, dammit! *You* have the file and *I* have the money!' Everyone realised that in the haste to do it again, we hadn't exchanged the money for the file. After several more attempts, the pressure got worse and it happened again, and after that Alan couldn't help but laugh when I asked him, 'You got the file?' The sun went down before we could get over the giggles and we found ourselves doing the scene over again in the morning.

The show was supposed to have taken place in Africa and there were cheetahs, mountain lions and leopards on the set nearly all the time. While cheetahs are the most easily domesticated large cats and usually quite tame, leopards aren't nearly as predictable. In one scene a man was supposed to be attacked and killed by a leopard, and the stuntman had a leather band covering his forearm under his shirt that the leopard was supposed to grab hold of with his teeth. The leopard's huge teeth went right through the leather and into the stuntman's arm, making huge puncture marks. Although there wasn't a lot of blood, the leopard's saliva apparently caused an allergic reaction in the stuntman and he had to be taken away in an ambulance. On one of my very first shows I learned that you could get injured and that you couldn't trust those who told you it was perfectly safe.

The Phantom pilot never sold as Roger, who was a great stuntman, didn't look so great in the episode that they chose, as he had to have his head in bandages, a week's growth of stubbly beard and a patch over one eye. When you do all these things to a slightly overweight middle-aged man, it doesn't help. Now, George Reeves, who played Superman in the TV version, wasn't in any better physical condition, but he never played Clark Kent with a stubbly beard, bandaged head and with a black patch over one eye.

Having quit my job as the reverberation unit salesman and installer, I no longer had the new Ford station wagon to drive or a regular paycheck. I was told by Mr Gilbert that he would have a check for me on the Friday following the end of shooting.

I was now driving my old 1951 Ford with the crashed-in grille and the door that wouldn't open on the driver's side because of a previous accident. Not only did my car have four bald tyres, it had a cracked block from overheating and water would get into the oil, which caused me to have to change the oil several times a week with used oil that you could buy from gas stations. On the way over to the office to get my check, I had a flat tyre.

I hadn't eaten in a couple of days and I didn't have any money to get the flat fixed, but I was counting on getting a check that day. I rolled into a gas station where I made arrangements to leave the cowboy work boots that they had bought for the show and given me to keep (what else could they do with them?) as security for the cost of a good used tyre. I figured I would cash my check and go back and pay for the tyre and retrieve the boots. When I got to Mr Gilbert's office, I was told that he was busy and to wait.

It was almost ten minutes to six on that Friday when he gave me my paycheck and I literally ran to my car and drove down Fairfax Boulevard to the bank. I double-parked in front of the bank and got to the front door just as the bank guard was about to close the door. He was nice and let me in. I got up to the teller's window and handed the lady my check. She looked at it and after checking on the account to verify available funds she sort of laughed, which wasn't very encouraging. 'I'm afraid that there isn't enough money in the account to cash this,' she said.

I was devastated and very hungry. I jumped back in my car and drove back to Mr Gilbert's office. He was still there and hadn't expected me to get to the bank in time. 'The check will be covered on Monday,' he said, afraid that I was going to punch him out or something. 'I hope you have food in your refrigerator,' I said. 'Why?' asked Gilbert. 'Because you just adopted me!' I answered with my stomach growling. Bob Gilbert took me to the Crossbow (where they knew him and, of course, myself) and talked them into cashing my check, which I cleverly endorsed 'without recourse'. I immediately ordered two cheeseburgers with everything on them.

Years later, when I was promoting the James Bond films in Manila, I received a telephone call from Gilbert. He was living in the Philippines and wanted to come up and say hello for old time's sake. Diane and I had the presidential suite with three bedrooms, our own private pool and a manservant at our disposal. It was a great contrast to the old times, and he enjoyed it, too.

GETTING AN AGENT

I had already tried to get an agent, having received a list of dozens of Hollywood agents from SAG, all listed in alphabetical order. I was a pretty persistent person and had talked to all that would see me. The only guy who was halfway positive was an agent named Herman Zimmerman. Herman told me that if I still wanted to be an actor after six months, to come back and see him. I think it was his way of weeding out the wheat from the chaff and putting those off that wouldn't have the tenacity to stick with it.

Several months after our first meeting and having done the two shows, I walked into Mr Zimmerman's office, looked him in the eye and told him, 'I have a SAG card, I got two lead heavy roles on my own and I have film on myself. Do you want to be my agent?'

Mr Zimmerman was obviously impressed as he said, 'Yes.' And with only a handshake, we began a business relationship that lasted until he died some 20 years later.

Herman shared his office with his wife Nellie, who was the agent for children. It was an upstairs cubbyhole, but it was on the famous Sunset Boulevard. Over the years, I moved several times with Herman, as Nellie went into the business of making precision parts for Lockheed, and Herman moved his office to Studio City so they would be close. The two of them were wonderful people, just like having an extra mother- and father-in-law. Occasionally, they would come out to our house when we had young children, and Nellie would bring one of her great carrot cakes. Diane got the recipe from her, as it was that delicious, and over the years Diane has added a couple of ingredients to make it even better. Diane calls her recipe 'Jaws Delight' because I love it so much.

Mr Zimmerman had to have a colostomy and Nellie helped him with it, making it possible for him to continue as an agent on a part-time basis. When Nellie died, Herman continued on for a while, but his heart just wasn't in it without Nellie and a couple of years later he died too.

Herman was my agent for over 20 years when he went into partnership with Joshua Gray and Steve Stevens. I am glad that he got to see me make it big, finally, with the first Bond film and the next Bond that I did. In between the two Bonds he saw me do four other films and it was exciting for both of us. I say that because my father never got to see me make movies and Mr Zimmerman was a father figure to me.

Joshua Gray has since died, also, but I'm still with Steve Stevens, as he and I both refuse to die!

MY FIRST MARRIAGE

While I was working at the Crossbow I met an attractive, but not so young, woman named Faye who approached me about buying an extra health club membership that she had for Vic Tanny Gyms. It was a lifetime membership, but the gyms eventually went out of business as they could not sustain themselves with gyms full of lifetime members that no longer had to pay anything.

Faye approached me about the membership by first asking me to dance and we became good friends, going to the gym together. Little did I know at the time that we would end up in what could have been a lifetime marriage, but like Vic Tanny Gyms our relationship wasn't based upon the right principles.

Faye had just ended a very long-term relationship with a man whose mother refused to accept their marrying, because her son was somewhat younger than Faye. My father had just died, and at the age of 20 I found myself on my own without many resources. Although I looked older and may have seemed older because of my huge size, I was, in fact, a young man not mature enough to even grow a beard.

I spent a few nights at Faye's apartment in North Hollywood before moving to Burbank. During the time I was selling the reverberation units for the Hammond Organ company I went with Faye in her car to visit her daughter Caron, who lived with Faye's ex-husband in a small house high in the hills near Universal Studios. Faye was helping her ex-husband to decorate and rent an apartment that was below the rest of the house. I heard the sound of an organ being played quite well next door, so I checked my lead file to see if this was a Hammond organ that was being played and with Faye to see who this was that was playing. It turned out that the neighbour, who *did* own a Hammond organ, worked for Disney Studios as a cartoonist, and I proceeded to get my sample reverberation unit out of Faye's car and walked over to the front door of the house next door.

Faye's car was parked against the kerb with the wheel turned in to keep it from rolling. Apparently, my getting the reverberation unit out of the car disturbed its motionless state, because between the time that I rang the doorbell and before the neighbour could come to the door, I saw her car begin to roll backwards down the hill. Fortunately, it didn't turn the corner or it would have really been a disaster. As it was, it only jumped the kerb, narrowly missing another neighbour who was working in his front yard and who looked like he was going to try and stop the car by waving his arms at it. The man dodged out of the way at the last minute and the car came to rest after smashing into a large wooden window box full of flowers.

The police were summoned, and Faye was trading insurance and other pertinent information with the man when she was suddenly placed under arrest for an old traffic ticket, which she claimed she had paid but the records indicated that she hadn't. I managed to borrow enough money from Joe Gianguli, the owner of The Rag Doll, and was able to bail her out that night. She had been body-searched and deloused and was not in a very good mood. I think she blamed me for making her car roll down the hill, but she soon got over it, and eventually I did make a sale to the cartoonist.

I did whatever I had to do on the side to survive. I had considered wrestling, but when I was selling the echo units for Hammond organs I ran into Jules Strongbow, former wrestler and wrestling promoter at the time. His wife had a Hammond organ and I picked the name out of the list, Mrs Jules Strongbow. There's only one Jules Strongbow, and I excitedly headed for his house with my echo demonstration unit.

I had just left the front door, disappointed that no one was home, and was putting the demo unit in the station wagon when Jules Strongbow himself drove up in his big Chrysler sedan. He didn't notice me as I approached the driver side and patiently waited for him to get out of his car. Seeing me, he remained in the car and lowered the window about an inch. 'What'ya want?' he asked gruffly. I suppose that when he saw a seven-foot two-inch giant standing by his car with a black case in his hands he thought that he had promoted one bad deal too many, as he was obviously afraid of me.

I quickly explained that I was there about his wife's Hammond organ to put an echo unit on it, etc. He said that she wasn't home and that he had nothing to do with her Hammond organ. He still hadn't opened the door, but by this time he saw that I was sincere and rolled the window down, as it was in the summertime, and he shut off the car engine and its air-conditioning. I then asked him about the possibility of getting into wrestling, and he tried his best to discourage me. 'You seem like a very nice young man,' he said. 'My advice to you is stay out of wrestling. It's a rough game and you could get hurt. Keep doing what you're doing,' he said as he exited the car and headed for his front door.

I felt that Mr Strongbow may have got a few new grey hairs that afternoon from the experience, and I decided to stay out of wrestling.

I ran into a young man named Larry Hayes, who was a singer, and he introduced me to some friends who wrote songs and owned and operated a recording studio. Bigfoot was a real craze at that time, and a song had just come out called 'Big Bad John' that had gone through the roof and to the top of the charts. Faye went with me to the studio, where they proceeded to try and get me to cut a record with the Bigfoot theme. I don't remember the lyrics, but I can tell you that this was a bad idea set to an American Indian war-chant beat.

Faye was getting bored and wandered off to have a drink in a nearby bar, as she felt that I was wasting my time. She was right, but these people had spent time coming up with the song so I gave it my best shot. (About a year later I was used to promote the song 'The Monster Mash' on the Lloyd Thaxton show on KCOP Channel 13 in Hollywood, which turned out to be a huge hit, so you never know about these things.) When we were finished, I couldn't find Faye so I drifted into the restaurant next-door to have a burger and something to drink.

I ran into a couple of girls who had gone to Baldwin Park High and were on the volleyball team. They were quite tall and, for whatever reason, they were living together in Hollywood. I joined them at their table and soon we were laughing and joking about old times at Baldwin Park High. It was all very innocent as I was still very shy. About that time Faye walked in and she became immediately jealous when she saw me with two tall girls my own age. She left with my car and I had to hitch a ride back to my place in Burbank.

Faye wasn't there when I arrived, and she had the key to get in on my car key ring. She finally pulled up in my car and she and I had a big fight, which resulted in her hitting me in the forehead with a big set of keys, making a bump which eventually turned into a cyst. It grew larger as I grew older and altered my appearance somewhat.

She was upset because I wasn't ready to marry her. Looking back at the situation with the wisdom of hindsight, I realise now that she was trying to prove to her old boyfriend and his mother that she could find someone even younger than him who would marry her. I'm not sure that this was a conscious decision on her part, but I wonder who the extra Vic Tanny lifetime membership was bought for.

Unfortunately, I decided that I could get past the close to 20-year age difference and we were married. My mother and sister and a few close members of the family attended and 13 long years of marriage began. I should have realised that what we had done was a mistake sooner rather than later, but I had been raised to abhor divorce and that people should find a way to work things out rather than start life anew. This proved to be a big mistake as things only got worse as time went on.

Faye was different in her relationships with people. She had an argument with her mother who had come out from Texas to live with her when her children were younger. Her mother apparently got homesick and left Faye with the kids and no babysitter. They had not talked to each other much since that happened, and I never met or knew her mother. Her brother Wayman was obviously cut from the same cloth as they were both Hendersons. I remember once, when Wayman got into an argument with his wife Theresa, he didn't talk to her any more than was necessary, though they were still living together as man and wife.

All my life I was very close to my family, but after my marriage to Faye it seemed that I was estranged from them. Faye seemed to be jealous of my time with them and didn't enjoy spending a lot of time with my family. Suffice it to say that everything wasn't all bad with Faye, but we never really had that special something going that it takes to make a happy marriage. To make things more difficult, she had, besides her daughter Caron, a grown son named Bobby who was almost my age, and when he was discharged from the Navy, he moved in with us.

Trying to live on $55 a week unemployment in between the rare acting roles was a very difficult thing indeed, and it was only made more difficult by having another grown man to feed. I remember Faye buying cans of vitamin soup that were on sale in a clearance at Bill's Ranch Market. The powdered vitamin soup was in cans about the size of coffee cans and she got them for about 25 cents each. They came in assorted flavours, like chicken, vegetable, tomato and split pea. The first two I didn't like and the last two I really hated. Believe me, none of it was good, as the taste was overwhelmed by the smell and taste of the vitamins and minerals that had been added. Unemployment day fell on a Thursday and by Tuesday and Wednesday we were always down to this vitamin soup. Thursday night was spaghetti night since there was enough money to buy hamburger to put in the pasta. Needless to say, the only steaks served in the house were round steak.

I tried doing odd jobs, even becoming a Fuller Brush man, only to find out that it probably was one of the most difficult jobs in the world. You first had to go into neighbourhoods giving out the sales brochures and then go back with your free samples and try to sell the items in the catalogues you had delivered earlier. If you were persistent and continued to show items, eventually you would make a sale. My territory was the worst. It was in a very hilly area with long, steep driveways that I would drag myself up, only to ring the doorbell and not find anyone home.

It was almost like the movie version of the Fuller Brush Man with Red Skelton, as there were also some lonely women that just enjoyed having company in the house and they would spend what seemed like hours looking at all the shades of lipstick we had to offer. Most people don't know that the salesmen have to buy those samples. Yes, even the vegetable brushes! Everything you sold the previous two weeks would be dumped in one big box at your front door and you had to sort through all your orders, matching the thousands of items and placing them in a bag with the order slip stapled to it. Then you had to deliver the merchandise and collect the money. Collecting the money was the worst part. The lonely housewives didn't always have the money to pay for what they had ordered or they had moved away, leaving you literally holding the bag (of items). When I got out of that business, I was surprised to find out how well I did, as my returned inventory was worth quite a lot more than I thought.

I tried to get Bobby, Faye's son, to help me by taking the responsibility of delivering the Fuller Brush merchandise, but he couldn't seem to find half the streets or anybody at home. I finally decided to have Bobby take a job that I could help him with and still collect my unemployment insurance. He got a job washing telephone booths and cleaning the bugs from the light box overhead and cleaning the windows, etc. We drove my old Plymouth station wagon and together we cleaned dozens of booths a day. It wasn't a bad job during nice weather, but when it turned cold it was miserable because you got soaking wet.

Another job that I had in the very beginning was being a prop man. I had met a real nice guy at the corner gas station where I hung out occasionally when they worked on my car. The owner of the gas station would let me charge gas and repairs, and I would pay him back whenever I got a movie or TV job. All the guys who hung out there were heavy drinkers, as was the owner. Their favourite drink was Hill & Hill Whiskey, which was one of the least expensive brands at that time.

I was always invited to take a pull off of one of their pints of whiskey whenever I was there, and one day they introduced me to Charles Duncan, who was a special effects man in the studios. His nickname was 'Drunkin Duncan,' and he lived up to his name. This sounds pretty scary when you consider that the guy was in charge of explosions and other special effects, like sending an arrow down a wire that is supposed to strike you in the middle of the chest area where it hits a metal plate covered with wood.

But although Mr Duncan drank, he was never, in my experience, really drunk. Somehow he had built up a tolerance for the stuff which allowed him to do his job and do it well. Mr Duncan had some special equipment that he rented out, like a fog machine he had bought from government surplus that could put out enough fog in an hour to cover up a small town.

He happened to overhear me talking to the owner of the gas station about how I was going to make payments on some major work on my old car and he asked me if I needed a job. I told him that I could sure use a job in between my acting roles, as the money from unemployment benefits just wasn't cutting it. Charlie took me down to Local 44 where he introduced me to the folks, and the next day I started my first job as a prop man at Columbia's Sprigg's Warehouse.

Normally, a prop man is the guy who is in charge of supplying, placing, and keeping track of all the props on a show. On an independent production, a lot of the furniture and other items are rented out from various rental companies that supplied props. This could be a great job. Prop men work outdoors on location a lot and get to do some travelling. The prop man is also the guy to see if you run out of cigarettes or want a candy bar. They also handle the gun props and blanks, etc.

My job as a prop man was totally different. The major studios like Columbia and Twentieth Century-Fox had their own props, which they kept in huge three or four-storey warehouses. I started in the wintertime and when I punched in it was still dark. The warehouse had a freight elevator and when you got off on a floor, there was a single light bulb burning in an area that was probably 10,000 square feet, maybe more. As you walked down the aisles of the warehouse, you would pull on long strings to turn more light-bulbs on to light your way. Everything you can imagine is stored in these places. Various kinds and ages of refrigerators, vending machines, television cameras, beds, books, paintings, tables and chairs.

My reason for being hired so easily became readily apparent. The chairs were hung from chair hooks which were suspended from the ceiling. Normally, it took two guys to bring the chairs down. One would use a 'chair pole' while the other wrangled the chair to the ground. Being so tall, I didn't need a chair pole and could do it by myself. The other obvious reason for hiring me was my brawn, as I could wrestle the big stuff onto dollies by myself and bring them to the truck that would be waiting at the loading dock on street level.

I eventually found myself working at Twentieth Century-Fox. They had an old guy there who was about to retire. He was invaluable because he knew where everything was in the monstrous dark tomb they called a warehouse.

They say that John Wayne started out as a prop man and then became an extra before becoming an actor. This was encouraging but, to tell you the truth, I hated it. It wouldn't have been so bad if I got to work outside, but coming to work in the dark, going home in the dark and working in a dark warehouse all day where you turned the lights off behind you as you made your way back to the freight elevator was horrible. I felt like a mole!

I called in sick to do a TV show, and when someone in the local saw it on TV I got called in to talk to management. The good news was that they wanted to give me a permanent job as a prop man and I would get a union card in Local 44. The bad news was that they said that I would have to give up acting on the side and that I was to take over the old guy's job and cata-logue the entire warehouse before he left. On one hand, it was a good oppor-tunity since Local 44 wages were about twice what the average person made per hour, and with full benefits, but it meant being in that cold, dank ware-house permanently.

'Well?' they said. 'What do you think?'

'I think that I want to be an actor and I am not about to give that up,' I replied sincerely. That was the end of my job as a 'prop man' or more appro-priately, 'warehouse man.'

Looking back at this decision, I wonder what would have happened if I had talked it over with Faye. I think she was looking for someone who could support her and now her son, too. She liked to go to nightclubs and have a few drinks and enjoy the entertainment. I wasn't making the kind of money that allowed us to do that, and the prop man job was one that would have made me a good provider.

I did have one job that was promising for a while. I installed screen doors for a local company, which allowed me to use my mechanical skills and to do a little selling. We got paid by the door and we got extra money for upgrading the customers to better quality doors, and also for the extras such as wood door stops.

I was doing all right at this, but soon discovered a large tract near Long Beach called Rossmore Leisure Homes where the doors were extra wide and required special order doors. There were some dairies in that area, so people wanted and needed screen doors, but because of the width of the front door they were very expensive.

I came up with what I thought was a brilliant idea. I could buy these custom-width doors 25 at a time for just a few dollars more than the standard size. I would throw a dozen doors in the old green Plymouth station wagon I had bought for this business and go out to Rossmore, and by going door to door with the screen doors in hand, I could show them and sell them on the spot. I was doing very well at being a door-to-door door salesman until the local competition turned me in to the city officials since I was operating without the benefit of a city business license. Considering that I had to have a business location, a bond and a license, I decided to sell the last of the doors and move on.

Screen doors sold well in the summertime when people wanted to leave their front doors open for the breeze and needed a screen door to keep out the flies. Consequently when the weather got colder the screen door company went on vacation and that was the end of my career as a door-to-door door salesman.

I was still driving the old green Plymouth station wagon when I drove over to see Herman at his Sunset Boulevard office. The old station wagon was a standard shift and the clutch had began to slip. The brakes would lose their pedal and you had to pump them up occasionally. I had left Herman's office and I was coming up La Cieniga Boulevard, which at that point is a really steep hill as it approaches Sunset Boulevard.

I got stopped by traffic and I kept my foot on the brake to hold the old Plymouth in place when all of a sudden the brake pedal was all the way to the floor and I was starting to roll backwards. I gave it gas and let out the clutch, which started slipping. Thank God no one was behind me and I managed to quickly turn the wheel as I rolled backwards and was able to roll into a driveway. I pumped the brakes back up, took a deep breath and started down the hill.

THREE

FROM *EEGAH* TO *THE WILD, WILD WEST*

had got acquainted with another actor named Buck Maffei, whom I met during those few days that I lived in Faye's apartment. Buck was about 6'10" and 400 pounds. I met him at a nearby restaurant and, in his desire to be a friend, he shared a potential employment opportunity with me that he was unable to take advantage of because of his excessive weight. He had also played a small role in the tag ending of *Klondike*.

Buck told me about a producer named Arch Hall who had a project called *Stringanza*. The producer had interviewed Buck, who liked the idea of playing the title role but worried about whether he could handle it. Deciding that I would be better suited for the role, Buck generously told me about it.

I went out to Arch Hall's office arcade and met with him. Arch was a very charming and affable gentleman, who had enjoyed a long career in radio doing a show with his wife Adalyn called *What's Buzzin' Cousin*. He had apparently saved his money and owned quite a bit of real estate, including a two-storey office complex located on the corner of Olive Avenue and Lincoln Street in Burbank. I noticed that one of his downstairs office units had a sign on it for rent, and when I found out it rented for just $35 a month, water included, I decided to take it.

We talked about the role in *Stringanza*, which was about a guy who lived on the island of Stringanza who had learned to stay young by drinking the blood of female virgins that he sacrificed for this purpose. It all sounded a little weird to me, but at that point in time I felt that beggars couldn't be choosey, so I listened to him describe the movie with feigned enthusiasm.

'EEGAH, THE NAME WRITTEN IN BLOOD' AKA 'EEGAH, THE LOVESICK GIANT'

I believe that Arch Hall sensed my disapproval of the *Stringanza* story, as he quickly formulated a new project that he had been thinking about called *Eegah*, the story of a caveman who is still living in a cave on the outskirts of

Palm Springs. In the story, the caveman, in search of food one night, leaves the mummified remains of his ancestors and ventures closer to town. As he crosses the highway with his rabbit in hand, he is almost run over by a young girl in a foreign roadster who faints at his huge presence. Eegah is fascinated by his new discovery and particularly by the way she smells as he sniffs her perfume. One thing leads to another and before long the giant has the girl captive in his cave. With the help of her boyfriend and father, she manages to escape. In the end the giant is killed, while Roxy, the girl Eegah fell in love with, looks on sadly and her father recites a quote from Genesis about 'In those days there were giants in the earth…'

Little did I know that one day I would be known around the world for my role as Jaws in two James Bond movies, and also for having been in one of the 100 worst movies of all time: *Eegah*.

Arch Hall was in a predicament, having made a little black and white movie that he couldn't get released called *The Choppers*, starring his son Arch Hall Jr. At that time, most of the drive-in movie theatres played double-features and every studio made their own companion, or second feature, to go with the bigger and better one. Arch Hall decided that he had to come up with a bigger and better movie in colour so he could distribute his own double-feature, using his own company, Fairway International Productions. He succeeded on one count as the movie was in colour. I am not knocking *Eegah*, as it was great practice for me and it was a phenomenal success at the drive-ins, considering what it cost. Some people say that it only cost $15,000, which is quite an understatement. That might have been what Arch Hall had to come up with in cash, but I know that he put his real estate and good credit on the line for a lot more.

Not to say that this was an epic production. To the contrary, it was the most disorganised film I have ever worked on. First of all, the raw stock wasn't purchased from Eastman Kodak like most normal films. Instead, short ends bought from studios and individuals were used, meaning that the camera had to be reloaded constantly because the film kept running out. Secondly, a man from a little local radio station was hired to do the sound, and I do not believe that he had ever done it before, since a lot of the first few weeks of production all had to be dubbed.

I remember being out in the middle of the desert, in the blazing heat of midsummer, and a man running towards us yelling something which we could not quite hear. As he got closer, it became apparent that he was a messenger carrying bad news from the laboratory when we could finally hear the words: 'Stop shooting! The film is no good!'

Apparently, some of the short ends were outdated and the colours were off considerably. The lab, however, was able to do a lot of colour correction and the result was low quality, but passable. I give Arch Hall credit. He had made the little black and white film *The Choppers* using new raw stock, had gone full union with the crew and director, yet had a product that he couldn't get distributed. He then came up with a little more cash and, taking a big risk, he made *Eegah*, which, when coupled with *The Choppers*, gave him a marketable double-feature booking suitable for drive-ins.

Arch's financial capabilities were extremely limited with *Eegah*, yet he made lemonade out of that lemon. He wasn't the only one who should take credit, though, as a lot of people realised along the way that this movie could not be taken seriously and instead made it very campy indeed, kind of like Mel Brooks' *The Producers*. It was this quality that allowed people to laugh along with it instead of just at it, making it into a cult movie that is still sold in video form to this day and is enjoyed even now by millions.

Some of the problems, like with the raw stock and the sound, were inherent, as were the problems caused by Arch Hall using Marilyn Manning as his son's love interest. Ms Manning worked for a local chiropractor who had one of the larger offices in Arch's business arcade. Whether Hall Sr and Ms Manning were having an affair is open to speculation, but one thing's for sure, he was very fond of her.

The problem was that Arch Hall Jr was about 17 years old and Ms Manning looked to be more like 25. Neither one of them had much acting experience and their 'Tom ... Roxy' dialogue when she pulls up at the gas station where he works is so over-the-top that it is only rivaled by the famous 'John ... Marsha' routine done by a man-and-wife comedy team, which became so famous on a record that it was played over and over on radio stations.

Mr Hall had been good to me, and when I was having a hard time paying the measly $35 a month for his office, he would tell me not to worry, that we would make this picture together and he would recapture the rent at that time. I remember when the film started, being able to move Faye and myself into an upstairs apartment that had a separate kitchen and bathroom complete with shower. It was still a studio apartment, however, with the bed in the living room.

I interjected a lot of humour into *Eegah*, adding things like taking a huge bite out of a roast as I was passing by the food server in a fancy country club while searching for my lost love. I also did a mime-type routine when I encountered a lovely female mannequin in a store window after hours in downtown Palm Springs. I kept bumping into the glass when I tried to go through the window to check her out. The scene where Eegah inadvertently goes into the ladies' room, causing the inevitable shrieks and screams, was also my idea.

I even had a chance to direct a very small scene in the cave when Arch Hall had a falling out with Ms Manning and couldn't go on, for whatever reason. I asked him if I could do some of the simple scenes that I knew would have to be shot while he pulled himself together, and he gave me permission to do that. The cuts in that sequence where you see my legs or Ms Manning's cross to the other side of the cave, and a few others where you see me scoop up the sulphur water etc, were directed by yours truly.

Arch Hall was the director of the film, though, and he managed to do the impossible. The scene where the car almost hits me was filmed with only the light coming from the real headlights of the little sports car. It's hokey, but like the first *Blair Witch Project* film, it gave *Eegah* a different, almost realistic look. Since Arch Hall died, others have tried to take credit for directing the film, but I can attest that either Nicolas Merriwether or William Watters (both Arch Hall pseudonyms) directed the film.

I learned a lot from the man about promoting movies. He and his son and I did a four-state promotional tour that was extremely successful in getting both attention and publicity for the movie, which resulted in huge box-office at the drive-in theatres. I remember leaving Burbank in Hall's brand-new 1960 Calais Cadillac, which is the only one I've ever seen that didn't have power windows or seats, or a built-in air conditioner. We pulled a small trailer behind for our luggage and Arch Jr's guitar and amplifier equipment. I knew when our first stop was at McDonald's in Barstow that we were probably doing the most cost-effective tour in the history of films, but I still enjoyed it.

At the drive-in theatres, Arch Jr would get up on top of the snack bar and lip-sync to the songs in the movie during intermission. Of course, all the teenyboppers would be screaming, as virtually nobody came to Cincinnati, Columbus, Dayton, Louisville, Huntington or Charleston to promote movies and it was a big deal to them. Of course, when I came out in my animal furs and carrying my huge club, they really started screaming and running as fast as they could.

This was the time of B-movies and cheapo monster and horror movies, and people were less sophisticated then. I remember being in Appalachia in a town named Bluefield, West Virginia. I think the movie tickets were still selling for about 50 cents there while everywhere else they were a dollar and a half. As we were driving away from that little town I heard a voice cry out: 'Eegah, don't forget me!' I turned in my seat to see a young black boy around eight years old running after the car and waving. 'Don't forget me, Eegah,' he yelled again, seeing that he had my attention.

Today that young boy must be nearly 50 years old and probably a grandfather, but I didn't 'forget him'. In fact, I can still remember him as though it were yesterday.

What I learned from Arch Hall was that newspapers and radio and TV stations all around the country have a need for stories, and if you walk in as one, they put you on the air or write it up. Arch had a lot of chutzpah; in fact, he was famous for it. They made a movie based upon his life story named *The Last Time I Saw Archie*. Arch Hall was played by

Robert Mitchum and the great con jobs that Archie did were the basis of the movie. When I say 'con jobs' I mean it in an innocent (well, almost innocent) sense. Arch was called on to work in the entertainment unit because of his experience in radio and movies. He sat around a lot and was bored, but he soon discovered that by carrying a pencil and a clipboard everyone was terrified of him because they thought he was a big shot writing down things that might get them in trouble. Arch found that with his clipboard and strange uniform he could get almost anything he wanted, including aircraft to fly in to see old friends around the country.

I parlayed my experience promoting *Eegah* on the road in four states, brazenly walking into newspaper offices, the same way Arch and I did, when I was by myself promoting *The Human Duplicators* in Chicago, Illinois and Toronto in 1964. *The Human Duplicators*, another low-quality movie, was launched successfully with lots of publicity, garnering four feature stories that came out the same day in the four major newspapers that existed in Chicago at that time. I remember the main headline of one story: 'Richard Kiel, big and bright!' It was written by the late Ann Marsters, who was a sister of either Dear Abby or Anne Landers.

Over the years, I used the same techniques to get stories in the *Herald Examiner*, the *Los Angeles Times* or the *Valley Times*. I remember walking onto the entertainment floor of the *Los Angeles Times*, trying to find a writer to write a story about me, and being pulled into the office of a young man from the East Coast, who had just signed on as a feature writer and wrote a fabulous feature story. The young man in braces was Charles Champlin, who later became the Entertainment Editor for their Calendar section.

Years later, when I did the Bond films, it was these instincts for promotion and marketing that helped me do well with the press, but it was Arch Hall that gave me the courage to go out there and do it.

Believe me, it's a lot easier to accomplish good press with a $35,000,000 film than a $35,000 one! All the experience I got from promoting those two low-budget films helped me later when promoting the big-budget films, earning me a reputation as a person who had the ability to do a good job with the press and media in promoting films for the major studios.

For years my little sister Georgann kept asking me, 'When are you going to do *Stringanza*?' I guess she was fascinated by the story and probably asked me that a dozen times. I have never been excited about doing horror or vampire films and it isn't because they are usually low-budget because I have certainly done my share of low-budget films. It's just that they are not my cup of tea and I guess because I don't enjoy them that much (except for *Love at First Bite*) I can't get excited enough to want to act in them. I acted in one film that I never did see called *House of the Damned*. I even co-wrote a horror script called *Dance of Death* which was later retitled *Nightmare-a-Go-Go*. I re-read it one day and although it had all the scary elements I had no real desire to pursue it as it had no redeeming qualities. So I trashed it.

But I think someone rescued it from the trash as I once saw a really bad movie on late-night TV that looked like that story.

SERVING MAN ON *THE TWILIGHT ZONE*

I was still in the middle of shooting *Eegah* when I got the call from Herman about doing *The Twilight Zone*. Arch Hall was very nice about it, having been an actor himself, and shot around me during the week it took for me to do what turned out to be one of the classic episodes, entitled *To Serve Man*.

I had been told that MGM and the producers had the right to use someone else to dub in my lines and that they probably would do that. I remember driving in directly from Palm Springs and reporting to MGM for hours and hours of make-up before beginning the long day of shooting. I was so tired from driving right from one job to another and going through hours of brutal make-up that when they gave me a chance to do the lines myself, I was not prepared and did not do a very good job when I read the lines of the 'Kanamit'. Ultimately they *did* use someone else to dub the voice of the Kanamit, and I wasn't surprised, just disappointed in myself.

People ask me how it was to work with Rod Serling and what kind of guy he was, and I have to report that, frankly, I never saw the man. I can only guess that he probably had script approval and that he did the intros and exits all at one time or in groups, as I have yet to talk to an actor who worked with him on the show.

This show is so popular that when I go out to autograph conventions the photo of me as the Kanamit character is one of the most popular photos that people want autographed. It is not one that I am the most proud of, however. Why? Simply because it wasn't great acting that made the show a classic, but rather a great story, good special effects and terrific make-up.

My favourite shows were ones where I got to talk and even act. I dreamed of playing a part where I was wearing a nice suit and telling jokes. One day I got to do just that in a show called *My Mother the Car*, starring Jerry Van Dyke. I played a guy named 'Cracks' who tells jokes constantly. I wore a black silk-and-wool suit and I thought that I looked terrific. They didn't even try to make me look big, and because I was going to be just a regular guy who tells jokes, I couldn't wait to see the show. The only thing I noticed right away was that the character I played didn't stand out because they didn't go all out like they usually did to make me 'bigger than life.' In other words, they didn't use extreme camera angles to make me look bigger or reverse shots on the other actors from my point of view to make them look small in comparison to me.

I learned along the way that the camera shooting a flat picture has a hard time seeing the difference between a guy 6'2" and a guy 7'2". The difference is in perspective or how much you have to crane your neck to look up to someone a foot taller. Camera angles are everything and I learned how to help directors make that work.

THRILLER – AND A FEW KIND WORDS FROM BORIS HIMSELF

Soon after finishing *Eegah* I got a call from Herman telling me that Universal wanted me to play the role of Master Styxx in an episode of *Thriller*, hosted by the famous Boris Karloff. And, again, because I would be playing an Englishman with a cockney accent and would be working with real English actors, they wanted the right to dub my dialogue, if necessary. I agreed, but vowed that this time I would be ready for them and that I would give it my best shot. The other actors turned out to be the outstanding character actor and former leading man, Henry Danniel, Torin Thatcher, and Lesley Howard's son Ronald. Everyone, including the leading lady, was actually English or Scottish.

I bought a book entitled *Foreign Dialects*, which broke down each syllable by vowel and consonants. Arch Hall tutored me and, because of his experience in radio and legitimate theatre playing various characters, he was a big help to me. He also let me borrow a company tape recorder, and I used all the techniques in the book to pull off a pretty acceptable cockney accent.

Because of all the practice, I knew all my lines and everyone else's as well. When one of the other actors would forget their lines, I could recite them for them verbatim. I probably was a pain in the **** to the other actors, but I must have impressed someone as Boris Karloff had some pretty nice things to say about me as a new up-and-coming actor in the promos for the show. And I was very pleased that this time they used my own voice with my cockney accent.

Over the years I found the *Foreign Dialects* book to be very helpful, along with a similar book by the same publisher called *American Dialects*. I must say that a lot of actors can hear a dialect and assume it easily, but I am not one of them and needed all the suggestions given in the book. I always wished that I had the kind of talent that some of these natural-born actors have, but, believe me, it didn't come natural and I really had to work at it.

That's why I admire people like Roger Moore and Burt Reynolds. Like me, they realise that they are not the greatest of actors like Al Pacino, Tony Hopkins, and Sir Laurence Olivier, and they do not take themselves too seriously. Some actors have been fortunate, like Stallone in *Rocky* or Brando in *The Wild One* or *On the Waterfront*, to find that perfect role that fits them, but most of us are just likeable personalities like the great Duke Wayne.

THE RIFLEMAN, OR, 'JUST TELL THEM YOU WERE BORN ON A HORSE'

Herman had told me that if I was ever asked if I could ride a horse to say 'Yes,' since most of the time all it entailed was riding to a hitching post and getting off or getting on the horse and riding out of the scene.

I finally got an interview for a Western. It was *The Rifleman* starring Chuck Connors. Jules Levy was the producer, and I was led into his office to find him sitting in a big chair behind a huge desk and he was smoking a cigar which, as he was not very tall, seemed almost as big as he was.

Mr Levy reached out his hand to shake mine without getting up and I noticed that he was very impressed with the size of my gigantic hand as his was certainly swallowed up in it. I didn't have to read from the script for the role. He simply thanked me for coming in and told me that Casting would be in touch with my agent.

Little did I know that he had his own agenda, which was predicated upon my huge size alone. When he did ask me if I could ride a horse, I took the 'Yes' one step further and said that 'I was practically born on a horse.' In truth, my only experience on a horse was as a little kid in Michigan, where I ended up sailing over the horse's head onto the ground when the horse suddenly stopped at a fence. I had never tried it again as my first experience was rather earth-shaking and I had no desire to repeat it.

Herman called me the next day and said that he had made the deal and that I was to report to Conejo Movie Ranch out in the west part of the San Fernando Valley. I read the script and was pleased to see that there was dialogue. I wasn't so pleased to see that my partner and I beat up the Rifleman in his barn by taking him on, two against one. I was even more more displeased with the description of us riding down the hill together, where we confront Lucas McCain and his son and, after threatening them, 'spin' the horses around and ride off over the hill again at full gallop.

I had spent the previous week at Pickwick Stables, taking a crash course in getting on and off the horse and trotting around the corral they had there. We were then allowed to go out of the stables on the trail that led into Griffith Park, where we could gallop the horses if we wanted to. Every time I tried it, I remembered my Michigan experience and found myself pulling the horse back to a medium trot. I decided to approach the horse wranglers and ask them if I could let my horse get used to me. I really wanted to get in some last-minute practice.

Getting on the huge horse, Whoa Nellie, that they had found for me, I trotted around for a while and finally got up the nerve to take the mount into a full gallop. I wasn't expecting the response that I got. I was used to the nags at the riding stable, but this horse was a well-fed, seldom-ridden, fine specimen who was champing at the bit to run across the beautiful meadows at Conejo Ranch. As soon as I touched his belly with my heels, the horse shot out like a Corvette car in a drag race, and my cowboy hat (which the studio had specially made for me) went flying off in the wind. I found myself hanging on for dear life while the horse moved effortlessly under me like a living locomotive. The horse wrangler brought me my hat when I finally brought Whoa Nellie to a stop, and he suggested that I have the hair person pin it on with hat pins so it wouldn't come off again.

I was terrified thinking about the scene that I had to do – and was glad to get the hat pinned to my hair so it wouldn't fly off and cause me to have to do the scene over, and maybe even over and over.

About that time the producer, Jules Levy, arrived and came over to where I was, asking if I had met Chuck Connors yet. I told him that I hadn't seen him. Jules smiled and told me to wait in my dressing room and go over my lines, and that he would come and get me when Chuck arrived, and that he had a little surprise planned for him.

When Mr Levy came and got me, I found out why I had been hired so quickly and easily. Someone had made a leather backrest and seat for Mr Connor's cast chair and had engraved it with the famous rifle and the name 'Rifleman' along with 'Chuck Connors'. Just a week or so earlier, someone had stolen the leather back-rest from this chair that Chuck dearly loved, and the 6'5" was furious and had put out a reward so he could get back his custom-engraved leather back-rest and do in the hombre who had stolen it.

Mr Levy, who was about 5'6", walked with me toward the 6'5" Connors, and when he got close he yelled out, 'Chuck, we found the guy who stole your chair back! And he called you an asshole.' Chuck spun around and looked up at me in disbelief. His expression changed from one of intense anger to one of understanding as he surveyed the situation. 'Called me an asshole did he?' I waited for the big man to take a swing at me, but instead he finished his statement matter-of-factly. 'Well, he was absolutely right.' He reached out his hand and introduced himself to me while everyone chuckled at Jules Levy's little joke. I was relieved to find that Chuck Connors was an intelligent guy with a good sense of humour, as I wasn't looking forward to taking him on.

The horseback-riding event turned out to be a little more challenging, however, as the wranglers were quick to get me back in the saddle so I could get used to riding. They knew that I was not only not born on a horse, but rather a complete greenhorn.

Thank God movie horses are high-spirited and well-trained. The director ran through our lines with us. Kevin Hagen (the actor who played the doctor in *Little House on the Prairie*) was the other bad guy, and we both had our lines down pat. We were instructed to ride up the hill and out of sight. When the director yelled 'Action,' someone would cue us and we were to 'gallop' down the hill, come around an oak tree and rein up at the fence. There we would do our lines, pull out our pistols, threaten McCain and his son and ride off back up the hill and over the horizon.

As I followed Kevin Hagen up the hill, I began to pray the 'sinner's prayer', asking God's forgiveness for lying about my horsemanship. Kevin turned his horse around and I lined up next to him. My heart was beating like a bass drum, and I thought it was going to explode out of my chest when suddenly the second assistant director gave us the cue and Kevin's horse bolted away like a shot out of a cannon. I found myself on the other cannonball beside Kevin as we bolted down the hill. It took all my willpower to not yank on the reins and pull the mighty steed to a stop. I wanted to rein him up so badly and the hill looked so steep as we flew down it towards the specks below that consisted of the oak tree, Lucas McCain and his son.

I fought to keep my eyes open but I couldn't. Fortunately, my horse did whatever Kevin's did and he was an excellent horseman. As we slammed to a stop, I dug my heels into the stirrups and opened my eyes. We were right on our marks. We did our dialogue, pulled out our guns, threatened the Rifleman and his son, spun around and rode off back up the hill and out of the scene.

'Cut – print!' was a beautiful sound to hear as that meant that we had done the scene in one take and I might never have to get on a horse again.

If you ever get a chance to see this show, you will see that my eyes are closed most of the way down the hill and my lips are moving in silent prayer.

VOICE LESSONS AND DRAMA COACHES

Bob Wood, the head censor at NBC, had become my good friend and mentor and he was determined that I improve my speaking voice by going to a voice coach. He sent me out to see a guy named Maestro Shapiro who lived in a West Hollywood mansion. The 'Maestro' taught opera and that just wasn't my bag.

I eventually found a woman named Gertrude Holmes, who lived in a more modest part of town. Ms Holmes had well-known stars like James Mason, Richard Chamberlain and Robert Vaughn, among others, for clients. All of these men had soft voices and she was helping them to develop more power and range in their speaking. I was kind of soft-spoken and needed more power and range myself, which Ms Holmes, and later on her daughter, Claire Holmes, helped me to develop.

I also would go to drama coaches when I had a particularly demanding role. I remember when I had the opportunity to try out for a lead role that required me to do a crying scene, I sought out Ben Bard, the former drama coach at Twentieth Century-Fox who had gone into private teaching when the studio star system disintegrated. Bard was a great teacher and was able to show me how to get into the crying mode through breathing techniques that put you on that same physical plane that usually comes from emotions within. I had already been exposed to the tear-producing technique where they blow menthol through a tube at your eyeballs causing them to well up.

Apparently I wasn't a very good crybaby, however, as the director cast someone else in that role, but it did help to give me confidence that I could break down and cry in a scene if I ever had to.

You can actually learn and earn at the same time when you are working in television and films. You can hire coaches and dialect experts to help you with specific roles. Over the years, I found that I could get good professional and specific coaching for better roles when I got them and that the learn-as-you-earn method worked well for me.

I was a very shy person and I still am to this day. You say, 'How is this possible? You're an actor!' Let me share something with you. Over the years, I have learned that most actors, singers and comedians are insecure and push themselves into role-playing in order to overcome their fears. The same is true of a lot of supersalesmen and politicians.

Lots of actors and actresses are shy. The difference is that when you do TV and movies, you get to do it over and over again if you don't get it right the first time. You can do a scene ten or even 15 times, if you have to, in order to get it perfect. Besides, you have help. You have a director to help you get the right concept and to deliver your lines with the perfect nuance. You have make-up people and hairdressers to make sure your nose isn't shiny and that your hair is combed. You have wardrobe people to make sure you don't have lint on your lapel and that your clothes are hanging right.

Unfortunately for others, I'm afraid you have to learn *before* you earn in most cases, but I had the advantage of being a physical giant who got parts first because of my size. This backfired on me one time, however, as a friend, Robert Barron, wrote a *Bonanza* episode for me and before starting work, or even getting a contract, I went to a drama coach and had him help me with the part, which was a guest-starring role. When the casting people called my agent to make a deal for me, it turned out that they wanted me to work on the same dates that I had already committed to work on *The Wild, Wild West* TV show. The drama coach had another large client named Dick Peabody – and he used the script I had left with him to prepare Mr Peabody for an audition for the role, which he then won even though it was written by my good friend especially for me.

THE WILD, WILD, WEST – OR ROBERT SAYS 'HE TALKS!'

I did my stint on *The Wild, Wild West* the same week that Dick Peabody was doing 'my' role on *Bonanza*. At the time I was upset that I couldn't do them both, but today I am glad that things turned out the way they did. *The Wild, Wild West* turned out to be a bit of a break for me as it was extremely well done, and I had the good fortune of playing the part of Voltaire with the talented actor Michael Dunn, who played the famous Dr Loveless.

Although the role I had on *The Wild, Wild West* was a good one, I didn't have one single word of dialogue. I was meant to be window-dressing for

Michael Dunn, as my job was to carry him around and to protect him from harm. I had to show every emotion with subtle facial expressions instead of using words. I had used this technique playing the infamous caveman Eegah, and I expanded upon it in this very successful Western series.

Years later, what I had learned would serve me well when I did the two James Bond films as Jaws. Jaws only utters four words in the two films, and they all are heard at the end of *Moonraker* when he toasts his new girlfriend Dolly with 'Well, here's to us!' Most people don't realise that is all I said in the two James Bond movies as my character had so much impact, both dramatically and at times humorously – but that's all I said.

Don't get me wrong. I enjoyed working on the show. Bob Conrad was a joy to work with, as was the late Ross Martin. The leading lady on the first show that I did was Leslie Parish, who had starred as Daisy Mae in *Li'l Abner*. She was a very sweet young lady, and I remember her befriending some little kittens she found running around the soundstage and taking them home with her. I felt a little jealous of those kittens. So even though I wasn't getting to talk in the show, it was a very positive experience.

The *Bonanza* role, on the other hand, which I didn't get to do, had lots and lots of dialogue. I was quite disappointed but made the best out of my situation. I remember one scene where I was supposed to sit quietly in the background while Michael Dunn and his real-life friend, Phoebe Dorin, sang and he played the harpsichord. I think it was part of Dunn's deal that they could do this as they had a nightclub act together and this helped to promote their act. I wasn't about to be shut out of the scene, however, and I got the prop man to get me a little leather bag with leather strings and filled it with licorice candy. While they were singing, I took the leather bag out of my coat and slowly pulled on the leather strings and opened it, taking one piece of licorice out at a time. I chewed the licorice with a big smile while tapping my even bigger feet to the music.

The next day when they saw the rushes, they realised that they were going to have to film close-ups of me doing these things so the audience could see them clearly. Of course, this enhanced my role and character tremendously. When I got called back for another round as the same character, Bob Conrad would kid me about my scene-stealing and my little leather bag.

I told Herman to tell the producers of the show that if they wanted to keep bringing me back they were going to have to give me something to say. I didn't want to continue in a non-speaking role as I was afraid of getting stereotyped as a guy who couldn't talk. Herman made the mistake of actually telling this to the casting people, who came back with the statement that the character wasn't supposed to talk, would never talk, and if I didn't do the shows, that I may never work for CBS again. I was pretty chagrined after honouring my commitment and missing the 'better' role on *Bonanza*. I felt they had no appreciation of what I did to make the Voltaire character more interesting, so I decided not to do any more shows and take my chances with CBS.

I was working on the television series *Honey West* with Anne Francis when my grandfather and uncle came out to visit the set. Anne Francis was so gracious and sat on the stairway talking to both of them for quite some time, and my grandfather, who was enamoured of Ms Francis having seen her on the big screen, was delighted to be talking to her.

In spite of my agent's upset with the casting people, I decided to take my relatives over to visit *The Wild, Wild West* set and introduce them to Robert Conrad and Ross Martin. Robert was very nice to them, as well, and mentioned that we had a show coming up soon. I said quietly that my agent had requested that I have some dialogue in the show and they'd said no, so I wasn't going to be doing any more of *The Wild, Wild West* shows. Perhaps it was just a coincidence (though I doubt it), but when I returned to the *Honey West* set, I had a message to call Mr Zimmerman. Herman was excited to tell me that they were rewriting *The Wild, Wild West* script and that I would talk.

I wondered how they would accomplish the transition, but if you see that show rerun, it was quite simple. Artemus (Ross Martin) says something like this to James West (Robert Conrad): 'Who's the biggest guy you know?' James says 'Voltaire.' Artie says, 'Well, he's back in action, and what's more, he can talk.'

Not only did I work for CBS again, but I also did another *Wild, Wild West* show, where I wasn't paired with Dr Loveless, called *The Night of the Simian Terror*. In that show I played a character named Dimas who was so much bigger than his baby brothers that his father put him with a scientist to raise with a bunch of gorillas. It was a great part with quite a lot of dialogue and a very sensitive scene at the end with my father, who was played by Dabbs Greer. I can't help but believe that Bob Conrad got on the phone when he heard about my dilemma and got them to re-write the script so I could talk in the preceding show, which allowed the producers to see what I could do, and that led to the subsequent role in *The Night of the Simian Terror*.

Bob was a great guy. He was pretty serious at that point in his life. He had already starred in a television series called *Hawaiian Eye*, where he didn't make any real money. It was customary in the business in the early 1960s to take a relatively unknown actor and make him into a star, but the other side of the deal was they didn't pay you a whole lot. The Screen Actors Guild minimum at that time was $315 a week and some of the studios were paying a package of $500 an episode, which included pre-purchasing your residuals, a practice that was declared unethical and outlawed by the union a few years later. The residuals didn't go on in perpetuity like they do now. As I recall, they became less and less with each re-run and stopped entirely after about five or six runs. No one knew that some of these shows would go on forever on cable and family networks. I remember Bob telling me how the amount of his take-home pay on *Hawaiian Eye* wasn't enough to answer the fan mail, and they wouldn't do it for him. But I also remember reading in the trades later on that, when Bob got to portray famous WWII ace Pappy Boyington in *Baa Baa Black Sheep*, he was getting paid $600,000 per episode and I was happy for him.

Some people say that Bob Conrad was an uptight guy with a big chip on his shoulder, like in the battery commercial he did. Some also said that he didn't allow bigger actors on his show because, like Alan Ladd, he wasn't very tall. I found him to be just an aggressive guy who knew what he wanted and had no compunction about going in and talking to the network when he was at odds with a time-slot they were giving him. In spite of his size, he had no problems with my being on the show, and I really appreciated his making sure that I was.

FOUR

JERRY LEWIS, PAUL BUNYAN... AND THE IMPORTANCE OF PUBLICITY

When I was at **Pickwick Books** in downtown Hollywood getting my copies of *Foreign Dialects* and *American Dialects*, I ran across a book in the sale bin called *Confessions of a Scoundrel* by Guido Orlando. I bought the book and, when I got it home and started reading it, I realised that it was a lucky or blessed moment for me when I decided to make that purchase.

Guido Orlando was a publicist who made his reputation by guaranteeing the clients he chose to take on that he would secure a studio contract for them within one year. The clients that Mr Orlando represented were usually beautiful women, mostly beauty pageant winners who had one thing in common, a very rich father or boyfriend. He explained how he flew one restaurant chain owner's daughter to every event that a playboy prince was going to be at, and how he managed somehow to get the two of them together in a photograph and would plant rumours that they were an item, which he backed up with all his photographs. The photo would turn up in every movie magazine and supermarket tabloid and, of course, the restaurant owner's daughter would end up with a studio contract, earning Guido a big fat fee.

The part of the book that caught my attention, though, was how Mr Orlando got started in the movie business. It all started for him when a friend told him about an audition he was going to for the part of Napoleon in a Broadway production. Guido went with his friend and couldn't help but notice that no one looked like Napoleon in spite of the fact that they were good actors. Orlando's friend didn't get the part or even a second call-back but Guido decided to give it a shot himself. He rented a Napoleon costume and got a mortician to put a wax nose on him that made him look like the French Emperor himself. Guido got the part and that started him down the showbiz road. He said that many of the other actors auditioning probably would have made a better Napoleon, but the director and the producers couldn't get past the fact that he looked like the character they were looking for.

Many, many times I used this technique to get cast in a television show or a movie. I always tried to look as much like the part as possible whenever I walked in for an interview. It worked time and time again! In simple terms: if they are casting the part of a banker you do not want to show up wearing Levis and a matching Levi jacket. On the other hand, if they're looking for a guy to play a prison inmate you do not want to go to the interview wearing a double-breasted suit.

'THEY WANT A GIANT INDIAN!'

I was working weekends at the Rag Doll Bar and Dance Hall, which was located at the corner of Lankersheim Avenue and Victory Boulevard in North Hollywood. It was just across the street from the famous Palomino Nightclub, which was on the opposite corner. The Rag Doll burned down a number of years ago and is no longer a neighbourhood landmark. The owner was Joe Gianguli, the uncle of the Pepsi man and his brother, my former employer Tony Farah. I was hired as a bouncer, doorman and ID checker for the same reasons I worked at the Crossbow, mostly because I was so big that nobody would challenge my authority, which meant there were very few fights or problems as long as I worked there.

Part of my job was to keep the regulars out of trouble, and one of these was the owner/trainer of the famous Lassie from the movies and long-running TV series. Rudd Weatherwax was a heavy drinker, to say the least, and would often be sitting at the bar when I would arrive at 8.45 in the evenings to assume my nightly duties. Because he was a good customer, I was told to call him a cab and help him out to it if he'd had too much to drink. As a result of my taking care of him in this fashion, we became acquainted, if not good friends.

One night he approached me proudly with the news that the series producers had bought another of his story ideas and that it was a five-part show that featured a giant Indian, which he said he had written with me in mind. Rudd asked me if I had any photos of myself that he could show the producers. I told him that I would bring some in the next night, which I did, and he promised me that he would take them into the studio the following Monday.

That Monday night I stopped by the club hoping to see him and find out if I had the part. Sure enough, he was there when I walked in and he immediately shared the bad news with me. He had shown them the pictures as he promised, and they told him that they were looking for a giant *Indian* – and that I wasn't an Indian. Rudd said he'd told them that I was a giant and it was going to be a lot easier to make me into an Indian than it would be to make an Indian into a giant. He said that they wanted to see if they couldn't find a giant Indian. I was a little disappointed, but not defeated.

I got in touch with my make-up friend Werner Keppler and shared the problem with him. He made arrangements with a hair person to sew two wigs together and make me an Indian wig and told me to come to his house on Saturday. He planned to sculpt an Indian nose on me using mortician's wax and take some pictures of me in the Indian wig and with the Indian nose.

I rented an Indian-type leather jacket and headband from Western Costume Company, along with some period-style wool trousers that would go with the jacket, and showed up at Werner's place to get made up. When the wig was in place and the wax nose was done, I looked like the famous Indian on the Indian nickel, especially with my Indian wardrobe on. Werner took some photos with a good camera and gave me the roll to get developed, which I immediately took into a one-hour photo place. I then headed for the Rag Doll hoping to find Rudd Weatherwax there so I could show him the new Indian me.

He was there and astonished by how much I now looked like a real Indian. He said that I should go in like that on Monday as he was sure that I would get the part. I explained that the nose was sculpted from mortician's wax and already beginning to melt from my body heat. I told him that I would, however, have photos in the get-up and make-up the following day for him to take to the studio on Monday. Rudd gave me his home address and I delivered the photos to him the next day.

On Monday night, I found him at the club and he was jubilant. It seems that when he showed the photos to the producers they were elated and said 'Now *this* guy is perfect.' Rudd explained that it was the same guy but with Indian make-up, wig and clothing. The producers called my agent, cast me in the role and had me go to their make-up guy to make a rubber (ie, more permanent) Indian nose.

Because of the help of my friends, and not giving up, I did this five-part show, which was made into a movie as well as being on television.

As an aside, we worked overtime hours on Thanksgiving Day. We went into what they call 'golden time' and on a holiday that meant you got four hour's pay for every hour you worked, as the holiday was already double pay.

The Lassie television series was owned by Jack Wrather, who also owned the Lone Ranger, the Gilbert Toy Company (chemistry sets, toy trains etc.) and the Disneyland Hotel. He was well known as a very conservative spender, and I was approached by the production people to forget about my extra pay and, if I did, they promised to use me again in the future. I thought that was colossal nerve to work people 17 or 18 hours on a Thanksgiving and not pay them extra for it. I held my ground and made them pay me, which they respected, and a few years later did an eight-part show for them, as well.

LANDING ON GILLIGAN'S ISLAND IN A RUSSIAN SUBMARINE

One of my fondest memories was doing the cult classic show *Gilligan's Island*. Everyone was a lot of fun and I enjoyed doing the show very much. I got a chance to do Russian dialogue with the help of my *Foreign Dialects* book. Some of it was dubbed, but my work with the book made even that work better as my attempt at the dialect produced mouth and tongue movements that matched the dubbing.

The only part of the show that doesn't carry good memories with it was when my character had to jump in the lagoon and swim off rapidly, as he is frightened by Gilligan and his cohorts, who are dressed as ghosts. It was January and the lagoon on the back lot of CBS Studio Centre was ice cold. I was wearing a Russian submarine officer's uniform, over which I was wearing a sheet, since I too was dressed as a ghost, trying to scare them off the island.

In order to look like I was going at 100 miles an hour through the water, they had me hooked to a cable that pulled me through the water while I moved my arms in a superhuman backstroke. Like a lot of shots in movies and television, this one required a half-dozen retakes. I was turning blue by the time we did the last take and my teeth were chattering uncontrollably. The prop man brought out a half-pint of brandy, which I gratefully accepted and chugged down as I headed for my dressing room, a warm heater and some dry clothes.

What was Gilligan like? Well, he was Gilligan. Bob Denver seemed to be a lot like Gilligan. Kind of bright-eyed and bushytailed. In fact, all the people that worked on that show seemed to be totally typecast! Tina Louise was like a movie star. Jim Backus and Natalie Schafer who played his wife looked and acted like they would be right at home in a fur coat and at the golf country club. Even Dawn Wells was like the innocent teenager she played. Years later I worked with Dawn Wells on a small independent movie and she looked better than ever. She must have really been a teenager when she did *Gilligan*. If not, she should start bottling whatever that youth formula is that she uses and start selling it.

GETTING LET DOWN BY JERRY LEWIS

It was about this time that a friend of mine, Tom Armstrong, who was a writer, wrote a television series idea called *The Brothers Hart*. It was a vehicle for me and my friend Bill Engesser, who is about an inch taller than me and about the same build. The series was to be a comedy about these two giant Hart brothers who join the Peace Corps in order to see the world and do some good in it. They have big hearts and small brains and, of course, the show was to be a comedy.

We were fortunate to get into Twentieth Century-Fox to meet the writer Hal Kantor and producer Marty Melcher to talk about the show. I blew it when some one mentioned that he was Doris Day's husband, and I said 'Sure, he is.' It was something the characters in *The Brothers Hart* would do, but it didn't go over too well with Mr Melcher, Mr Kantor, or the agent who got us in to see them.

One day I talked Bill into crashing the gate with me at Paramount Studios by just walking back in with the actors having lunch across the street at Oblatt's. We had no problems as the guard decided that two seven-foot giants must belong in there and he made no effort to stop us. We were looking for the Jerry Lewis set where they were producing *The Nutty Professor*. We found it, and it had a big sign that said 'Closed Set – No visitors Allowed!'

We walked in and saw that Jerry was rehearsing a scene with the Les Brown Orchestra. There were a lot of people standing around that played dancers in the scene and they immediately surrounded Bill and I to see what we were doing in the movie as two giants. Jerry heard the rumblings of the crowd and looked over in our direction to see what was going on, and I thought to myself 'Oh crap, we're in trouble!'

Jerry walked over and started doing a funny routine with us, then he walked away and called someone over and in a minute the guy was heading our way. Before we could beat it out of there, the man caught up with us and asked who our agent was. We told him and he was writing it down as we went out the door.

That afternoon we got a call from Herman that Jerry Lewis wanted us to do a bit in his picture. It wasn't much of a part, but it was a good credit to be in a Jerry Lewis movie because at that time he was hugely successful. Paramount's stills man had taken a picture of Bill and I talking with Jerry and they included it in their *Paramount Magazine* with the caption: 'A couple of interesting characters in Jerry Lewis' new picture, *The Nutty Professor*.' The picture in the magazine was almost better than the part, as Bill and I just played a couple of guys in a gym whom Jerry runs into for a few seconds.

Our friend Tom Armstrong thought that we might be able to parlay this connection into getting *The Brothers Hart* television series off the ground with Jerry Lewis' help. I didn't think there was much chance of getting Jerry Lewis to help us with Tom's project, so I was surprised, and delighted, when Tom was able to make an appointment for all of us to meet with Jerry the following week.

We sat in the outer office at Paramount waiting to be taken in to see America's top comic film star. We were holding our breath when we were finally escorted into a private office. There, Jerry sat at a typewriter, typing away with a cigarette hanging out of his mouth and the music so loud it would make your head split. Jerry reached over and shut off a switch, and suddenly the room was stone silent except for Lewis' loud voice almost yelling out, 'What do you want?'

Everyone was stunned, including myself, but I did manage to mutter out 'Help!'

'What?' he asked. I managed to say it again a little louder, and more understandably this time. Tom Armstrong picked up the cue and pulled himself together to pitch Jerry on how we were looking for help in getting *The*

Brothers Hart series produced and on the air. He briefly told Jerry about the premise of the show and gave him a couple of thumbnail sketches of possible episodes and handed him additional materials.

Jerry, to everyone's surprise, responded very favourably to Tom's pitch and ended up saying that he always wanted to do something different – how he had even thought about doing a show about an ugly girl – and, yes, he would definitely be able to help us. Jerry said, 'I'll call you soon.'

At the end of the interview we were all about as shocked by this positive response as we were in the beginning when we encountered the loud music and the sudden silence when Jerry turned it off. As we were walking out, Jerry said to Tom, whom he had identified as the spokesperson for our trio, 'Look, if you don't hear from me, don't hesitate to call. I get busy and sometimes I forget, so by all means call me.'

We waited for a week for the call that would change our lives, but it didn't come. Tom decided that it was time to take Jerry up on his suggestion and he called him again and again for several months without getting a return call.

I wasn't surprised, as many stars have a lot of pressure on them to do all kinds of things, and I surmised that Jerry had changed his mind about wanting to get involved in our project. He may have run the possibility of the show by some network executives and found that they were cold towards it even with him involved.

I kept right on working during those months, but Bill and Tom were devastated by the failure of the TV series to materialise.

Years later, I found out that this was a time when Mr Lewis was going through a lot of allergy and pain problems and that his medication may have caused him to say something he didn't mean to say. I know from my own experience, having spent a lot of time trying to help friends make it in their singing careers or as actors, that you have to stop spending so much time trying to help everyone else and focus on your own career.

My only hard feelings about all this came years later when I was to be on the Danny Thomas show in a sketch with Lucille Ball, Danny Thomas and Jerry Lewis. I met Danny Thomas and Lucille Ball and everything was obviously a 'go' until Jerry Lewis walked in and saw me. He immediately said something to Ms Ball which I couldn't hear. She then whispered something to Danny Thomas, who was shaking his head in disbelief. I could hear Danny Thomas saying, 'But he's perfect, look at him.' I couldn't hear what Lucille Ball said to Danny Thomas, but I didn't get to do the show.

To this day, I don't know what was said, and no reason was given for my not being hired. Of course, both Danny and Lucille Ball have passed on that bigger stage in the sky, but whatever it was, it doesn't matter as I have had a wonderful career and part of it included being in a Jerry Lewis movie.

ROUSTABOUT WITH ELVIS PRESLEY

Being in the film *Roustabout* was another of those career moves that I made because I felt it was an important film credit. I played a carnival strong man in a travelling show owned by a woman played by Barbara Stanwyck. My scene with Elvis Presley was so brief that if you blinked you would miss me.

Elvis is dancing down the midway at the carnival and he stops from time to time at an attraction as he dances and sings away. I was carnival dressing that allowed him, along with the sword swallower and the snake lady, to get from Point A to Point B in the movie and give him an excuse to sing while he does it.

People ask me what he was like, and I should say that 'I don't really know', as the only conversation I had with him was between takes when he introduced himself and shook my hand. All I can say is that he was very polite to someone who was a nobody at that time playing a bit part in his movie.

I had actually met him before at the Rag Doll when I worked there as a bouncer/doorman and he came to see his Memphis buddy, Lance Legault, perform at that club. Lance was a great performer, almost in the same rockabilly style as Elvis. I remember Lance's rendition of the song 'Such a Night It Really Was', which used to go on and on in the tradition of a dance marathon, and the rock 'n' rollers loved it.

Lance went on to be a serious actor playing the Colonel on *Magnum P.I.* and the killer in *Coma*, among many other important roles. He used his great voice to do the promotions for network television shows and many national commercials. Lance raises thoroughbred horses on his ranch near Tehachapi, where he spends time with his beautiful family, and he is still in the business with occasional acting roles and many voice-overs in commercials.

PAUL BUNYAN 'LIVE'

I ran into a young fellow named Ron Kinchella, who had a brother who worked at one of the big radio stations in Los Angeles, KFWB, which at the time was a boomingly successful Top 40 station with the usual 'standup' rock and roll format. Roger had changed his name to Roger Christian and was making big money. Ron was determined to break into the business, too, and shared his plan with me.

He was going to a radio and television engineering school in Burbank that prepared students to take a federal test which, if passed, gave the student a federal license to be an engineer at a radio or television station. All radio stations that had a directional antenna, or were over a certain amount of power, and all television stations had to have someone on the premises with this type of license at all times when they were broadcasting. This meant that they had to have at least two engineers and sometimes three if they were on the air 24 hours a day. To avoid this, stations would hire announcers that had these licenses as back-ups to their regular engineers. This provided people who had one of these licenses with a way to break into the business in small markets – and, if they were talented enough, to gradually move into larger markets.

At that time every television market in the country had children's shows with live hosts who would also do the commercials. *Bozo the Clown* was one of these programmes with a local host in every market. The *Popeye* cartoons also had a local host in every market. In addition, many markets came up with shows and hosts of their own.

I had been working on an idea for *The Paul Bunyan Show*, as I felt that this, along with cartoons, would provide the format for a children's show for a major market. Hosts who worked in major markets made very good money and I was looking for something steady and substantial like that.

I decided also to go to this engineering school and use the license to get my show started in a small market and then move it to a larger market such as Los Angeles. The tuition for the school was $600. To put that in perspective, the price of a new car in 1963 was about five times that amount. It would be like $3000 today, and for me that was a lot of money.

I figured that if I was going to pay all this money to go to this school, I better work hard and be a good student so I could not only pass the test, but do it in as short as time as possible. There was a lot of math involved, and I had not taken any higher math courses in high school like Algebra, let alone Algebra II or Trigonometry. I had avoided the higher math courses and opted for subjects that might be practical in my father's business, such as office practice, business law, typing, book-keeping and, of course, Speech I and II. Conquering the math involved in this course was the biggest accomplishment in my life up to that point. It was an extremely difficult course and I decided to really buckle down in order to pass it.

My hands are huge and it was difficult to write all the small numbers. I also tend to be a little sloppy when I write and I had to turn ruled paper sideways and keep all of these numbers in columns in order to do these problems accurately. I paid extremely close attention and used painstaking care when I worked out all of these mathematical problems.

In addition to tests on theory and circuit configuration, all of the students had to take a 75-question math test and pass it before you could take the federal examination. The day after we took the math final, we all came back from lunch and took our places at our desks. School started each morning at 8.00 am and ended about 10.30 each night, with just two one-hour breaks. It was a six-day schedule to boot, and extremely exhausting.

Bill Ogden, the owner/instructor at the school, had been an instructor in the military, and he used intimidation to keep you at constant attention. For example, Mr Ogden had two plaques on the wall in the classroom. One said 'OIC' and the other 'RTDQ'. When he caught someone daydreaming, he would ask them a specific question about what he had just explained. When they got it wrong and Mr Ogden had to explain everything all over again, they would invariably say 'Oh, I see!' And Ogden would yell 'Join the club' and point to the 'OIC' plaque.

Federal and state tests have something in common in that they seem to use trick questions and answers to fool people. One of their favourite tricks is to ask, 'Which of the answers below is the most correct?' And in a five-answer multiple-choice test, all of the first four answers can be correct, with answer number five being, 'All of the above are correct' – which is the 'most correct' answer and therefore the only one counted right. Ogden wanted to prepare us for this, and when one of the students fell for the trick, he would point to the other plaque, 'RTDQ', and yell, 'Read the damn question.'

Right after lunch on the day of the 75-question math final, Mr Ogden said very loudly, 'Kiel, I'm mad at you!' I was terrified. What had I done? 'You aced my math final,' said Ogden, 'and no one has ever done that before. It must be too easy! I guess I'll have to make it harder.' I drew a sigh of relief. I couldn't believe it. I had made a perfect score in what I thought was going to be the most difficult part of the course.

I do remember in my senior year of high school taking an aptitude test which rated me highest in mathematical aptitude and suggested that I should pursue a career in science or engineering. Of course, as my high school education was practically over, it was too late for this information to do any good.

Needless to say, I passed the federal examination for the Federal Communication Commission's First Class Radiotelephone Operators License the first time I took the test. When Ogden's nephew, who taught the nightly math class, left the school to take a job at Cal Tech, I was hired to take his place.

Having the engineering license in hand, I proceeded to send out applications for employment to various television stations on the West Coast. I used a different approach than most people. Rather than just sending in a resumé, I instead sent a package with my concept for the show, along with a large paper circle with a string attached to it and a weight on the end.

I instructed those receiving my concept for *The Paul Bunyan Show* to pin the paper circle, representing my head, on the wall in such a way that the weight on the end of the string touched the floor – explaining to them that by doing this they could see how tall I was. I also enclosed an outline of my huge hand. Looking back at this, I can truthfully say that these kinds of simple hokey ways to get people's attention work much better than some of the more traditional and slick methods that I was able to use later when I had more resources. I finished putting together about two dozen of these packages and mailed them from Bill's Ranch Market, an all-night supermarket which had its own Post Office.

I went to bed expecting that in a few days I would hear from some curious programmeme director who might be interested in me as his combination children's show host/back-up engineer. I wasn't expecting the phone to ring at 8.00 am the next morning. A voice inquired 'Paul?' to my sleepy 'Hello.' 'Is this Paul Bunyan?' 'Paul who?' I responded, taken off guard by such a quick response. 'Paul Bunyan.' 'Oh, yes,' I responded. 'This is Paul Bunyan speaking.' 'What is it going to take to get you up here?' the man asked.

I wasn't at all prepared to hear from anyone just a little over eight hours after I sent out my packages, and to this day I do not know how the mail in Burbank got to Medford, Oregon the next morning, but it did.

'I don't know,' I said. 'What did you have in mind?' This wasn't what the man on the other end of the line wanted to hear. I had sent out my movie and TV credits along with my concept, and I am sure that he was afraid that I would want more money than a small station in Oregon could afford, so he was hesitant to make me an offer.

'Why don't you come on up and we can talk about it?' said the man. Little did he know how difficult that would be for me with my old car, but I said, 'Sure, I'll get up there soon and we can discuss it.'

I put the phone down and got some coffee, and as I began to slowly wake up, the phone rang again. 'Richard Kiel?' said a deep voice on the other end of the line. 'Yes,' I said, 'this is Richard Kiel.' 'Bob Geller here,' said the voice. 'I'm the programmeme director for KHSL Radio in Chico, California and we are interested in doing something with you at the Chico State Fair as Paul Bunyan.'

I had no real interest in breaking into radio, let alone working at a fair as Paul Bunyan for a radio station. 'I don't know,' I said. I was really looking to do my Paul Bunyan show on TV, and I hadn't thought about personal appearances.

'KHSL owns a television station, as well,' said Geller, 'and a radio station in Redding. Doing this would give us a chance to meet you and maybe something could be worked out in regards to your doing your show for us at our TV station. Right now, however, I am trying to put together a promotion for our radio station at the state fair and I thought you might fill the ticket.'

My first thought was that Chico was somewhere up in Northern California, which was a lot closer to Medford, which was in Southern Oregon, and perhaps I could kill two birds with one stone and get paid for doing it. I made a modest financial arrangement with Bob Geller to be Paul Bunyan for KHSL Radio at the Chico State Fair and started looking for lumberjack boots and a red checkered shirt to go over long red underwear and a lumberjack type hat.

Paul Bunyan (for those readers who may not know) is part of American folklore, and – along with his blue ox Babe – the subject of many larger-than-life stories. In the photo section there is a shot of me being Paul Bunyan, complete with a wooden axe, taking pictures with youngsters and oldsters alike at the fair. It was a big success, and I soon found myself in the office of Bud Stulpnagel, the programme director for KHSL-TV. I was also introduced to Bob Pope, the station's engineer, who couldn't believe that I also had an engineering license. KHSL Radio was located in the same building as the TV station and, being a directional radio station, they both required having someone with the kind of license that I had to be on the premises at all times. KHSL-TV and Radio already had a couple of announcers that also had the license, but having one more to back up the real engineer couldn't hurt.

Mr Stulpnagel, being an a actor at heart, wanted to play Ole Olafson in my show and he decided to try and hire me if I was willing to take the position of merchandising director, which was the only job that was available immediately. He promised me that as soon as they could find a sponsor for the show, I would also become Paul Bunyan on Saturday mornings. I was to be paid the whopping sum of $500 a month to do all three jobs, but I considered it a learning experience and a step toward doing the same show in a larger market perhaps a year later for $5000 a month or even more, so I took the job.

After selling the large items we owned at a garage sale and packing everything else into cardboard boxes, which were shipped by Greyhound bus to Chico, Faye and I made the trip from Glendale to Northern California on that same bus. A single night in the one and only hotel in town was all it took for me to get situated and on the first morning I was there Bob Geller sent me with a salesman to try and sell Bill Bowman, a local soft-drink bottler, on being the exclusive sponsor for *The Paul Bunyan Show*. The man was already bottling Canada Dry and Squirt, but he had a contract to introduce Dr Pepper into five Northern California counties. Bowman decided to sponsor my show, and as a result of that commitment the salesman took me to Newton's Auto Mart, where I was furnished with a green two-tone Cadillac sedan which was about nine or ten years old.

Bobby, Faye's son, had decided to go to Ogden Radio School with our financial help, and he passed the Federal test on the first try and landed a job at a small radio station in Mt Shasta, California.

During my time as Paul Bunyan, I drove around Chico with a sign that started on the front fender of my car and ended on the back fender which stated: 'KHSL's Paul Bunyan in a giant value automobile from Newton's Auto Mart, 1616 Park Avenue, Chico, California.' I did supermarket appearances for Dr Pepper all over Northern California's five counties and was very popular. Dr Pepper provided six-ounce sample bottles that I was able to hand out at supermarkets. Some of those kids could drink a dozen bottles or more.

When I first started at the station they didn't even have a video tape recorder or VTR, and I had to do my show live on Saturday mornings at 8.00

am. We invited kids to come on the programmeme from all five counties that the station and the bottler served, and it was good PR and marketing for both the soft drink and the station.

I had to get down to the station early in the morning and make sure the old tube-type cameras were turned on ahead of time so they would be warmed up and ready to go when the show started. We only had one cameraman and two cameras, so the cameraman had one set up as a static camera and moved the other one around while the engineer would switch from one to the other. I had a professionally done theme song recorded in Hollywood by a singer friend named Larry Hayes. The staff announcer, Bill Windsor, who opened the show with a wonderfully deep voice ('It's *the Paul Bunyan show...*' etc), went on to become a network announcer at NBC. Faye did the various puppets and did them quite well, including Babe the Blue Ox. It was difficult for her because she had a very small, quiet voice, but she managed to do Babe with a lot of humour.

Doing a live show could be a disaster as kids would arrive late, and frequently sickly, from the long winding ride, sometimes even throwing up. We gave every child a six-pack of Dr Pepper and one little girl dropped hers on the cement studio floor at the beginning of the show, creating havoc until we mopped up at break.

It was a lot of fun doing the show. I asked the kids the same kind of loaded questions that Art Linkletter would ask on his national show *Kids Say the Darndest Things*. Such as, 'If you could be anything you wanted to be, what would you be?' You would expect kids to say, 'A doctor, nurse, or school teacher,' which they did, but sometimes they would let the dark side show and say they would be a worm. When asked why, they would say weird things like, 'So I could go underground and hide!' Another loaded question was, 'If you had a million dollars and could buy anything you wanted, what would you buy with it?' The typical heartwarming answers would be, 'Buy Mommy a new washing machine!' or 'Daddy a new car!' But every now and then one of them would reply with their secret desire, like, 'I'd buy a whole bunch of candy bars.'

Sometimes they would say things that they thought would please me, or maybe because they didn't want to be greedy. I remember one little girl, when asked what she would buy if she had a million dollars, replied with a big smile, 'A Coke?' My sponsor was Dr Pepper, but that didn't matter to her because as far as she was concerned all soft drinks were Cokes. Fortunately, my sponsor had a good sense of humour and laughed his head off.

Sometimes the answers weren't quite as innocent. There was one young boy who, when asked what he wanted to be when he grew up, replied, 'A policeman.' I followed up with the usual, 'Why do you want to be a policeman?' 'So I can catch the robbers.' He went on to tell me, 'You better be nice to me, my father's the head detective on the Chico police force and he's recording this show!'

I should have left well enough alone, but I followed up again just like Art Linkletter would have done. 'Why do you want to catch the robbers?' I asked. 'So I can get the money,' replied the youngster. 'You can't keep the money,' I replied. 'I can't?' exclaimed the boy in a very disappointed tone. 'No!' I said. 'You have to give it back.' 'All of it?' asked the boy, sincerely. 'Yes!' I said, 'all of it!' I couldn't help but wonder how much ribbing his detective father would get over his son's final remark, when he said in total innocence, 'Well, I'd keep a dollar.'

Fortunately, I was in good standing with the Chief of Police, who would help me with all the parking tickets I'd get at KHSL, which had no parking lot and meant you had to park on the street and feed the meters.

My sponsor, Bill Bowman, liked to drink at the time and was a huge, over-weight fellow. Every time he would walk into a bar, he would loudly roar 'Kazork!' This had become his trademark, so I came up with a contest to write the best story about a 'kazork', with the winning boy and girl each getting a new bicycle. The station would put the best stories in a pile on my desk, and I would read them on the show. One particular Saturday morning I was reading a typical letter for the first time and it went something like this, 'Once there was a kazork that was different from all the other kazorks because they had tails, and this kazork was very unhappy because he didn't get any tail at all.' You can imagine how hard it was to keep a straight face with that one.

Chico was a college town, and the college kids were my biggest and most loyal audience as the show had a cult following with the students. They enjoyed the campy way we treated Paul Bunyan, who told outlandish stories with the help of cartoons while his puppet buddy, Babe the Blue Ox, made fun of him by saying things like 'Come on Paul, nobody's going to believe that!' They also enjoyed the conversations with the kids and the goof-ups that came out of doing a live show.

Every weekend I made personal appearances up and down the valley and into all the mountains, from Lake Almanor and all the way to Weaverville, a small former mining town in the Trinity Alps. We even got up to Mt Shasta to visit with Faye's son Bobby and to see the radio station that he worked at. I think it was kind of a culture shock for him; all of his friends were in Southern California and unless you snow-skied there wasn't a whole lot to do in this small tourist town.

I think it was hard for Faye to do the show and go with me on all these personal appearances. As Paul Bunyan, I was instantly recognisable and loved everywhere we would go. No one seemed to care that she did the puppets and Babe the Blue Ox.

All in all, however, it was a fun time. The biggest problem was that the owner of the station, a widow, let her stepdaughter supervise the station for her when she wasn't around, which was a lot of the time. The stepdaughter and the other women at the station were a clique that you either catered to or you did not succeed in your job. I was a young man of 24 and wasn't about to butter up what I considered a bunch of old ladies. They were actually women about Faye's age and weren't looking for anything more than compliments and innocent schmoozing.

Because of my unwillingness to be a charming liar and tell the stepdaughter how great she looked each morning, and my failure to write an Ole Olafson role for Bud Stulpnagel to play on the show, I was soon on my way out the door. I suppose that my refusal to share some of my personal appearance revenues with the station to help offset my huge $500-a-month salary was another reason.

For me, the bitter reality set in when the News Director got upset on learning that I was making as much as he was and he had been News Director for at least five years. When I told him I only made $500 a month, I thought that I was complaining, but he was devastated to learn that I made so much. As soon as the station got a videotape recorder, I quickly made a recording of the show, complete with the puppets and cartoons, and headed for the bigger markets where I could make some real money.

I got into my 'Giant Value from Newton's Auto Mart' Cadillac Fleetwood sedan – with that big sign on each side I was able to buy it cheap – and headed back to Los Angeles. Faye now had her own car which we had purchased while working at the station and we drove back to Southern California separately.

Our house in Redford, Michigan

Mom and Dad in love

Me, with my dog Queenie

My first bike

My first time on a horse

Me with Grandpa Baylis, my mother's grandfather

Me, Brook Tilley and Louis Guida

Me, Uncle Art and Donny Brown

My mom's father and mother

Dad the dude

Dad, his mom and my mom

One of dad's fancy cars

As our family got bigger, with my sister Georgann…

....so did our house

Why we moved to California

Mom, Sis and I on the way to California

Our first 'house' in California. At least my sister seems to like it

Going fishing with Dad

Starting to think BIG

Little Genie age 10

Big Genie much later

My sister Georgann and nerdy me

Little Sis getting the mail at our second-hand store on Garvey Avenue in South San Gabriel, California

Georgann and I in front of our very pleasant house in north El Monte, which Mom and Dad sold to go into the appliance business

The car I drove through the garage door

Mom in back of our store, getting ready for Halloween

Mr Greeley, my freshman English teacher, who encouraged me to get into public speaking

Selling refrigerators

Our store in Baldwin Park, California

Trying to be 'bad'

Klondike with J Patrick O'Malley

The late Herman Zimmerman, my agent for over 20 years

Master Styx in *Thriller*

Eegah

Serving Man in *The Twilight Zone*

As Paul Bunyan, during the first promotion for KHSL Radio in Chico, California

My ex-wife Faye, who operated the puppets on *The Paul Bunyan Show*

With my 7'3" friend Bill

With Jerry Lewis in the original *Nutty Professor*

As 'Big Frank' in 1965, in the process of doing five supermarket appearances per day

As a giant Indian in *Lassie*, with John Provost

The Man From U.N.C.L.E., with Robert Vaughn

The Wild, Wild West with Robert Conrad

The Wild, Wild West with Michael Dunne Conrad

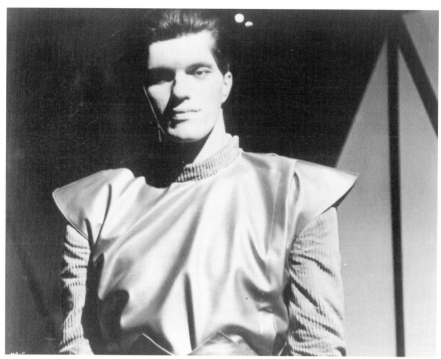

Dr Kolos in *The Human Duplicators*

As a Russian submarine captain in
Gilligan's Island

I was a teenage monster in *The Monkees*

As Samson, breaking everything in *The Longest Yard*, with Burt Reynolds

A picture which Burt
Reynolds took

Meeting with then Governor Jimmy Carter

Diane, the year we met

At my 20-year class reunion. Diane is 22

Renewing our vows, almost 20 years later

U.N.C.L.E., THE MONKEES
AND REAL ESTATE DEALS

On the way back to Los Angeles, we stopped at TV stations in Oakland, Sacramento, San Jose and Fresno, California. There was interest at all of these stations, but I really wanted to see if we couldn't get situated in the Los Angeles market before accepting anything anywhere else.

Within days after our returning to Los Angeles and renting an apartment in Glendale, I had a couple of interviews set up at Los Angeles TV stations. As the appointments weren't for a couple of days, I decided to stop by Ogden Radio School and see my friends there. The date was November 22 1963, a day that would go down in infamy as the day President John F Kennedy was murdered in Texas.

While I was in the office talking to one of the secretaries, we all heard the shocking news. I had called my agent the day before and let him know that I was back in town. I called him to talk about the Kennedy shooting, and he said that he was so glad I'd called since he had just received a request for me to do a small role in a television pilot at MGM. The show was the pilot for *The Man from U.N.C.L.E.*

The studio drove me to the Lever Brothers' Soap Factory facilities right off of the Santa Ana Freeway in an industrial area of Los Angeles. As we arrived at this vast industrial facility, which was composed of huge pipes and boilers, and drove through the guard gate, I couldn't help but notice the Nazi-type uniforms on guards that were waiting to go to work on the production. It was more than just a little eerie, considering the events of the day, and I wondered if there wasn't some giant conspiracy underway to take over our great country.

It turned out to be just a television pilot starring Robert Vaughn, who was such a close friend to President Kennedy he couldn't do the scenes that were scheduled for the day, necessitating some quick changes which meant bringing in some people like me and others in order to do an action scene instead.

I did the small part in the pilot and, when it sold, I had the opportunity to interview for a much bigger role in an episode later on.

All my interviews with programme directors about *The Paul Bunyan Show* were cancelled because of the emergency 24-hour-a-day coverage of the aftermath of the Kennedy assassination. Television programming on all stations was cancelled, too, and it took a few weeks for the programme directors to get everything sorted out and back on schedule. The momentum that I had going was brought to a halt and I never was able to get my appointments reaffirmed. In the meantime, I found myself back at work in episodic television and really didn't have a lot of time to schedule new appointments. The small role in *The Man from U.N.C.L.E.* turned into a chance to play a much larger one after the pilot sold, and I ended up working a lot in television that year. The national tragedy of the President's assassination inadvertently changed the direction of my career, and I never did get back into the market of hosting a children's show.

The interview for the bigger role in *The Man From U.N.C.L.E.* was with five guys in a small office at MGM. 'We're looking for a guy who can pick up one man, throw him over one shoulder, knock out another guy and throw him over the other shoulder and throw them both into a Dempsty Dumpster! Do you think you could do that?' 'Sure!' I said. 'Come here!' – motioning to the five men – 'Which one of you wants to go first?' They all remained seated. 'No, that's okay,' one of them said. I got the part, and it was the beginning of a steady stream of work. If you ever see a re-run of that episode, you will laugh at how I accomplished those physical tasks with the help, of course, of the director Alvin Ganzer.

BREAKING INTO THE STUDIOS

People, including media interviewers, frequently ask me: 'How did you break into the movies?' I usually answer them humorously, waving my arm across in a sweeping movement and saying, 'I just broke right in and became a studio.'

In truth, breaking into the movies is not easy, and I want to share with you some of the tricks and techniques that I had to use to get inside these inner sanctums of movie-making.

The big studios were the hardest to get into. They not only had guards at all entrances, they also had very strict policies. Warner Bros was probably the hardest, as Jack Warner was a tough guy, and someone had managed to steal a large boat and trailer off the lot once in broad daylight, which made him very mad.

One of my techniques for getting in was to rent a Western costume and sit in a restaurant across the street from a studio that was making Westerns at the time. When the actors wearing Western costumes would go back into the studio, I would walk with them and the gate guard thought that I was just one of the returning actors from the Western movie or TV show and would never stop me.

The smaller studios were easier as most of the productions were independent and that meant that there wasn't the kind of tight security the big studios had. I found that I could make friends with these guards when I would go in and out on legitimate interviews and I got to know a lot of them by name. I remember one of the guard friends at Producers Studio even telling me that there was a science fiction movie about to start production and they were starting to cast it. He told me that the producer, Hugo Grimaldi, had just gone to lunch, and he described him in detail for me before letting me go in. I found the producer in the commissary and sat at a table across from him. Of course, he noticed me right away and asked me who my agent was.

Shortly after meeting Hugo Grimaldi, I got word from my agent that the director wanted to see me. When I arrived in his office, I was disappointed to find out that he was interested in my playing the part of a doorman at a mansion owned by a scientist.

Other things were happening in my life at that time. A good friend of mine whom I had helped get into movies, Bill Engesser, was working for the Morrell Meat Company, appearing on Los Angeles children's shows and appearing at supermarkets as 'Big Frank', the man from Morrell. He arranged an interview for me with the chairman of the board.

The chairman had invented the famous 'Little Oscar,' the character for the Oscar Meyer Company, and had been hired by Morrell Meat Company to come up with something successful for them. At the time I was committed to doing the Greater Ohio Scouting Exposition for the Boy Scouts in the Columbus Ohio area, an event arranged by an Ohio television station which had responded to my Paul Bunyan brochure. Also, the programme director for the station in Columbus was going to be talking about me coming there to do my Paul Bunyan show, and they were flying me in.

The Morrell Meat Company wanted me to come early, stop in Chicago and meet the chairman of the board before going on to Columbus. I did this and was approved enthusiastically by the chairman, but told that I would have to go to Ottumwa, Iowa to meet the working Vice-Presidents. They flew me to Ottumwa in the chairman's private plane and, after meeting with the Vice-Presidents, I was told that I was hired, but because it was not coming through an agent, they wanted to pay me ten per cent less than my friend Bill made.

That was a little disturbing, but worse yet, they didn't want to give me a new Ford Thunderbird convertible like Bill was driving, but rather the standard company car, which was a four-door Chevrolet Bel Aire. I okayed the salary but held firm on the car, as I felt that Bill and I should be on a par. I found out they were getting Bill's Thunderbird for free from the Ford Motor Company and, due to a change in Ford's policy, they couldn't get a second one.

I told them that they were already saving money without the agent and that, instead of the Chevrolet Bel Aire, they should step up anyway and furnish a comparable car to the Thunderbird. I told them that I would prefer something bigger like a Pontiac or Oldsmobile convertible. They said 'No way,' and that if I changed my mind, the job with the four-door Bel Aire was open. In the meantime, they wanted me to go to the company clinic and give blood for a tuberculosis test. I told them 'No way,' and that I would take the tests when they came up with an acceptable offer.

They sent me back to Chicago on the train, which I actually liked better because I got to ride in the Pullman car, which had big swivel seats that were quite comfortable.

I did the Greater Ohio Paul Bunyan Scouting Exposition and found myself in the office of the TV station in Columbus Ohio, talking to the programme director about coming to work there. We were just getting through the small talk when the programme director's secretary busted into the meeting, saying that I had an emergency phone call. I picked up the phone and was surprised to find myself speaking with one of the Vice-Presidents at Morrell Meat Company.

Apparently, they were in trouble with the chairman for not making a deal with me, and they tracked me down to tell me that the job was mine with a Pontiac Bonneville convertible, but they had to have their answer right now. I said 'Yes,' knowing that a bird in the hand was always better than two in the bush, and I didn't make the move to Columbus, Ohio.

After a two or three-week training period in Southern California, where I drove around with my friend Bill watching him be 'Big Frank' and talking about old times, I was told that I would be sent to the Oakland, California plant to be Big Frank in San Francisco. In the meantime, Mr Hugo Grimaldi, the producer of *The Human Duplicators*, had met with his writer and decided that, instead of the doorman part, which I had turned down, they wanted me to play the lead role of Dr Kolos.

I told the Morell people that I had this commitment to do this movie and would have to do it before making the move to San Francisco. They reluctantly agreed, knowing that I was not one to buckle under pressure.

It was a great part, full of sensitive moments. I played an android who is sent to Earth on a mission to duplicate top scientists and officials so the aliens could take over. One of the people that I am supposed to duplicate is a beautiful blind girl named Lisa, played by Dolores Faith. Dr Kolos is so taken by her that he cannot bring himself to duplicate her and, in the end, is destroyed for that failure.

It was a low-budget movie, but very good practice. The movie had a great story but really hokey special effects. Unfortunately, I was convinced by the director that Dr Kolos needed to deliver his lines somewhat robotically, since he was an android. I obliged, and the ultimate effect was to make me sound like a bad actor. After all, Kolos wasn't really a total android or he wouldn't have had feelings about the beautiful blind girl and wouldn't have shed the tear that brought back Lisa's eyesight when Kolos had to leave her behind, knowing he would be destroyed.

The writer, director and producer were happy, but I learned a great lesson about speaking my piece when I knew I was right and not letting the director or producer talk me into something that I knew wouldn't work. Many years later, I used that experience when I was making the second James Bond film. I was also reminded that I didn't appear nearly as big as I could in films unless the director used special camera angles. A good example of these angles working correctly is the scene in *The Longest Yard* where I am lifting weights and Burt Reynolds recruits me for the football game. I was standing on an apple box and the camera was looking up at me from a very low angle, exaggerating Burt's point of view. When the camera was looking at Burt from my point of view, it was high above me, although I was still standing on an apple box, and it was shooting down on Burt across the back of my head. The result: he looks tiny and I look much taller, like a giant man.

I found that some directors were open to my suggestions to shoot my scenes like this and others were not. That's why in some movies I seem so much bigger than life and in others I do not. I really didn't care if directors accepted my suggestions or not as it helped me to look like a different actor in each instance. That's why I'm not always recognised in my more conventional roles like Captain Drazac in *Force Ten From Navarone*. I just look like a very big man and, with the costume and the beard, I look nothing like Jaws in the James Bond movies.

BIG FRANK, THE HOT DOG MAN
I finished *The Human Duplicators* and reported to the John Morell Meat Company's offices in Oakland, near Jack London Square.

The Oakland people were not enthusiastic about my being there, and neither was the advertising agency that was in charge of the account. They felt that they were being forced to take a programme that had been developed in lowly Los Angeles and that such a programme would never work in the Bay Area, as they call San Francisco, which they felt was an entirely different market. I had no idea that there existed such snobbery from people who took great pride in being second and third generation San Franciscans.

Don't get me wrong! I absolutely loved the Bay Area, all of it, from the big beautiful city with its bridges and high hills all the way to its suburbs like Walnut Creek and Concord, where I lived, and from places like Pittsburgh and Antioch on the river to Sausalito and Tiburon to the north of the city. I liked it there so much that I busted my butt to make the promotion a huge success. The advertising agency hated the promotion, having been forced to abandon the one that they had come up with, which was the Morell Meat Company 'Happy Hearts Club, where we put our hearts on every package'.

One of the advertising agency people was doing a children's show on KTVU in Oakland called *The Kookie Kastle Show*. They advertised Morell hot dogs and lunch meat on this show and another from San Francisco called *The Mayor Art Show*. Both of these people made appearances for Morell Meat and their 'Happy Hearts Club'. I knew down deep that they hated the promotion, resented me and would do everything they could to make the promotion fail and make me look bad. But I succeeded in making the promotion a huge success, as children love 'giants' and whenever I appeared, however briefly, on these children's shows to announce my weekly appearances, thousands of children would show up with their parents.

I was doing five supermarket appearances a day and driving all over the Bay Area to do them. I would leave the house at 6.30 am with the top down on my convertible, put the top up as I went over the bridge to do an appearance in the city, and find myself putting the heater on when I got to the fog in South City. I loved it, even though it meant having to wait until the traffic died down and usually eating in some family-style Italian restaurant before heading home.

The powers that be up there would not let the programme be a success, however, as they claimed that the extra cost of the promotion was not paying for itself. They expected that my weekly expense should be immediately offset by an increase in sales sufficient to generate the profit it would take to do so. They did not consider the long-term PR benefits.

In Los Angeles, the salesmen had been trained to demand putting five of our Morrell Meat items on sale in the newspaper ad the week of an appearance. They were able to get the stores or supermarket chain to do just that. In the Bay Area this wasn't happening and I asked to go with the salesmen who said it couldn't be done so I could show them that it could. I had no problem getting the clients to do this as all you had to do was ask. The salesmen, however, were order-takers with no initiative other than to write down whatever the meat buyers requested and no more.

At one appearance at an amusement park near the ocean there were thousands of kids, and they were pushing and shoving to get their free picture and balloons. I was afraid that some of the smaller children would get hurt or even crushed, and I stopped handing out pictures to yell at the bigger kids, who were pushing, to stop. It was at this moment that I saw that the advertising people had a camera on me to apparently show Ottumwa what an ogre I was. And I knew that, no matter how hard I tried, they would never let this popular promotion be a success in the Bay Area.

I was told that I was being transferred to Memphis and then on to Cincinnati, and I was very disappointed as I very much enjoyed living in San Francisco. I decided to return to Southern California and go back to being an actor.

Again, that door closed and, as my wise mother would have said, 'Better doors opened'. My career in television and, even better, movies was just about ready to take off.

MONKEYING AROUND WITH THE MONKEES

One of my favourite experiences in my career was doing *The Monkees* show. I got to be a gay interior decorator and rock 'n' roll singer complete with long hair, granny glasses and the obligatory paisley shirt. Oh, I almost forgot. I start out as a monster.

The most fun part was being able to ad-lib along with the guys, and I had a ball doing all the dance-type goofy stuff to music and all the other crazy things that the Monkees and their friends did. My rendition of the gay interior decorator was really out there and today it wouldn't be considered politically correct. But in the era that it was done, it was considered humorous. And it was funny.

I saw first-hand how the Monkees, who were really talented, were also over-worked and underpaid. Their contract included the TV show, the records (without additional revenue), plus doing concert dates. I was sitting talking to them when their producer told them what time their rehearsal would start that night after the shooting of the TV show, and one of them asked, 'When do we get to eat?' They were told that they could order pizza in if they didn't want to wait until they got home. I had the feeling that they would probably have to pay for their own pizza.

The show was only on the air for a couple of seasons. Not because it wasn't popular or getting high ratings, but because the four guys wanted more money, and the producers wouldn't give it to them. Today things are different. Stars of successful shows get their contracts adjusted in spite of pre-agreed options in their contracts, and half-hour sitcom stars make as much as $750,000 an episode, or even more.

The Monkees have several songs in the Top 200 of all time and they did it in just a few years. I believe that the producers and songwriters could afford to be stubborn because they had already made enough money and figured their stars would cave in. Unfortunately for the fans they didn't and that brought the show, the records and the concert dates to a screeching halt.

I'm glad to see that they have all done well in their lives since. My wife Diane had a crush on Davy when she was in her early teens, and when I saw that they were playing in concert in San Bernardino California, we went out to see them and she got to go back stage and meet them – and of course, Davy himself. When Davy sang the song 'Day Dream Believer' he dedicated it to Diane, which made it a very memorable night for her. And she's still a Day Dream Believer.

I DREAMED OF A PREGNANT JEANNIE

It was about the same time that I was in *The Monkees* that I got to play a role in another of television's most popular shows, *I Dream of Jeannie*. We shot part of it at the old Columbia TV ranch, which was located right in the middle of a residential district a couple of blocks from NBC Studio in Burbank. The interiors were shot at Columbia Pictures in Hollywood.

I played the role of Ali, an old boyfriend of Jeannie's whom she winks up to make Tony jealous. There was a scene where I carried Barbara Eden in my arms, and I was told to be careful as she was about six or seven months pregnant. If someone hadn't told me she was pregnant I would never have known because she'd really kept her weight down.

She had been in an earlier television sitcom called *How to Marry a Millionaire*, where she played a character called Loco Jones, and I thought she was one of the prettiest women on earth. I really was excited about getting to swoop her up in my arms; excited, that is, until I was told how pregnant she was. And the day that I was to do this, her now-former husband, Michael Ansara, was there visiting the set. Michael Ansara wasn't quite as big as I am, but he's a pretty big guy and he played a lot of fierce Indians in his career. We didn't finish that scene that day and it was put off until the next morning. That night I had dreams – or should I say nightmares – about carrying Barbara and dropping her. Just before I woke up, I remember seeing Michael Ansara's unhappy face coming after me.

The next day everything went fine, and I had no problem carrying her and doing what needed to be done. If only the person who warned me to be careful had said nothing, I would have been just fine.

Larry Hagman was a real nice guy to work with and I remember calling him sometime later when some of my relatives wanted to visit a show and *I Dream of Jeannie* was real popular. Larry said, 'Sure, you're welcome to bring them out, but we're going to be rehearsing a bunch of pick-up scenes that we want to film the next day and we won't be in costume.' I said that would be fine and brought my relatives in to see the rehearsals. My cousins were elated as they watched the show regularly. Unfortunately, my aunt wasn't such a fan. When I introduced her to Barbara and Larry, she turned to me right in front of them and said, 'When are we going to meet some stars?'

SELLING LINCOLN-MERCURY CARS

I passed a dealership one day that was called Cinema Lincoln Mercury, and its logo had kleig lights shining into the sky like at a movie opening. I thought this might be the perfect place to begin a career selling cars. My father had sold Ford-Mercury cars in Michigan and had done quite well at it. Funnily enough, he had also taught math at the Henry Ford Trade School prior to that, as he was once a tool and die maker until he was injured at work and took the job teaching.

It's funny how we inherit things through our genes and how my own life paralleled my dad's. He probably would have become an actor had he lived in California in his youth. He was a sharp dresser and even looked like a famous actor of the time, Otto Krueger. Yes, Dad might have been an actor but, unlike me, he would have been a leading man.

I did real well selling Lincoln-Mercury cars. I partnered with a guy named Dick Buckley, and together we sold more cars than anyone else at the dealership. Separately, I won many of the sales contests, including a console model colour TV, lawn furniture, and even a trip for two to Hawaii. While there, Faye found a real estate agency on the main boulevard that was offering three-acre lots on the big island for just $1260 cash. She found a deal on a local airline that allowed us to go to that island and check out the property for about $25 each. We flew over and, frankly, I wasn't too impressed as the lots were near Hilo and about five miles into what was literally a jungle.

People had built homes and were living there, but you had to catch water on your roof and store it in tanks since there was no running water available. It rained so often that this didn't seem to be a problem, and people even had swimming pools. The lava soil was fertile and covered with wild orchids and banyan trees. People would run out to greet you if you slowed down in front of their house as though you were some long-lost friend. I believed at the time that they were exhibiting the 'Aloha' spirit, but learned that they had to pay to get the electricity extended out to their property – and when another house connected onto their power line, they got some of their money back.

We eventually bought three of these lots for cash and I sold cars like crazy to pay for each of them. I even interviewed at Pfleuger Lincoln-Mercury in Honolulu and was offered a job there. Traffic was heavy, and the only affordable housing (in the $20,000 dollar area) was way out at Makaha Beach, and I decided that the round trip through traffic would be too difficult. We also found some lots on the big island of Hawaii, overlooking the ocean at Kalapana (black sand) beach, that were only $3000 each. They were long, skinny, one-acre lots, and we bought three of them with the idea of living there ourselves one day. The three lots together made for a nice rectangular lot with privacy.

The nice thing about working for a new car dealer at that time was that, if you sold at least eight cars a month, you got your demonstrator free and they even paid for the insurance. My first demonstrator was a silver Park Lane four-door hardtop with a black vinyl top. It had power windows, power seats and a tilt wheel. The first thing that I did was to take 'my' new car to a drive-in restaurant so I could show it off. Faye wanted to take a trip to Palm Springs and visit an old girlfriend so she could show off 'our' new car and brag about our Hawaii property.

We stayed at the Motel 6 in Palm Springs, which was literally $6 a night at that time, but the only phone in the room was a pay phone, and you had to put in quarters to make the little black and white TV work. The rooms were air-conditioned, though, and the pool was heated with a fantastic view of the surrounding mountains. Faye's girlfriend immediately noticed the dealer plates and broke Faye's bubble by calling 'our' car a 'loaner car.' She apparently had test-driven cars for a couple of days and thought that was what we were doing. Over the years, she learned that I always had a new 'loaner car.'

It was about this time that Faye and I bought our first house. It was one of those houses you see in Los Angeles that hangs on the side of a hill. This house hung over a park in South Pasadena, while the house itself was on a street in an area of Los Angeles called Montecito Heights. It was a brand-new two-storey house with new carpeting and fresh white walls. It had a built-in oven, plus garbage disposal, and we were in seventh heaven. We soon noticed that the bread board had carving marks on it from a knife and found out that the builder had gotten into financial trouble so he rented some of the houses out to provide income to help cover his payments until the houses were sold. This was against the rules of his lender, and they foreclosed on all the houses and allowed us to buy the house directly from them through a realtor for $22,000 with only $2000 down. This sounds strange, but it was 1967 and you could buy houses then for what a Toyota Camry costs today. The payments, including taxes and insurance, were only about $175 a month.

I had bought Faye an almost-new Mercury Comet coupe at a sale the car rental companies held. It only had 7000 miles on it, and she was very proud of it. We had paid cash and decided to sell it in order to come up with the $2000 for the down payment we needed. An old couple who were retired and on Social Security were trying to buy the car but couldn't get financing. I approached my bank with the idea that we would co-sign for them, as we really wanted this new home badly. The banker replied that he could just simply loan us the money instead and then we wouldn't have to sell Faye's car.

We bought a second house a few months later on that same street from the same lender and at the same terms. The lender had foreclosed on it, and it needed to be freshly painted inside and the rugs cleaned. The realtor suggested we offer $20,500 on this one with $1,500 down and no payments until 60 days after escrow closed. I borrowed the $1,500 from our friendly banker, completed the painting and carpet cleaning during escrow, and the day escrow closed, it was rented out for $500 a month. I collected the first and last months' rent and a cleaning/security deposit for a total of $1,100.

Because we didn't have to make a payment for 60 days, we had two $500 rent payments come in and only had to pay about $165 out of that for our first payment, so we were able to pay back the bank loan and have money left over every month from the rental income. We bought a third house a few months after that at the same terms, and about a year later we were offered a fourth one across the freeway that had been foreclosed on by the same lender. This one had a baby grand piano in it, which I traded in on an electric player piano for our house.

In 1969 I went to work for a Toyota dealer located at the base of the hill below and found that I could sell Toyotas as easily as cracking sticks. How's that you ask? How could I even fit into a Toyota? I couldn't, and that made it easier. 'Go ahead and take it for a spin,' I would say. 'No, you drive it,' they would reply. 'I can't,' I would say. And they would have to drive it themselves. Well, a four-door Toyota Corona with automatic transmission was only $2231 at the time and was built like a Swiss watch, making them very easy to sell. I sold 27 of those little cars in one month, taking every other weekend off. The average commission was about $100 each, and back then, $2,700 a month was a whopping big salary. In addition I was winning sales contests, getting an Accutron watch and a home beer bar to go with my colour TV, electric player piano and my outdoor lawn set, which was on the upstairs deck overlooking the park.

The same realtor came up with a deal on a five-unit apartment complex high on a hill overlooking downtown Los Angeles in an area called Echo

Park. The units were actually individual houses that ran up the hill with about 50 yards of steep steps between them. At the very top of the hill and steps was a large house that had a big downstairs area with a separate door. The lender had foreclosed on the five units and was willing to completely renovate them with their own crew, putting in new electric and all new plumbing fixtures. They would also paint inside and out and put on new roofing material.

The five units were offered to us for $35,000 with $3500 down and 6.6% interest, with the same deal of no payments for 60 days so we could rent them out and cover part of the down payment. We bought the five units and turned the top house into two rental units. By the time the lender was finished renovating we had them all rented.

MAKING THE MOVIE 'A' LIST, OR, 'IF THIS IS THE BIG TIME, WHO NEEDS IT?'

I was doing real well selling cars and investing in real estate, buying repossessed houses from lenders and getting them fixed up again so they could be leased out to cover my payments. I also found that I could buy large parcels of land, divide the parcel into four pieces and sell two or three of the parcels for what I paid for the whole thing.

My agent called to tell me that the famous director, Otto Preminger, wanted to interview me for a new movie that he was making called *Skidoo*. The movie was to be a comedy and it literally had the kind of cast that made *It's a Mad, Mad, Mad, Mad World* such a big success: Jackie Gleason, Carol Channing, Groucho Marx, Arnold Stang, George Raft, Peter Lawford, Cesar Romero, Mickey Rooney, Slim Pickens, Burgess Meredith, Frank Gorshin, Frankie Avalon, Alexandra Hay, John Phillip Law, Fred Clark, Robert Donner, football star Roman Gabriel, and a young actor who had just won a Tony Award on Broadway named Austin Pendleton.

I was excited just thinking about working for the director of such prestigious films as *The Man with the Golden Arm*, *The Cardinal*, *Exodus*, and older classics like *Laura* and *Forever Amber*. I was warned by some of my actor friends that Preminger had a bad reputation, for being very nasty with actors. I wasn't worried though. I always knew my lines, was never late and because of my size was never picked on.

My decision to go ahead was confirmed when I met the famous Mr Preminger. He seemed extremely charming and seemingly humble, almost as though he was reading my mind regarding him. He told me that he had followed my career and thought very highly of me as an actor and that he would be very pleased if I would accept this role in his movie. Wow! I thought. This guy is nothing like his reputation. Nobody had ever talked to me like that before. I reckoned that everyone was mistaken about him and were just exaggerating his difficult demeanour.

Boy, was I wrong!

With the financial security of getting this role and a contract for a couple of months' work, I went ahead and borrowed the money from the bank to buy the five unit-housing complex in Echo Park. The role itself was that of a Trusty who, along with Frank Gorshin, another Trusty, makes a deal to help new prisoner Jackie Gleason get together with Michael Constantine and Austin Pendleton to hatch a plan. The meeting takes place in the prison mess hall where we are all eating prison stew. Before we did this big scene, I had occasion to watch the infamous Otto at work, and I began to understand why my friends had warned me about him. He would not allow the young starlet, Alexandra Hay, nor the older Carol Channing, to wear any make-up. In fact, nobody in the cast was made-up. This didn't bother me, as I was fairly young at the time and didn't have to worry about bags and dark circles, but I couldn't help but notice that these leading ladies were going around in tears most of the time.

I had a simple little scene to do where Frank Gorshin and I bring Jackie Gleason to his cell. We had to walk down a long hallway at the old Lincoln Heights Jail, escorting Gleason in front of dozens of jeering inmates who were waving their arms through the bars at Gleason, who was the new jailbird in town. Otto had tried a few takes before lunch, only to be informed by the script supervisor that the inmates were wearing watches on their wrists that were waving wildly at Gleason as he came down the hall. Otto was upset with the extras about this and yelled at them. We shot the scene over and over, but none of the takes was to Otto's liking. To be fair, perhaps some of them didn't work because of the camera moves and the like, but Otto was becoming very unpleasant.

In the movie business, they have a rule that the director does not talk to the extras. If he does, they become actors, with their pay being about tripled. Preminger was becoming very angry. He was not getting what he wanted, and you couldn't help but notice that he spurted out saliva when he barked his orders to the assistant director, who passed them on to the extras playing prisoners in the cells. Up close his skin was transparent or translucent, as though you could see right through it, and he really looked weird, like some kind of angry, spitting, white frog.

At first I was amused by all this, and during lunch I watched Mr Preminger deal with the press, and he was the same charming guy that interviewed me. He wasn't spitting saliva and he looked human again. After lunch, we went back to the hallway scene and after hours and hours of doing it over and over, he finally seemed happy; or, at least, he wasn't so angry. The script supervisor, a woman who was used to working with him, was trying to get his attention all during the scene by pulling on his shirt sleeve.

Preminger responded by literally pushing her away, as though he was getting what he wanted and was not about to be distracted by some 'stupid woman'. After he finally yelled 'Cut, print,' he turned to the script supervisor to see what she wanted and the lady whispered something in his ear. After hearing what she had to say, Preminger literally exploded, yelling at the top of his voice at the extras: 'You idiots! You have your watches on again!'

(They had put them on before going to lunch and had forgotten to take them off again.) 'I will not pay you for today! I am not afraid of the extras' union.' It was a very nasty scene and, finally, after the little man fumed and fussed for a while, we did it over and over until he finally called it a night.

I was more than a little taken back. I had never heard a director get so personal before, calling people 'idiots.' I figured that this was probably an unusual event caused by the circumstances, but I remembered seeing Carol Channing and Alexandra Hay all red-eyed like they had been crying, and I began to not like this director.

When we finally got around to the mess hall scene, I realised that shooting scenes over and over and over was Otto's typical style, and so was yelling at people. He insisted that we all actually take huge helpings of the stew into our mouths and that we talk with our mouths full, and he made sure that we swallowed every big bite. Over and over we shot the scenes, until we were all beginning to feel sick and bloated with the canned stew. And all the time Otto is barking out instructions to us, the saliva is spurting from his mouth and all over our stew.

Preminger then started to pick on Austin Pendleton, whom he claimed was screwing up every scene. Keep in mind that this young actor had just won the prestigious Tony Award for his work on Broadway. 'You want to be an actor? You must act!' he yelled at Austin, with saliva flying everywhere. His skin took on that strange translucent quality as he concluded, 'You stink!'

What I saw happening was appalling. Apparently, Austin Pendleton had overcome a stuttering problem through therapy, and because of the intimidation and verbal abuse, he was beginning to stutter again; quite badly, in fact. He tried to reason with Preminger, who was shaking his head in disbelief. Austin was stuttering uncontrollably by now, turning to Jackie Gleason and saying to him, 'I don't un-un-understand the mo-mo-motivation…' And Gleason said to him, 'The motivation is to get it done and get the hell outta here!'

I could tell that by then Jackie Gleason just wanted to finish this picture and go back to Florida and play golf. I wanted to finish it myself so I could get my money and pay back the loan the bank gave me for the down payment on the apartments.

The next day we were all on hold because Preminger must have known that we would all be sitting on our toilets getting rid of all that Dinty Moore canned stew that we had been forced to eat the day before. When we came back, Otto decided to be nice. Austin was able to get through the scene without stuttering and we finally heard those wonderful words, 'Cut, print!'

The premise of the movie was that Jackie Gleason is a former hit man for the mob who is forced out of retirement and goes back to prison to do a final job of killing someone who's in there. The comedy is supposed to come out of the fact that someone puts LSD in the prison food and we all act bonkers, doing very bizarre things that are supposed to be really funny. During the bizarre episode, I had a scene where the Frank Gorshin character slaps the

Beany character (that's me) across the face to wake him up from his LSD wacko hallucinations. Preminger proceeded to show him how to do it, with the saliva sputtering all over us, and then actually slapped me hard across the face.

In the movie business, nobody really hits people. You just make it *look* like you're hitting people, and with the right camera angle and the sound effect, you can't tell the difference. I guess that it was this little man's big chance to slap a big guy like me in front of everyone and get away with it.

I'm a pretty cool-headed guy and I have learned in life how to control my temper and walk away from senseless fights, but after watching this jerk abuse people for weeks, I was not my usual calm self, and I put my nose in his face and in a hoarse whisper told him: 'If you so much as touch me again I'll f***ng kill you!' He got the point and, because he sensed that I really meant it, he never did anything or said anything that might possibly upset me from that moment forward. In fact, I got called back to do some looping on the movie, and as I was walking to the sound stage he stopped to give me a ride in his car.

I went to the cast party and was surprised to see that he had a beautiful wife who was a lot taller than he was. Everyone was dancing but Preminger and his wife. At that time, I was drinking heavily and, with a few too many drinks in me, I decided that I would repay this guy for all his abuse by dancing with his wife. She was a very good dancer and we were just starting to dance when I felt someone tugging at my arm. It was Otto reclaiming his wife. For a moment I felt a little sorry for him and what I had done, and I soon left the party before anything else might happen.

The film opened at the Bruin Theatre in downtown Westwood. It played for just a few days before closing. I remember going to see it there with about a dozen people in the audience. The scenes that were supposed to be humorous were very difficult to watch because they were just too bizarre and also because, at that time, drugs such as LSD were not the subject matter for jokes. Preminger actually hired the Green Bay Packers to do one of the hallucination scenes. The entire line of these huge football players suddenly were naked and the patrons were looking at seven or eight 300-pound butts, bare-ass naked on the screen.

Needless to say this comedy was not as funny as it was shocking, and you could see the strain on all of the actors' faces, who couldn't help but show that they were not having fun doing this movie. One by one the people in the movie theatre began to leave and, when the end finally came, there was only one other man in the dark room who was brave enough to sit through the entire movie. Paramount Studios not only shelved this movie, I don't think it ever went to video. Thank God!

Some years later, I learned that Johnny Andriasano, the former boxer and referee who choreographed the boxing scene in my very first show, *Klondike*, had allegedly been humiliated by Otto Preminger in front of everyone and as a result committed suicide.

DIVORCE – AND REMARRIAGE

Faye found a little cabin in the mountains in a place called Cedar Pines Park near Crestline. It was small and quaint, but it had an adjoining sleeper cabin so you could have friends up. I loved that cabin. It had nothing in it of value except an old refrigerator and stove, which nobody would steal, and the furniture was old and funky so you didn't have to worry about damaging it. The cabin was real cheap and it needed some fixing up, which we did on my weekends off. It was during the repairs that Faye met a guy named Bob Gardner, who was a handyman and helped us with the remodeling.

Then we bought a 40-acre ranch in the high desert with a house on it and a corral for horses. We sold off 30 of the 40 acres to family and friends and created a one-and-a-quarter-acre pond for swimming and fishing. I bought a Toyota Landcruiser station wagon with four-wheel drive for $2700, so I had a new Toyota to drive which was not a loaner car.

About that time, Faye bought an old truck and hired Bob to put some big, metal-framed picture windows she found at a salvage yard into the walls of the biggest house in our Echo Park complex. The house overlooked the lights of the city and the new skyscrapers that had gone up in downtown Los Angeles. This increased the amount that the big house would rent for and made the long hike up all the steps bearable for people that would rent it. She also put Bob Gardner to work helping her convert the underfloor area of the two houses closest to the street into small student apartments. She didn't get any building permits to do this.

I no longer sold Toyotas, having gotten a real estate license, and was working for a broker selling lots in three subdivisions in Big Bear Lake. I was doing exceedingly well selling real estate, and the realtor found a couple more houses that we could buy and fix up. At this point, we had three rental houses and now the eight units in Echo Park. Bob was now working full-time for Faye and was fixing up the old ranch house in the high desert or working on the apartments. He got a free place to live and was paid a living wage.

I was driving a new gold-coloured Cadillac convertible with a white top and gold seats. It was perfect for showing lots in the summertime with the top down, and I would use the Toyota Landcruiser four-wheel-drive station wagon in the winter. I sold building lots in the three subdivisions in Big Bear for the broker and then in three more subdivisions in the Fresno foothill areas. I made good money and enjoyed working outdoors. Eventually I progressed to selling large parcels of land in the area where we had the ranch in the high desert.

When the lease was up on the convertible, I found that Cadillac no longer made the larger De Ville convertible and the El Dorado was too small for me to drive. The dealer made me an offer on a Fleetwood 75 limo that had jump seats in the back but no dividing glass between the driver and the rear passengers. I believe they call this a 'Texas' limo. It was perfect for showing the high desert property, and I had a two-way mobile phone installed in it, so it was pretty impressive at the time, which was 1972, when hardly anyone had a phone in their car.

The only problem was having to collect the rent at the units in Echo Park, as I had to park the limo in front and climb up the steps to collect the some-times past-due rent. I felt like the stereotypical rich landlord when, in fact, I was not.

There are a lot of flakes out there renting houses and not paying the rent, and I ran into my share. There are also a lot of young girls and women who try to use their feminine wiles to get away with not paying the rent. This is compounded when you're driving a Fleetwood 75 limo. It wasn't unusual to be called by a young woman who was late with her rent and to be told that the toilet was 'blooping' – and yet when you would go there you could find nothing wrong with the toilet and the young lady laying around in her sleep-wear. I had to be hardnosed and collect the rent, and since I was doing so well selling real estate, it occurred to me that it was time to get out of the rental business and simplify.

Faye, on the other hand, was enjoying all this. She liked fixing things up and decorating. She didn't have to earn the money to buy the rentals and provide the funds to fix them up, and she didn't have to collect the rent or deal with the repairs; that was my problem. It got to a point where she thought that all of this, and our wealth or net worth, was mostly her doing, as she considered herself the brains behind the remodeling, which to her was everything. She seemed to forget how many nights I spent painting walls and repairing ceiling tiles after a long day of selling cars.

Faye's son Bobby had left the small radio station in Mount Shasta and had gone to Salmon, Idaho. After he left Salmon we didn't hear from him for over two years. I don't understand how a son could worry his mother like that by not contacting her for so long, but on the other hand, Faye had not related to her own mother by going to see her or inviting her out to see us for all the years we were married. In fact, I never even met her mother during those 13 years.

When we finally did hear from Bobby, he was doing very well and was driving a late model Cadillac coupe. He had become a short-order cook and had a new job in the Los Angeles area at Bob's Big Boy restaurant. He soon bought a brand-new red Volkswagen Beetle and a brand new motorcycle. He had a girlfriend and seemed very happy. But something happened between Bobby and his girlfriend and the manager of the restaurant, and he and the girl broke up. Bobby had moved out and was sharing an apartment with another young fellow when we got the news that he had hooked up a garden hose to the tailpipe of his VW and had committed suicide by asphyxiation.

By the time we got there, his body had been picked up by the coroner and we made funeral arrangements with a funeral parlour and cemetery out in the desert on the way to Palm Springs, where Faye wanted him buried. His motorcycle was covered by death insurance, and the funeral director took it as partial payment. Faye's brother Wayman took over the VW payments and drove the car for several years. The funeral director came in from Banning to pick up Bobby's body from the coroner, and he stopped at our house to get some papers signed. Bobby's body was in the back of the station wagon in a body bag, and I was furious at him for coming to our house and exposing Faye to such a scene. I managed to sign the paper and get him on his way before she came out and saw her son in a body bag, which she no doubt would have insisted on opening.

Although the marriage was already coming apart this was the beginning of the end, as Faye never really got over the death of her son. She would hear sounds that she identified with him trying to contact her. She spent most of her time thinking about him, and what she might have done, and started sleeping in the spare room. It seemed that she wanted to be by herself even though she was living in a house that she shared with me. It was a very difficult time for her and, of course, for me as well.

Finally she started to throw herself back into more remodeling as a way of covering her pain. She found a four-bedroom cabin in Big Bear that was on four small lots. The cabin was a large two-storey affair that didn't have electricity to it and the lights and electricity were furnished by a gasoline-powered generator. She was working on fixing up this cabin when the generator caught on fire, burning down the generator shed. The insurance company claimed the cabin was under-insured and, because of the type of policy, it reduced the payout for damages because of the age of the building and the generator. We decided to bring the electricity in and started the process of putting new siding on the cabin since a good part of it had been damaged by the fire. The guy that Faye hired to do the siding didn't put tar paper under it to keep the cold wind from blowing through in the wintertime and we – I – had to go to court to make him do it over.

The underfloor apartments that were created without permits were discovered by the City of Los Angeles building inspector, who called to arrange a meeting with me. I guessed he wanted a bribe, but he never would say so, and I wasn't about to bring it up for fear of getting in trouble. It turned into a nightmare, as the units were cited by the inspector and declared uninhabitable. I had to hire an electrician to bring the wiring up to code in both underfloor units, which only rented for $65 each at that time to students. I also had to hire a plumber to vent the little sinks and especially the toilets.

I appealed the decision by the City and was able to show my progress until the final correction couldn't be made and it was one that they required. The ceiling height had to be eight feet in order for the underfloor units to be brought to code. There was no way to do that so I told them that 'I could appreciate such a building code better than anyone, being so tall myself.'

I brought up the fact that many of the City's public buildings had ceiling heights that did not meet code. I cited examples that I had found at Los Angeles International Airport. I told the panel that we only rented to short students and I produced letters from these 'short' students that pleaded for their right to live in these economical little units. Finally, I said that if they would raise the height of their public facilities to meet the code, I would raise the height of the ceilings in these underfloor apartments. The members of the Housing Advisory Appeals Board looked at me like I was crazy until I said that in each instance this wasn't practical or even possible and asked for a variance, which I was promptly granted.

I told Faye that I wanted her to stop the remodeling routine and that I wanted to sell the rental properties, cash in, and simplify our lives. To compound things, Bob Gardner had stolen some of our cheques while he was alone at the ranch and cashed them night after night at a local bar. I refused to make them good, and he was in trouble with the bar and the law, so he wasn't around any more.

Things came to a head when Faye had a couple of men come out to the desert ranch from one of those 'helping hand' places that sent out recovering alcoholics. I came out to the desert ranch when I was in between projects and found these guys waiting to go to work who were officially on the payroll. I found some things for them to do and, when Faye finally arrived, she was furious that they were doing what I had told them to do. She barked orders at them and treated me like I was some kind of employee myself.

I was furious and took her into the house and proceeded to paddle her butt. She left in a rage and drove straight to Barstow to the sheriff's station, where she tried to get the local police to come out and arrest me. She wasn't injured, other than her enormous pride, and the sheriff found the whole thing kind of amusing, asking her what she had done to deserve a spanking. She apparently gave them a piece of her mind and, returning to find that I was still there, she left in a huff.

I WASN'T A SCHMOOZER

I suppose that some people would say that I dropped the ball by not staying in touch with all the contacts I have made over the years with famous people like Burt Reynolds, Dick Van Dyke, Clint Eastwood, Robert Wagner, just to name a few. It's just that I respect my own privacy and that of others. I run into these folks from time to time and I enjoy seeing them again, but after my experience with Jerry Lewis, I decided that I didn't want to impose upon major celebrities or movie stars. Besides, I had seen too much of the 'hangers-on' in my early days of acting, visiting Eddie Fisher's house where his brother Bunny and all his friends would hang out with nothing to do but play silly games like seeing who could throw the most cards into a hat or who could make up the funniest and dirtiest caption for picture stories in magazines, etc.

I also remember going to Red Foxx's house and meeting his family members, who were interested in doing a mock-up beer commercial with me in hopes that they could sell the idea to a bottler and make some money of their own. Nothing ever happened, I didn't even meet Red Foxx, but I saw my first projection TV, which at the time had a terrible picture.

I have never tried to put the arm on people I have worked with like Burt Reynolds or Clint Eastwood to try and get work or invest in my projects, because I knew how it felt when people tried to use me to get somewhere in the business.

Some actresses or would-be actresses will use anyone to get a part or get ahead in show business. To be fair, it must be said that the same thing would be true for their male counterparts. I started writing screenplays in 1965, and soon learned that if you had a small production office and a business card that identified you as a producer, you could take advantage of some of the thousands of young naïve girls that arrive from small farm towns in the Midwest every day, looking for that big break that will bust them into the movie business. It was something that I didn't have in my heart to do, but I saw it being done on a daily basis.

I remember the time when I was asked to be in a show honouring Ed Wynn. Because I had done *The Man From U.N.C.L.E.* television pilot and the other subsequent show where I had a featured role, I was selected to be in a skit with Robert Vaughn, David Janssen (*The Fugitive*) and Gene Barry, who was doing *Burke's Law* at the time. *Burke's Law* was a detective show about a wealthy investigator, played by Gene, who drove a Rolls-Royce and always had a beautiful girl at his side. Each episode seemed to feature three gorgeous females that hung all over the star.

That night, after the tribute was over, I went to the cast and crew party and noticed that Burke (Gene Barry) was surrounded by beautiful babes just like on his show. His wife was patiently watching all this while Gene was definitely taking it all much too seriously.

Back in the sixties, I did *The Roar of the Greasepaint* with Joel Grey and Cyril Ritchard in order to have done 'legitimate' theatre and not be looked down on by certain casting directors who thought that if you hadn't worked the boards you were not an actor. I also played one of the sons in *Death of a Salesman* at LA City College. While I was doing *Greasepaint*, I saw a very handsome and most excellent black singer named Jack Crowder bragging about how he didn't go out with black women because they hadn't experienced the finer things in life and how he preferred the company of white women. One of the chorus girls, who was beautiful and black, seemed to have a crush on Jack, but he would have little to do with her.

A few months later she appeared on a new television show called *Star Trek*, and I couldn't help but laugh to myself, as Nichelle Nichols knew when she was doing that play that she was going to be a regular on the show, but kept it to herself for all the same reasons talked about in the story with Gene Barry. She didn't want to be used and, well, Jack just missed out, didn't he?

A few years later, I did a show with Robert Wagner that featured Jaclyn Smith. I don't remember whether it was *It Takes a Thief* or *Switch*. She was so naturally beautiful with her perfect white skin and her long gorgeous hair. Most of all, she was very nice and a real lady. At the time, she was married to a young actor named Roger Davis who had made some successful real estate investments, including a small Beverly Hills mansion which he lived in with Jaclyn.

Not long after I worked with her and met him, I did a movie with Roger called *Flash and the Firecat*. His co-star was a young model named Tricia Sinbarra, who was a long-legged blonde and a 'real looker' as they would say where I came from. Roger allegedly stepped out on his wife to spend his nights with his co-star and I do remember Jaclyn coming out to the set in what appeared to be an attempt to try and snap him back into reality.

Although Roger had been one of the stars of *Dark Shadows* and had replaced the late Pete Duel in *Alias Smith and Jones* for a season or two, he had not starred in any films, to my knowledge, until getting this role in *Flash and the Firecat*. The movie was definitely a B-movie, or even a C-movie, and went unnoticed by the film industry. After the break-up of her marriage to Roger, Jacylyn went on to do *Charlie's Angels* and much more. Ironic, isn't it?

After I did *The Longest Yard* with Burt Reynolds, he invited me to go to Savannah Georgia with him and some of the other co-stars for the opening of the movie. Burt had the studio purchase the entire penthouse section of a 747 airplane. The penthouse was an upstairs part of First Class where they had a lounge that you reached by climbing up a spiral staircase. By purchasing all the seats in this area, we were insured privacy so we wouldn't have all the people on the plane asking for autographs.

While we were up there, the flight attendant asked Burt if he would mind if the flight attendant from coach came up to meet him since she was a big fan. Burt said that would be fine, and the first class stewardess went back to get her. When the flight attendant was shown into the penthouse area and saw Burt, she immediately jumped into his lap and threw her arms around him and proceeded to plant a big kiss on him. We watched as Burt started to unbutton her blouse, and she shot up like she had just been invaded by a red-hot poker. 'What do you think you're doing?' she exclaimed. 'What do you think *you're* doing?' asked Burt.

I realised in that instant that Burt was showing her that, although she felt it was all right for her to treat him like a sex object, she was appalled when he did the same thing to her.

I've come to the conclusion that any intelligent and sensitive actor or actress will always be wondering if someone is really interested, or is it because they are a movie star? Because of these considerations I have not taken advantage of my position as a 'movie star' and I do not invade other actors' privacy.

After the episode out at the ranch, I didn't see much of Faye. Wherever I was, she was somewhere else fixing up and remodeling things. It was a lonely time for me, and when I met a saleslady who was living in Big Bear and selling lots for the same broker, we started spending time together.

Elsa was just a few years older than me and had a teenaged son. We had something in common in real estate, but very little in common in other things. Both she and her son were avid snow-skiers and I got the shakes just looking down the slopes, as skiing was something I had never learned to do.

Faye finally discovered that I was having this relationship and was determined to put an end to it by threatening to commit suicide. I wasn't ready for that, and I broke off my affair with Elsa. I didn't want to have to deal with another suicide in my life.

Elsa moved to Palm Desert and I only saw her once after that, and it was fairly obvious, I think to both of us, that I would only be repeating my first mistake. I continued to work and live a life of loneliness until something happened that would change everything.

A LITTLE TOUCH FOOTBALL WITH JOHN BRODIE AND THE BOYS, AND 'THE LONGEST YARD'

After my experience with Otto, I was pretty turned off by the movie business and decided that, since I was doing really well in real estate, I would quit pursuing showbiz. I had just made a sale of 240 acres at $1000 an acre and was going to be getting a five per cent commission on the sale at a time (1972) when you could buy a new home for cash for about twice the $12,000 commission. I figured if Otto Preminger represented making the 'Big Time', who needed it?

A movie was being cast, however, that caught my interest. It was called *The Longest Yard* and was going to be directed by Robert Aldrich, who had directed *The Dirty Dozen* and *Whatever Happened to Baby Jane.* Two of the 100 most classic films of all time. Aldrich was considered a 'man's man' director, and I thought maybe I would give the 'Big Time' movies one more try. Unfortunately, Aldrich was also a former All American football player himself, and I couldn't get an interview because I wasn't a former football star.

My agent had associated himself with two other agents in order to cut costs since he was nearing retirement. One of the other two agents, Steve Stevens, had been a casting director and had cast a picture or two for the producer of *The Longest Yard*, Al Ruddy. Because he knew Al, he was able to get me in to meet him, with the hope that Al would then get me in to meet Robert Aldrich.

Al Ruddy was the original producer of the first *Godfather* movie, having optioned the film rights to the novel. Because of the huge success of *The Godfather*, he had the biggest office on the Paramount lot and virtually had the ability to do any project he wanted to do. This allowed him the freedom to do a movie script that he had written the original story for. He hired Tracy Keenan Wynn, Ed Wynne's grandson, to do the screenplay. Tracy had written the critically acclaimed *Diary of Jane Pittman*, which brings me to the point that *The Longest Yard* was originally a more serious piece and only because of people like Burt Reynolds, Aldrich and the supporting cast did it turn into the audience romp that it was.

To my benefit, Al Ruddy is about 6'8" and was not used to looking up at people. I think he found me somewhat intimidating, as the first thing he said as he stood up from his huge chair was 'So tell me, what the f***k's happening with you lately?' Remember, I had sort of dropped out of the movie business after my encounter with Otto and hadn't done anything lately. The Good Lord gave me just the right words to say to Al as I responded quickly: 'I'm here talking with you, Al, and that's what's happening with me lately.'

Al liked me immediately. After all, I was one of the few people that he could look in the eye without bending down and I probably outweighed him by 100 pounds. A meeting was arranged between myself and Robert Aldrich as a favour to Al. The casting lady, Joyce Selznick, a tough broad from New York, was against it as she had already turned me down, and I could tell that Aldrich was against it from the moment I walked into the room. I had been warned that only former football players were being cast in this film because apparently he felt it was just as important to get the football right as the acting.

He immediately asked me about my football experience. Anticipating that this might happen, I had put together a line of patter which included my playing in high school and that I got together with Brodie and the boys occasionally to play a little touch football in the park.

'John Brodie?' he asked me. 'You play touch football with John Brodie in the park?'

'Yes,' I said, looking him straight in the eye.

'I'd like to see that,' said Aldrich, obviously not believing me. 'Let my secretary know when you're going to play the next time and I'll come over and watch you in action.'

'Sure' I said. 'I'll let her know.' I'd also anticipated this, and through one of John Brodie's friends I'd actually made arrangements with a mutual friend to get to play touch football with him and the boys at the park.

Sensing that my claim was probably a charade but respecting my perseverance, Robert Aldrich laid it on the line. 'Richard, this is not going to be a fun movie. First of all, we are going to be in a little tank town in Georgia that consists of motels and restaurants. There's absolutely nothing to do there. We're going to be popping helmets and cracking heads nearly every day, either scrimmaging or playing real football. There's going to be a lot of hurt and a lot of pain. Do you think you can handle the pain?'

He was really serious and obviously trying to discourage me. He must have had a bad experience with an actor or two on *The Dirty Dozen*. I decided to take a chance and I pulled out all the stops and shifted into my best acting gear.

'Is it all right if I hurt them?' I asked with a kind of lunatic grin on my face.

'No, of course not! We don't want anyone getting hurt,' he replied seriously. 'It's just a movie!' To this day, I am not sure whether he completely bought my act, but he sure seemed to.

I called the mutual friend and made arrangements to play a little touch football with Brodie and the boys that weekend and then called Aldrich's secretary to give her the time and the place. She came back on the phone to let me know that Mr Aldrich, unfortunately, was going to be out of town that weekend and would not be able to be there. Fortunately for me, I didn't have to be there either, and the rest is history.

I did have to report for a round-table reading where all of the actors read their lines with the other actors so that the director could confirm his choices. You were pretty sure that you had the part if you got to go to this reading but it wasn't for sure yet. In fact, Wilford Brimley (the Quaker Oats Oatmeal man) read that day and was replaced for some reason by Michael Conrad.

I sat down next to a weight-lifter with bulging muscles and was handed a script with the name 'Sampson' handwritten on the front. I looked for Sampson in the script and found that he was actually George 'Sampson' Granada, a former Mr Florida and of course a weight-lifter. I looked over at the weight-lifter's script which had Bruno handwritten on the cover and checked out the part of Bruno. He was a big strong guy who worked in the prison slaughterhouse killing the cows and bulls with a sledgehammer.

'I think I have the wrong script,' I said to the assistant passing them out. 'Isn't he supposed to be Sampson?' I asked, pointing to the weight lifter. 'No,' said the assistant. 'You're Sampson, he's Bruno.' I wasn't about to argue as I liked the part of Sampson better, but I still thought he was making a mistake.

I read Sampson and the weight-lifter guy read Bruno. We were both cast in those parts.

I arrived for the production a few days later than some of the other actors and found myself in the little motel town that Mr Aldrich had so aptly described. Not only was there nothing to do there, there were no king-sized beds left in town. The studio quickly put together something big enough for me, and the next morning I reported for work at the maximum security prison in Reidsville, Georgia. The only thing that made me feel different from a real prisoner was that I had a plastic pass card with my picture on it identifying me as one of the actors, which meant that, unlike the real prisoners, I could go home to my motel each night.

I found myself being escorted through multiple gates and being taken to the prison 'sewing shop' where I was to try on my uniform. There were a number of women there who were bustling about in their high heels and short skirts. Most of these women were pretty young, and they all were quite busty and well-decorated with vivid lip colours and heavy mascara. Standing there with my uniform in hand, I asked where I supposed to change. 'Right here,' I was told by the guard. 'Here?' I asked. 'In front of all these women?' 'Women!' laughed the guard. 'These aren't women! They're guy gals!'

While everyone laughed, I took a closer look at them and, sure enough, they all had on wigs and they were all wearing falsies that gave them their busty look. Thank God my uniform fit and I was able to get out of there without having to hang around. It was more than a little weird getting hoots and cat-calls while I stood very briefly in my skivvies and hurriedly pulled my prison pants on.

These same 'guy gals' were allowed to strut their stuff around the prison in those days and were also the cause of many fights and even killings in Georgia State Prison, until we left some input that was to at least cause some changes in that primitive, if not cruel, prison system. You can see some of the characters that I am talking about in the actual film, as they were featured as the prison 'cheerleaders' in the movie. You can also see some of the real guards in the movie as they were used as part of the cast, as well.

I remember one guard in particular who looked like he had the head of a bulldog grafted on his huge body. He would check our plastic pass cards each day as we moved into the prison through the main entrance. This guy seemed to have no emotion as he checked each card; no personality, no small talk, nothing. After being there a few days and watching this big automaton-type person at work, I made everyone laugh by pretending to knock on his forehead with my knuckles, asking, 'Anybody home?' Fortunately, he laughed and so did everyone else, including some of the convicts and other guards.

The prison was also segregated when we filmed there, and I understand that this has since changed. There were 50-something guys in each cell block, and cell blocks were either black or white and not mixed. This was done for a reason, I suppose, but it sure seemed strange.

One day I forgot my plastic identity card and left it in my locker. I was chastised by the production assistant, who insisted that I get it before going out of the prison to have lunch in the visitors' area, which was where the visiting families would eat and visit with inmate relatives or friends. I made my way back to the dressing room area, explaining to each guard I encountered that I needed to get my plastic ID card before going outside for lunch. As I moved across the yard, I saw the gate open at the other end and a cell block of black prisoners were allowed to pass through, and all 50 of them were headed in my direction. Now, I had been there for only about three or four days at that time, and not everyone in the prison knew that I was an actor. Wearing the official convict uniform made me look like every other prisoner and, from a distance, of course, I do not look so big.

I think that I did some of the best acting in my life that day, as I moved through 50 black rapists, killers and child molesters going in the opposite direction at a maximum security prison. As they got close to me, I pulled my 7'2", 345-pound body up as tall as I could, and I tried to look as tough as nails. I must confess, however, that I never forgot my pass again.

A strange turn of events happened that inadvertently made it possible for my part to be enlarged. The weight-lifter guy had been upset because his weights hadn't arrived on the plane; he would check his muscles every day and get angry because they were shrinking. The movie company bought him a chrome-plated set in Miami and had them shipped in. Aldrich was right about the football scrimmaging, as it was tough. I ran laps around the track in order to try and get back in shape, but every night I was sore from all the blocking and hitting in the practice scrimmages. The weight-lifter got hit hard and it bruised his body, sending him into a tizzy. We were all holding round-trip airline tickets and the story I heard was that he borrowed a car from the motel manager and drove towards the airport until it ran out of gas, then he hitched a ride and took the next flight home. This left a hole in the script that had to be filled with something and I think that I turned out to be it.

The Longest Yard became a real blessing for me in more ways than one. First, Robert Aldrich was exactly the opposite of Otto Preminger, and he knew how to get the most out of actors, especially male actors. I discovered Aldrich's secret of success first-hand when I was filming the scene where Schokner (the bald-headed character who goes around doing karate stances) breaks my f***ing nose! I had some ideas on how to make the scene more interesting and I added a couple of ad-lib lines and some funny facial expressions. After working in my last film with Otto Preminger, I halfway expected Aldrich to start screaming at me like Otto had at Austin Pendleton. Instead, I heard 'Cut, print, atta boy, Kiel. That was great!'

Robert Aldrich was famous for his 'atta boys'. In fact, his camera operator kept track of them in chalk each day on the side of the main close-up camera. His other famous way of letting you know that he liked what you had done was to say, 'Give the boy a Goodbar.'

I was pleased. I hadn't made the 'Goodbar' grade, but I was satisfied with an 'atta boy'. Aldrich approached me and said, 'Richard, I love what you were doing, but I didn't say cut. I want you to do the scene again, and this time do even more of what you were doing and don't stop until I say cut.'

The scene was with Robert Tessier (Schokner) and Burt Reynolds himself. The three of us were being given carte blanche to extemporise to our heart's content. I did a lot of ad-libbing, making a big deal out of the fact that I think that Schokner broke my nose on purpose. Burt reacted perfectly, making the scene hilarious, first getting Schokner to apologise, and then again when he resets my broken nose. I ask, 'How do I look?' and Burt says, 'You look better!' – then to the crowd: 'He looks better! Don't you think he looks better?' And everyone agrees, making me very happy.

This time, when Aldrich said 'Cut, print,' there was no 'atta boy' or 'Give the boy a Goodbar.' Instead, he announced to the entire cast and crew, 'That was a terrific scene, and I think that Richard deserves a big hand for his performance.' And he starts clapping, with everyone joining in, of course.

What a difference that moment was to make to the rest of my career. I thought to myself, 'So this is the big time! Not so bad, after all.' When I think of the contrast between these two famous directors, Preminger and Aldrich, I cannot help but realise how true the old adage is that 'You can get so much more by using a carrot instead of a stick.'

Robert Aldrich was an unusual director in other respects, as well. He always shot with multiple cameras. If he was doing a close-up or a medium shot, he always had a second camera running for back-up, which meant we didn't have to do scenes over if a camera malfunctioned or the cameraman did a jerky pan shot.

When Aldrich was doing action scenes like the football game, he used many cameras. When we worked outside, the cameras were mounted on Land Rover vehicles. These Land Rovers had been equipped with dozens of mounting brackets where cameras could be installed at different heights. The beautiful thing about this was that the Land Rovers could be quickly moved and the camera brought into place in just seconds, and we didn't have to wait for the usual half hour while the camera made a move. Time is money in our business, and the cost of an additional camera and the film involved is small potatoes compared to the daily cost of actors and other payroll. I learned from watching this, and I also applied Aldrich's principle of using incentives like praise, atta boys and Goodbars to get what he wanted, instead of fear like so many other directors and producers.

While we were filming, I took part in demonstrating a prison rehabilitation system developed by California-based Narconon. It was a programme designed to teach the inmates how to deal better with employers, and wives, and was very successful. After the movie was over, I went with Neil Brown, the head instructor, to the state capital in Atlanta to meet with Governor Jimmy Carter. We discussed the need for positive rehabilitation programmes with him. He was receptive and even made an appointment with us to meet with a state senator who was on that committee.

They had counsellors in the prison but they apparently were political appointees that got paid to counsel while they were also going to college, as the only counseling we saw was the handing out of a Bible, and the book *The Power of Positive Thinking*. Although this particular Senator seemed to have little concern for the rehabilitation of the men who found themselves in prison, he did have a relative of his own in prison who he hoped we could help on an individual basis in some way.

A lot of changes took place as a result of our filming at the prison. The guy gals were no longer able to parade around in drag and segregation became a thing of the past.

One day while I was cashing my check at Universal Studios I heard someone call out to me, 'Richard!' I looked over toward the voice and saw a stranger. 'It's me, Tom Roche!' said the man. I couldn't place him until he said his nickname, Bankrobber, and I realised that this was a guy that had gone through our communication programme that Neil had taught. One of the grips had told him that when he got paroled and needed a job to look him up and he would try and get him a job in the studios. Living with his sister and working at his brother-in-law's restaurant hadn't worked out so here he was working at Universal Studios.

It made me feel good to know that at least in a small way we had been part of something positive.

A NEW WIFE AND A NEW LIFE
The best thing about doing *The Longest Yard*, besides getting a chance to act, was meeting my present wife, Diane. We have four children, three grandchildren and have shared a worldwide bunch of experiences together.

Our meeting was one of chance or perhaps destiny. After a week or so of working on the film and coming home to an empty motel room in the little town of Glennville, Georgia, one of the other football players and I decided to ask the production company if we could borrow a car and go to Statesboro on Saturday night, as we were both bored.

I was still married to Faye at the time, if you could call it that. I had become the typical unhappily married man who isn't really sure whether he wants to get into another relationship. I tried to grin and bear it, but it was getting tough. It seemed that wherever I would go, Faye would be somewhere else doing her own thing. There were lots of friends and relatives who enjoyed the desert ranch and the mountain cabin. When I would arrive, she would usually pack up and head for one of our other properties. I had been naïve and just assumed that Faye and I would have children, not realising that, with two grown children already, she didn't want to go through that again. We had thought about adopting sometime in our marriage but, thank God, we didn't go through with it. I could tell at the County Adoption Agency that Faye wasn't really very enthusiastic about adopting and I just let it drop.

My friend and I cruised around Statesboro, which is a small college town where Georgia Southern is located. Asking around about the hot spots, we finally found ourselves in a rock 'n'and roll disco called The Flame. He and I were standing at the edge of the dance floor, watching everyone dance, when I noticed a very pretty and very young girl standing next to me. 'You sure are tall!' she said with a smile. I thought that she was awfully young and so very short (5'1½"). I said, 'And you're kind of cute.'

Not for me, I thought. Too short. Too young. She probably wouldn't like me anyway. We began a conversation, however, and I soon realised that we saw eye to eye on a lot of things, although we weren't anywhere near the same size or age. That night we did a lot of talking and she shared her heart with me in such an honest way that it touched me as no one ever had before.

The next day we went on our first date to Savannah. The city is one of the oldest in America and is near the Atlantic Ocean. We went to Tybee Beach, which isn't far from Savannah, and discovered that there had been a near-hurricane recently. It was freezing cold as we walked along the beach, and we each had a cup of coffee from a little stand, trying to warm up. The wind was blustery, and we decided that it wasn't the day to spend at the beach.

We found a restaurant back in town called the Pirates House, which is located on the Savannah River. The restaurant is about 200 years old and is located next to an area that has been restored. Old clapboard houses with fancy trim have become law offices and others real estate or dentist's offices. It was like becoming Tom Sawyer and stepping back in time with Becky Thatcher as we walked down the little streets and visited this old and famous restaurant.

We must have looked like a classic romantic couple seeking a private nook when we entered and waited to be seated early that Sunday evening. The Captain's Room was vacant except for us, with a wonderful, cosy fire roaring in the corner fireplace. They didn't serve liquor on Sunday in Savannah Georgia, but it didn't matter as we were intoxicated with each other, and that weekend I fell very much in love with a girl who was too young and too short, but turned out to be just right.

The first thing I noticed about Diane that was so much different from the other women that I had met or dated was that she was so grateful for everything you did for her. In contrast, I could never make Faye happy. Faye's birthday was close to Christmas, and one year I got her a Cadillac El Dorado convertible for her birthday and a mink coat for Christmas. She was very disappointed in the El Dorado, reminding me that she had wanted a Lincoln Mark V, or whatever, and she exchanged the dark mink for a white one.

Diane, on the other hand, was delighted when I put new tyres on her seven-year-old car that she was paying for by working two jobs while she was going to school. Diane was coming to see me every day and I noticed that her tyres were kind of bald, and while we were eating at a restaurant, I had the gas station next door replace the tyres and fill the gas tank without telling her.

At the restaurant she enjoyed her first T-Bone steak and made me feel like a king being able to buy it for her. Diane had grown up poor in regard to material things; several of the houses she had lived in only had an outhouse. Things like fresh whole milk, butter and cheddar cheese were unheard of in her family, who were used to powdered milk, margarine and processed cheese, which when they got that was a real treat.

Although Diane was from a very small town she stood out from the other girls in rural Georgia. She was a very smart young lady, and somehow her working in the college town gave her a more well-rounded idea of life. In all of our years together, there hasn't been anyone who didn't truly love Diane. They may have disliked me for whatever reason, but they could never dislike her.

Somehow Faye found out that I was bringing Diane back with me and was at the airport waiting for us to appear. She stalked us wherever we would go and told me that she would never give me a divorce. This all came to a halt when I asked her if she would give me a divorce if she could have whatever she wanted. I told her to write out a list of the things she wanted and that she could have everything that she felt she was entitled to and had put on the list.

The city house, desert ranch, a couple of rental houses, the Echo Park apartments, the Big Bear Lake cabin, all the furnishings and several pieces of property in Hawaii that were paid for were all on her list. She let me have the vacant land that had mortgage payments attached and no income, and once a couple of these were paid off later, she even reneged on those. When it came time for me to get my personal things, I found that she wanted my type-writer which I used for my writing. I had taken typing in high school and, even though I wasn't a great typist, she had no typing skills at all.

It was a good bargain, and I have no regrets except that it made beginning a new life with Diane harder than it should have been for her. But like it says in the Bible in Proverbs, 'It is better to live in an attic with someone you love, than in a mansion with a nagging woman.'

After the divorce, Faye tried to renew her romance with the somewhat younger man whose mother didn't want him to marry an older woman. Unfortunately, for her, it didn't work out. I couldn't help but think that for all those 13 years that we were married, she was still carrying a torch for a guy who ended up not being suitable for her in the long run. It's funny how life deals us the cards it does. But one cannot fully enjoy the spring without first experiencing winter.

Diane and I started out with over $40,000 in short-term debt from my first marriage, a few hundred dollars and a car with big payments, but we turned it all into a wonderful life. It hasn't all been perfect, we've hit a few bumps in the road along the way, but with our love for each other, the love of our family and for our family, we have made our life together very special.

SEVEN

BACK IN THE MOVIES

It turned out that *The Longest Yard* wasn't going to be the only time that I bypassed the casting director to get an interview and a part. My agent, Mr Zimmerman, told me about a very good part he was submitting me for. There was a casting breakdown that he said described the role of Moose Moran as being a doorman at the Golden Gate Casino, who was nearly eight feet tall and half that wide. The part was in a movie of the week which was going to be starring William Shatner, who had done *Star Trek* by this point, and I was excited since it looked like another potential career-maker like *The Longest Yard*.

Herman reported back that I wasn't big enough, and that they were going with Ted Cassidy – Lurch from *The Addams Family*. I had lived through many years of people mistaking me for Lurch and wanting me to sign Ted's autograph. It was a difficult time for me as I was getting bombarded with these kinds of requests and having to deal with them while he was making all the money for actually doing the show.

I remember years later, after Ted had died, trying to get directions from a lady as to how I could get to Santa Cruz with my family. She totally ignored my protestations that I wasn't him, that he was dead, etc. 'You're him!' she insisted. 'Yes, you are!' I ended up giving her Ted's autograph so I could find my way to Santa Cruz before it got dark as I was desperately lost. I could imagine how she must have felt the next day at work when she showed everyone the autograph, only to be told that Lurch was dead.

BYPASSING CASTING WITH A REGISTERED LETTER

Anyway, I knew that Ted Cassidy wasn't nearly as tall as I or as big, and I shared that information with my agent. The next day he told me that now casting was saying I was too big. Something was wrong and I knew it, so I decided to take fate into my own hands. I wrote a letter to the producer, Doug Heyes, and to the director, Bill Bixby, saying that, like the character

Moose Moran, I had in fact worked as a doorman at a nightclub. I told them of my height and weight and all my television and movie experience, including *The Longest Yard*, and sent the letter certified, return receipt requested.

I informed them that I had not been able to get an interview and that I would not be upset if they didn't cast me after meeting me, but that I felt I should have a chance to meet them and that they should have the opportunity to meet me, as well. The next day, Herman called me to say that he had heard directly from the producer's secretary and that they wanted to meet me right away.

Both Doug Heyes and Bill Bixby told me how much they liked my letter and handed me a script to study for a few minutes before reading a couple of lines for them. I read the scene and said that I was ready to read for them. They were favourably impressed with my reading and said that if they could make a deal with my agent, they would see me soon in front of the Golden Gate Casino, playing Moose Moran.

I don't know exactly why I said what I did, because normally I would hold out for as much money as possible and not let anyone, including my agent, see me sweat. In this case, I did know that the casting directors, for some unknown reason, wanted Ted Cassidy to get the part and were keeping me on the outside. I also knew that they would be dealing with my agent, so I piped in with, 'Oh, you don't have to worry about my agent, he's real easy!'

At that very moment the casting lady popped through the door and, much to her surprise, saw me standing there. 'This is Richard Kiel,' said Doug Heyes. 'He's perfect for Moose Moran, and if you can make a deal with his agent, he's got the part.' Before the casting lady could get over her shock, Doug hit her with his concluding remark, which by its very words left her without any way to continue shutting me out. 'You shouldn't have any problem, Richard says his agent is real easy.'

I did the *Barbary Coast* Movie of the Week for just $1500 a week since I didn't want to give casting any way to try and shift them back to Ted Cassidy. The made-for-television movie's ratings went through the roof, doing so well that Paramount sold it as a new series for the upcoming season. For the first time in my career, I was a regular series star under contract.

It was a great feeling getting a cheque in the mailbox every Thursday that was so big you could hardly spend it all. Diane and I bought a new Chevrolet Caprice Classic convertible, candy apple red with a white top and interior. We took a ride with our new baby son, Richard George, all the way up to the Yosemite area where we visited Yosemite Lakes Park, a subdivision where I previously sold real estate. We came back through Kings Canyon where the snow started to fall on us as we drove through the giant redwood trees. Our little boy started to giggle with glee as the snowflakes fell on his face, and we reluctantly put the top up as it was beginning to get cold.

Unfortunately, the *Barbary Coast* television series was not enjoying the enormous success of the Movie of the Week that spawned it. 'Why?' you may ask. It wasn't hard to figure out. The television series had different players both in front of the camera and in back of it. The producer, Doug Heyes, was replaced with former *CHIPS* producer Cy Chermak, and Dennis Cole was replaced by Doug McClure. I am sure that Cy Chermak was and is a very capable producer, but he sure was different from Doug Heyes, who literally dressed in cowboy boots and cowboy hats. Perhaps if Heyes had continued on as producer the show would have been a success. Of course, we'll never know.

The late Doug McClure was a great guy and even more charismatic than Dennis Cole. Doug and I became close friends while working on the show as, coincidentally, he too had an unsuccessful first marriage to a woman named Faye and a great new marriage to a gal named Diane, so we had something in common. Doug was fighting a drinking problem, starting with wine during the day and progressing to the harder stuff in the evening. Like a lot of alcoholics, he was an easy-going guy who would rather resort to a drink than confront his problems head-on.

Because of Shatner's huge success on *Star Trek*, the producers and the network were coddling him and taking care of his every need as quickly as they came up. I remember a network assistant who was working on the show telling me that people would tune in just to see Bill urinate. Well, perhaps *she* would tune in to see that, but regular television viewers, like my mother, couldn't understand the show as it was now being shot.

The way *Barbary Coast* was written, Cash McCall, originally played by Dennis Cole and now by Doug McClure, was supposed to be the star of the series and the character played by William Shatner was supposed to be his sidekick, kind of like James West and Artemus Gordon in *The Wild, Wild West*. The two shows had a similar format in that the sidekick would use disguises in the show. The difference between the way Shatner played his disguised characters and the way Ross Martin played them was significant. You, the audience, always knew it was really Artemus (Ross) in disguise as he made no attempt to fool the audience. On the other hand, Shatner's disguise and make-up was so elaborate and totally convincing that no one knew it was him, including the audience, which confused the hell out of normal folks like my Mom.

Not only that, every shot of Shatner's character took hours to do, even if he was just walking down the wooden sidewalk. McClure, on the other hand, found himself with five pages of tough dialogue to do, sometimes at eight o'clock at night, and many nights he would end up sleeping in his motor home because he finished so late. Shatner got a phone installed immediately in his motor home, while Doug had to wait for weeks to get one. It was things like this that bugged Doug and I believe thwarted the success of the show. Anyway, it only lasted 13 weeks, which was a shame as it was a great concept.

Prior to signing up for the series, I had done a promotional tour with Burt Reynolds for *The Longest Yard* and was asked to go to Tallahassee with him, Lee Majors and Larry Zonka to do a fund-raising stint for Florida State's football team, which was on something like a 30 – 0 losing streak. It was a lot of fun to fly in a private jet with Burt and the boys and to be escorted from the airport to the football stadium by motorcycle cops with red lights and sirens. I was asked to say a few words that night in the football stadium and it was really disconcerting, if not scary, to hear your words echoing back to you a few seconds after you said them because of the loudspeakers causing a delayed echo.

On the way back, Burt told me that he was going to be doing another movie soon and that there was a part in it for me. When the movie, *Gator*, was announced, we were in negotiations for the *Barbary Coast* television series and I had Herman call the casting people doing *Gator* to find out when I was supposed to work. We wanted to fit the role into the three weeks or so that I wouldn't work on the series, as they only wanted to guarantee me ten out of the first 13 episodes. The casting director on *Gator* was very short with Herman, telling him that they didn't know what he was talking about. We signed for the *Barbary Coast* series without trying to make any accommodation and I figured that Burt had changed his mind.

I wasn't even on the show a week when the *Gator* people called Herman to let him know that they wanted me for their movie. He got the dates and told them that he would see what he could do. Herman suggested that I talk to Cy Chermak about the possibility that I work in the movie during the three weeks that I wouldn't be working on the series. Cy protected his own interests and said, 'Hmm, you're on a ten out of 13-week guarantee. Well, there is an option for us to use you for 13 weeks and I just exercised it!'

That wasn't what I wanted to hear, but it did mean three more cheques on Thursdays so I couldn't complain. Burt wasn't very happy about the situation. He'd done me a favour and got a part written into *Gator* for me, and I decided that the least I could do was get my old friend Bill, who had helped me get the job as Big Frank, to take my place. Bill did a great job and it's hard for me to explain to people that it wasn't me, as it's one of their favourite roles that 'I' played.

I can't know exactly how black people feel when people think they all look alike, but I have some idea since I have been confused with the guys who played Lurch, Herman Munster and the wrestler Andre the Giant, who played a great role in *The Princess Bride*. To some people, we all look alike as all they see is size. Just like to some people who can see only black.

I used to suffer from some of the same stigmas that black people do as people used to think that really big people are all dumb and bad. This was in part caused by the movies, which used big actors to play the dumb Frankenstein monster who kills the little girl even though he didn't mean to. Or the similar role that Lon Chaney Jr played in *Of Mice and Men*, where he kills a little girl by accident. I remember standing in supermarket lines before I was well-known and a little girl or boy who might be naturally fascinated with my size would smile at me, and if I smiled back, their mother would invariably snatch them up protectively.

I've worked hard to try and change those stereotypical images. Contrary to what many people believe, size has nothing to do with intellect or moral character. Hitler wasn't particularly big nor was Napoleon, but they wreaked their share of havoc on the world. In fact, I co-wrote and co-executive produced a movie years later called *The Giant of Thunder Mountain* where the main storyline revolves around this kind of prejudice.

NOT ENOUGH BULK FOR THE HULK

Not long after I did the *Barbary Coast* series, I was interviewed by the Marvel Comics people to do what was to be two movies of the week, which would serve as the introduction or pilot for *The Incredible Hulk* television series.

I was hired to play the role and was fitted for the full opaque green contact lenses and reported for work the first day on location. It took quite a while to get the green stuff put on by the make-up department. I remember that it was in the evening and the wet sponges were very cold, and they were dabbed everywhere from the waist up and from your shorts down; you could see legs through the shredded pants so they had to make them green, as well.

We finished at about four in the morning that first day, and I remember the make-up person handing me a jar of Abolene, which is a commercial make-up remover, and a couple of towels to take to my trailer. I tried my best to wipe most of the green make-up off but a lot of it was in places I couldn't reach and it was about to be dawn so I decided to drive home before the traffic got heavy and finish the job there with the help of my wife, Diane. We had just purchased the new convertible that had a white interior. By the time I got home the seats were no longer white.

The worst thing, though, was that the fluid they used to put in the full contact lenses apparently absorbed into my cornea and was causing a halo effect with rainbow coloured multi-circles of lights appearing around every streetlight, tail light and all the headlights coming towards me as I drove home. I've only seen out of one eye since birth and, consequently, it is very difficult for me to wear contact lenses as my good eye doesn't want anything stuck in it. Doing a show like this, you could expect to have these lenses put in and taken out dozens of times a day.

I arrived home, green and with a terrible headache. I jumped in the tub and tried to get the rest of the green stuff off, but with no luck. A lot of it did come off and the tub was stained green as a result. I fell into bed to wake the next morning on green-stained sheets. When I reported for work the next day, I told the production people that they would need to get me a motel room each night and that I would need a bath brush, if not a cute little assistant to get the green stuff off me in the tub at the motel. They graciously accommodated me and that day we filmed the scene where the Hulk carries a woman out of a burning building that explodes. This scene is shown at the beginning of each episode. I drove home experiencing the same circles around every light, and the rainbow colours were still there when I turned off the light and went to bed.

The next day, I received a call to let me know that I was on hold and would not work that night.

I talked with Diane about my concerns that my one good eye might get damaged if I continued doing this show. I could see it going on for years and I wasn't sure how I could deal with that. I also told her that everyone on the show wants it to go on forever, and here am I hoping that it stops soon. What should I do?

The following morning, I got a call from the producer who told me that the Marvel Comics people were not happy with me as I did not have the kind of muscles that the cartoon character had. They were right! In spite of the fact that I probably weighed 325 pounds, I was big and tall but definitely not a body builder. We had signed a contract to do two Hulk movies for television, and the anticipation was that these two TV movies would turn into a series. The producer offered to pay me for the two movies if they could replace me with someone with bigger muscles. They cast Lou Ferigno, who was perfect for the role, and he didn't have the same problems with his eyes that I did.

As a result of not doing the series, I was available to do other television shows and movies such as *Silver Streak* and James Bond. And I got paid for *not* doing the two TV movies so I was happy.

RIDING WITH RICHARD PRYOR AND GENE WILDER ON THE SILVER STREAK

Prior to doing the James Bond films, I was already off and running careerwise. As a result of the success of *The Longest Yard* and the exposure I got on *The Barbary Coast*, I was getting interviewed and called back for major motion picture roles.

I was interviewed and called back twice for *The Black Bird*, which was a comic remake of *The Maltese Falcon* and starred George Segal. The part would eventually go to Lionel Stander, who played the helpful butler on *Hart to Hart* with Robert Wagner and Stefanie Powers. My agent was shocked that they would consider Lionel Stander for the same role I was vying for. What he didn't realise was that they cast Stander because he was an interesting type, and they were considering me for all the same reasons. I believe that's why I got cast in *Silver Streak*. The killer on the train didn't have to be seven feet tall and weigh over 300 pounds, but it made him and the scene with Gene Wilder more interesting.

While I was working on *Silver Streak* I developed a hernia in my groin area. I noticed it on the weekend when I was taking a shower at a motel out by my mother's second home, which was on a lake in the desert. By this time, we had our little son RG and we would leave him with grandma at her home on the lake so they could enjoy each other's company, and we would get a motel room for a night or two so we could spend some time alone. I had carried the luggage up the two flights of stairs and I guess that's what did it.

On Monday morning I was supposed to break through the door of the train with a fire axe, and I saw that they had a real fire axe and the door I was supposed to crash the axe through was a real door. I mentioned to the assistant director that I thought I had just developed a hernia and was a little concerned about having to put the axe through the door for real. He sent me to the studio nurse, who was very young and as embarrassed as I was when I pulled my pants down for her to inspect my groin area. She immediately got on the phone and sent me to a small hospital facility to be seen by a doctor. The doctor examined me and wrote a note to the studio saying that I had a hernia and that they needed to be careful how they used me until it was repaired. I went back to work and smashed the door down with the axe in one take, much to my relief.

One of the grips heard about my situation and came to me to recommend a doctor in Long Beach who specialised in hernias and used a new technique (everyone uses it today) which allows you to return to work the next day. I had the surgery done and was better than new.

One of the things that I enjoyed about working on *Silver Streak* was working with the director, Arthur Hiller. He was a really neat guy and we talked quite a bit. I always studied the directors I worked with, and how they were different in one way or another, in the hope that one day I would get to direct something myself. I asked Arthur one day, 'What would you say is the secret of being a great director?' Arthur had done *Love Story* and certainly had a flair for doing things right. 'Richard,' he began, 'if you have a good script and a good cast, the rest is pretty easy.'

Years later, as I just mentioned, I got a chance to act as co-executive producer on a film project that I co-wrote, *The Giant of Thunder Mountain*. I hired a consultant who had directed films with John Wayne, Jimmy Stewart and many other big name stars to help polish our script and oversee the production with me. This allowed us to hire a very young, up-and-coming director who had done only lower budget films before. I knew that this advice I had received from Mr Hiller was good advice and I worked very hard with the director and the consultant to hire the right cast. With good professional actors in every role, the film went like clockwork and my curiosity about what it takes to be a good director paid off.

BOND – AND BEYOND

I was working on *Silver Streak* one day when I got called to the sound stage phone by the assistant director. I knew it must be my agent, since my wife Diane had been instructed to never call me at the studio unless it was an outright emergency.

Herman was excited, even though he was trying hard not to show it. 'Cubby Broccoli wants to have lunch with you tomorrow!' I said 'Cubby who?' He replied: 'Cubby Broccoli, the James Bond producer,' with a grin that could be heard over the phone. 'He wants to have lunch with you at the Polo Lounge of the Beverly Hills Hotel. See if you can get permission to have a long lunch tomorrow and call me back right away.'

I immediately ran the situation by the assistant director, who wasted no time in giving me a yes. Maybe *I* didn't know who Cubby Broccoli was, but he sure did.

The next day I drove the convertible into the hotel drive with the top down. I was grateful that Diane and I had bought a new car as I remembered the days when I was invited to dinner at this hotel and parked my old beat-up car as far away as I could so nobody could see it. This time I pulled up for valet parking and made my way towards the Polo Lounge. The *maitre d'* informed me to take a seat as Mr Broccoli would be along shortly. A few minutes passed by very slowly as I awaited Mr Broccoli's arrival. I couldn't break the habit of being on time even if everyone else thought it was fashionable to be late. I was early and I hoped that it didn't make me look too anxious.

A well-dressed rotund man approached my table and I arose to meet the famous Cubby Broccoli. He was right out of the movies as he had a some-what gravelly voice and he talked a little bit like Marlon Brando in *The Godfather*. 'Cubby' didn't waste any time getting down to business and over lunch he proceeded to tell me about the character he was considering me for. First he told me that the director's secretary had seen me on the *Barbary Coast* television series, which was then running in England, and thought the director should see me. Cubby went on to say that, because he was coming over to the States on other business, he decided to meet me himself.

He also told me that they had already considered David Prowse, and, seeing that this didn't register with me, he explained that David Prowse was the guy in the Darth Vader suit in the *Star Wars* film, then being produced in England. My excitement at the possibility of being in a Bond movie began to dim slightly; it didn't take much of an actor to be in a head-to-toe suit, especially when James Earl Jones was saying all the words. 'The character we have in mind,' said Cubby, 'will have special teeth, either like tools or like a shark. They will be made out of shiny steel and he kills people with them.'

'Oh, no!' I thought. 'No wonder they're considering the guy in the Darth Vader suit. This is a monster part with a monster that has horrific teeth and he goes around killing people with them.' For a moment I thought, 'Here I am, working in a major motion picture playing a killer on the train who talks and has scenes with Gene Wilder. Why consider playing a monster role?'

Quickly, before I said anything, another thought passed through my mind: 'This is a James Bond movie. Why not try and make the most of it. You know how much you love James Bond movies...' As a compromise, I spoke some pretty brave words considering the eventual outcome. I had learned from experience that it is important to play a part in a way that you feel it will work for you. 'I believe you need an actor for this role, Mr Broccoli,' I said matter-of-factly. 'If I were to play the role I would want to give the character some real-life idiosyncracies. Let him have a certain vulnerability to offset the bizarre teeth.'

Mr Broccoli took movie-making very seriously, and he thought about what I had said for just a brief moment. I was approaching this role awfully seriously myself, and he liked that. 'What are you doing after you are finished working today?' he asked. 'Nothing,' I said. 'What did you have in mind?' 'I would like for you to come by my house. Meet my family and a few friends.' Mr Broccoli gave me some easy directions as his house wasn't very far away from the hotel, and he paid the bill and I left for the studio.

I called Herman from a pay phone and told him about the lunch, the teeth, and the meeting at the Broccoli home. He was, of course, ecstatic.

AN OVERNIGHT SUCCESS – AFTER 17 YEARS

Mr Broccoli's home was in the older section of Bel-Aire and it was an estate on about five acres, I would guess. This is in an area where lots this size are unheard of. As I was ushered into the house, I noticed a pool in the backyard and a pool house that was bigger and nicer than where I was living at the time. Mr Broccoli introduced me to his wife, Dana, at least one of his daughters and a man who I believe was one of the writers. I should have been taking notes, but I was more impressed with the cordiality that I was being greeted with everywhere I turned. Over the years as I got to know Cubby, I came to know him as a man who didn't like to waste a lot of money. But as a man who treated everyone with respect – and those he worked closely with like family. He was a family man and his family were a part of the approval process. I think we hit it off because I was also a family man and because I approached movie-making like a business, just like Mr Broccoli.

I almost blew it again when I was sent to London for wardrobe fittings and to a dental technician's office out by Pinewood Studios to get the teeth designed and made just prior to production. I was to leave from LAX about 12 noon on a Saturday, and we left our home in Covina early enough for Diane to drop me off at the airport in Los Angeles by 11.00 am or even a little earlier. What we didn't count on was unusual traffic that was unbelievable. The traffic was backed up for at least ten miles before you got to the airport turnoff and was like a parking lot, allowing us to proceed at about two or three miles per hour.

I remember that we finally got near the airport at very close to 12 noon. We were just crawling along and I considered jumping out of the car and running the last mile, suitcase in hand. Fortunately for me, the plane was late and I made it by the skin of my teeth. I've often thought about what would have happened to my career had I not made that flight. Well, of course, I did make the flight and I found myself coming back about a month later with Diane and RG, who was then about 18 months old.

The production company had put us into an apartment near the American Embassy, which was in a very upscale part of town on Upper Audley Street. I think this happened because the production offices were on Audley and someone knew of this flat. It was a nice apartment, but too expensive for the living allowance that Mr Zimmerman had negotiated, which was $500 a week. As I remember, this flat was renting for about $400 a week, which left us just $100 for groceries, cabs and all other miscellaneous expenses.

I am grateful for going through this experience and having to go on a budget in London, as I soon discovered how reasonable things were in America compared to England. A quart of milk cost as much as a half-gallon does here. The same was true for a half-pound of butter which cost about the same as a pound in the US. A six-pack of beer was about two and a half times the price. I often wonder how the English survive, when they pay half their income in tax and pay twice as much for everything, including having to buy a license from the government in order to watch the 'telly.'

The apartment served us well, however, as it was close to everything downtown, and Diane and I got to see a lot of London on our days off. The only problem for me was the cost and the fact that I had about a one-hour drive each way to the studio every day. To compound that problem, many days I would make the drive early in the morning through traffic only to find that I wasn't used, and at the end of the day I had to make the return trip through traffic back to London.

Our first filming on location was to take place in Sardinia, which is an island in the Mediterranean just off the coast of Italy. We found ourselves staying at the Calle de Volpe Hotel, which was built by the Aga Khan and was outrageously expensive. They charged per person and this included a full charge for our 20-month-old baby. When I got the bill, I literally went berserk. Diane calmed me down long enough to give me a chance to come up with a plan.

First, I approached the production office with my bill and told them that I hadn't intended to invest in their picture when I took the job. They laughed but realised that it was unreasonable to expect me to pay such an enormous bill with what they were giving me as a living allowance as the bill was three times as much. Fortunately, they doubled my living allowance to $1000 a week, which took care of two thirds of the bill.

I asked the director how much he was paying for his room and found that it was only 30,000 lira a night while I was being charged 100,000 lira a night for our room. That's when I found out that they charged per person, including the same amount for the baby. I went to the hotel manager and did my 'Mama mia' routine, telling them that it was ridiculous to charge so much, especially for a baby. The manager told us that our room was a little bit bigger than the director's so we would have a place to put the crib.

I told the manager that, since we were paying the price of three rooms, I wanted three rooms just like the director's, and the manager looked at me like I was crazy. 'Why do you want three rooms?' he asked. 'You don't need three rooms!' 'You're right,' I said. 'I want three rooms because it's cheaper! Three rooms like the director's would total 90,000 lira a day and we're paying 100,000 lira.' I think he lowered the bill to 60,000 lira a night, and this, along with the increase the production company gave me, made everything work out just fine.

The Calle de Volpe Hotel was absolutely beautiful but because of its location you couldn't drink the water. It was about the colour of urine, if not darker, and it foamed! It was hard enough to try and bathe in it, let alone think of drinking it, so you had to buy bottled water. Bottled water was expensive, as was everything else. Orange juice was $4.50 a glass and that was over 25 years ago. The wine that we were paying $6 a glass for was 30 cents a bottle at the supermarket. I didn't care what the people at the hotel thought when we brought cases of water, juice and wine in through the lobby. Let them think of me as a cheapskate with a reputation like Jack Benny had. I am sure it saved Benny tens, if not hundreds of thousands, of dollars over the years.

When we got back to London, we were informed that we would be going to Egypt soon and that I was to get the necessary 'jabs' as they call them in Great Britain. We decided to give up the apartment while we were gone and

I asked my driver if he could find us something out by Pinewood Studios so we could move in when we got back.

The production manager did not want Diane to go to Egypt because she was very pregnant with our soon-to-be daughter, Jennifer. When I insisted that she was going, they wrote me a very officious letter stating that it was 'foolhardy' of me to consider such a thing and that she should stay in London. I had a meeting with the production manager and he began to tell me about the horrible conditions in Cairo. 'There are people dying in the doorways and there is garbage and sewage everywhere!' I promptly told them that I didn't think that I even wanted to go to such a place. 'Oh,' he said, 'you'll be fine! We'll make sure that you have food that's been shipped in and bottled water. We'll be staying at the Sheraton in Cairo and it's a very nice hotel. Don't worry, we'll take care of you,' he said. 'Good,' I said. 'Make sure you take good care of my wife, too.' Having said that, I left the room.

Diane wasn't able to get all the 'jabs', as you couldn't get them if you were pregnant. She flew on ahead of me in the chartered jet the company arranged for because I had some scenes to do before going on to Cairo. When I arrived at the Sheraton in Cairo, she told me about her problems with the bottled water. She had ordered Evian water and when it came up to the room she noticed that the aluminum foil had already been removed from the top of the bottles. She refused to accept them that way and had a terrible time getting the hotel to send up bottles that allowed her to remove the foil. Later on while we were staying there, I saw one of the hotel employees refilling Evian bottles with water from the tap.

Another problem Diane was having was that some Egyptian man was calling her room telling her that he was in love with her, which was pretty incredible since she was about five months' pregnant. She'd hang up on him but he kept calling. I guess he figured that she was in Cairo by herself and maybe he could get a passport to the Western world through her, but as soon as I arrived, the calls stopped.

She told me that she had to stop going to the restaurant because all the waiters and waitresses were taking RG to the dessert trays and giving him anything he wanted. RG is blonde with sky blue eyes, which the Egyptians were fascinated by.

The thing that I remember most about Cairo is all the car horns honking day and night. They have some kind of a law there that says if you get into an accident because you didn't honk your horn, you are at fault. Consequently, everyone honks all the time. The traffic is unbelievable in Cairo. The pedestrians do not have the right-of-way. To the contrary, drivers seem to try and hit little old ladies and women with babies crossing the street, as they scurry out of the way.

Life is cheap in Egypt, and the drivers did not slow down as they whisked us through the narrow roads in the middle of the small town of Giza, which was full of people walking alongside the road. One of the production people told me about being here some years before and how their driver had struck and killed a young boy. He said that one of the local Egyptians that was working with them talked to the parents and came back to say that they had it all worked out. If the production company would give the parents $500, they would forget about it. He said that he was appalled: $500 for the life of their son? The Egyptian said that they had too many sons already but they did not have $500, and that was a fortune to them.

Later, as I worked with Roger Moore and Barbara Bach in the Valley of the Kings, I noticed that the soldiers were driving the curious children away by throwing rocks at them, just like they kept away the wild dogs that Egypt is so famous for.

One day we were eating the safe food off the catering truck, and the flies were so bad that you had to use alcohol wipes to wipe your mouth or suffer up to 20 flies all around your lips where any food had been. An older Egyptian woman was watching us while she nursed a little baby. When she took the baby from her breasts, the flies, dozens of them, were all over the milk around his mouth. She made a futile effort to shoo them away, but they were right back on the baby. The day we left to return to London, we were delayed for hours outside the airport. The flies were incredible that day, and we all clapped when we got the good news that we were finally leaving. I believe the curse of the flies still affects Egypt; you cannot get away from them if you have the slightest vestige of food on or near you. Even a cookie crumb will bring them by the hundreds.

I do not want to discourage anyone from going to Egypt or Cairo. The Sphinx and the pyramids are awesome, and I'm really grateful that I got a chance to see them. The Temple of Karnak at Luxor with its big columns and all its statuary is glorious and immense, as is the Valley of the Kings and all the monuments there. Taking the boat across and down the Nile every day to go on location was beautiful.

I remember laying down to take a nap on the base of one of the columns and looking up at the roof of the monument, where I saw a beautiful painting of a large eagle painted in vivid colours under the overhanging roof. It was protected from the wind and rain and the colours were so bright it looked like it had been painted yesterday. It was so beautiful.

On the other hand, I also remember the people lined up at the porta-potties because of dysentery caused by the food and water. One time I was inside one being sick myself and to stop people from trying the door and banging on it, I stuck my feet out under the door, which was cut about six inches short of the floor for ventilation. I was sick with nausea (a nice word for my condition), like almost all the cast and crew, and was given some pills to take for it. We were staying at the Winter Palace Hotel in Luxor and you could hear people retching in every room as you would walk down the hall to your room. One night I was feeling very bad and I got up in the middle of the night to take my pills. I opened a bottle of cold soda to take my medication with and something in my head told me to hold the dark brown glass bottle up to the light before drinking from it and I saw a tree of fungus inside. I have a weak stomach as it is, and that was it for me.

How do you get sick when the production company is flying in all the food and juice on location and you are being careful to only drink the bottled water with the foil seal intact? At that time, the ice was made with the water you weren't supposed to drink and the salad greens were washed in it. So if you used ice in your beverages or ate salad, you could get sick. They say that when people from other countries come to the US and drink our water, they get sick from the chlorine. I understand that today they have new hotels in Luxor that have water distillation systems, and these things are no longer a problem. The same is supposed to be true of the new hotels by the pyramids. That wasn't the case when we were there. I remember that the only thing you could eat at the hotel was yogurt and honey. Somehow nature (or God) designed these things to be safe in their natural form.

The other beautiful thing about Egypt was the people. When we came down the Nile in the boat and got off at the hotel, there were a lot of vendors selling goods at the dock. We were very tired, as we had been delayed along the way at the airport, and we just wanted to check in to our hotel room and get out of the heat. One young vendor was selling feverishly. He could speak the languages of all the tourists, whether they were French, German, Italian or English. He saw our little boy with his sky blue eyes and he brought out a little robe that was the same colour. We told him that we would be back and started to move on when he placed a sky blue necklace around little RG's neck that matched his eyes. We insisted that we would come back, which we eventually did, but he said, 'No, this is my gift to your beautiful little boy.' I tried to at least pay him for the necklace, but he was sincere. It was his gift.

We took the tour from Luxor to the Temple of Karnak one night and we were amazed as we rode in the carriage to see people by the hundreds sleeping in dug-out little caves in the hillsides along the road. The young children would swim in the side canals that were used for the irrigation of crops. There were living organisms in that water that would get into their bloodstream through their eyes, nose and mouth and, because of these parasites, these children wouldn't live to be twenty. It was hot and they swam there anyway.

When I worked at the pyramids, I made friends with a man who was in charge of protecting these antiquities from us and other tourists. He was very nice and extremely intelligent, having completed college. We would talk every day, it seemed, as I enjoyed learning about the country and its problems. I learned from him how they could send people to other countries to train as doctors, but how it was so difficult for the doctors to find the medications and equipment in Egypt that they had been trained to use. We were fortunate to have a doctor on staff who came equipped with most of these things.

One day the man invited me to his son's 16th birthday party, and I told him that I would try and attend. I mentioned it to production and they said by all means, it was important for me to go, as this man could make things hard or easy for them. The production company provided a car and driver for Diane and I and we purchased a sports bag for his son on the way. It was a most interesting experience. While driving to the address we were given, the driver was able to go through places which cabs are forbidden to take people to. We passed by the Necropolis, or City of the Dead, and it was overwhelming to see tens of thousands of people living in a cemetery filled with monuments that were small crude houses built out of stone. People were living in these little imitation houses without the benefit of running water or sewage. We also passed by the bazaars with meat and chickens hanging outside without refrigeration. I couldn't bear to think of how many flies must be feeding on that meat, flies that were spawned out of the refuse at the City of the Dead. It was bizarre.

The car took us to a neighbourhood which could be best described as a tenement, not unlike the worst in the Bronx. I told the driver that he must be lost when he drove us down an unlit alleyway-type drive, as I couldn't imagine this government official living in a neighbourhood like this. The driver assured me that this was the right address, and I realised that he was right when I saw our friend come out of a doorway to greet us. We walked up a few flights of steps and entered a tiny apartment where a number of people were gathered inside to celebrate the 16-year-old's birthday.

The brother-in-law was there with his wife and, like my Egyptian friend, he was very intelligent and easy to talk to. The living room was the size of a tiny office. When we had to use the toilet, we found that there was a door that led to a commode that had to be flushed by pouring water into it. Noticing that there was nothing else in that room, I inquired as to the location of the bathing facilities. I was told that there was a common shower facility down the hall. There was no separate kitchen, and the food was prepared in the parents' room. The 16-year-old boy shared a room with his older sister.

Diane, being pregnant, was always thirsty and when she asked about water, they went to an alcove that opened to the outside and produced an earthenware vessel that cooled the water through evaporation. I tried to signal to Diane not to drink this water and I realised we should have brought bottled water with us. She gave me a look that said she did not want to offend these people and that she was very thirsty. I kept my mouth shut, but I couldn't help but wonder if she would get sick from drinking unbottled water. So far, she was the only one that had not been sick and she was being very careful to not use ice or eat any salads. She was determined to prove that they were wrong in insisting that she not go to Egypt. God must have protected her that night in his infinite wisdom and knowing that she was pregnant because she did not get sick.

I had been warned not to admire anything at this man's house, as it was their custom to give you anything you admired. It was also their custom to not take no for an answer if you tried to refuse their gift. I made the mistake of noticing a Koran they had on the wall and mentioning how pretty it was. Today it ranks among our fondest souvenirs of our trip.

We returned to London after a harrowing plane trip. It was ironic because Roger Moore had a few glib remarks when he said goodbye to the rest of the cast and crew as he was flying back to London on Air France. 'Well', he said, 'in a few minutes I'm going to be in France, and you're all going to still be in Egypt.' He had no idea how true this would turn out to be, and I doubt if he knows what happened on our flight, which was with a local airline, *not* Air France. Somewhere along the way, while they were serving dinner and we were wondering whether we should drink the water or stick to imported wine, the plane took an unexpected plunge. I was in the rest room and was thrust against the ceiling. Out in the cabin the food trays hit the ceiling, as did anything else that wasn't buckled down.

Our son was sleeping in a couple of seats with the arm rests up across the aisle from Diane. The plane plunged down for about 20 or 30 seconds, which seemed like an eternity because it appeared that we were all going to die. I managed to get my head out the door and heard Diane emphatically asking the flight attendant or someone to hand her our son. Suddenly we bottomed out and the plane leveled out again. No one finished lunch as it was all over the ceiling, the floor and the seats. I don't think anyone was hungry after that, and if they were, they stuck to a liquid diet. We couldn't help but think of Roger Moore eating caviar and drinking French champagne on Air France.

When we arrived in London we were all hungry, and I was glad to see our driver waiting for us when we got out of customs so we could stop at a drive-through fast food place on the way home. 'By the way,' I asked, 'were you able to get us a place near the studio?' 'Yes,' said the driver with a funny grin on his face. 'How close?' I asked. 'Real close,' he replied. 'Thank God,' I thought, 'this will save me two hours a day in traffic.'

Little did I know that the location of our 'flat' would save me much more than two hours a day. We drove into Buckinghamshire and I noticed that we were heading for Pinewood. Surprisingly, we drove through the gates and into the studio, and before I could ask where the driver was taking us, we stopped in front of a two-storey brick cottage. 'This is it,' he said, almost chuckling to himself. We got out and he opened the door to the main room, which had a huge fireplace that already had a nice warm fire burning in it. 'I got some things in for you in the fridge and some groceries are in the cupboards. I didn't know for sure what you liked, but the main necessities are there like milk, butter, sliced meats, bread, beer, coffee, tea, orange juice and some assorted cereals. I hope you find it satisfactory.'

In the meantime, Diane was checking out the kitchen and RG was up the stairs checking out the bedrooms. 'Dad!' RG exclaimed. 'We have our own bedroom upstairs and you can see everywhere out the window!' Diane came out of the kitchen. 'It's very nice,' she said, complimenting the driver on his excellent selection. 'It used to be the stable keeper's cottage when Pinewood was a residential estate,' said the driver. 'It's been vacant and I was able to get it for £400 a month.' The driver knew we were trying to reduce our living costs from £400 a *week*, and he had a Cheshire Cat grin on his face because he was so proud of himself.

'It's perfect,' I exclaimed, glad to be out from under the big bucks rental we had, although it had given us a chance to enjoy London.

'And that's one of the sound stages where you'll be working,' he said, pointing to a stage door about 20 yards away.

'You're kidding!' I said as I realised I could walk to work. 'I'll still be on standby to take you to the grocery store or wherever you want to go, Mrs Kiel,' he continued, smiling as he, too, was free of that long round trip each day; he and his wife also lived near Pinewood. 'Just call me.'

This arrangement turned into a wonderful thing for me and my family. They no longer had to bring me into the studio just in case they needed me as they had me 60 feet away, and I was put on standby call day after day after day. This meant that I could sit on the big couch and read books by the fire and spend great times with Diane and RG.

It was during these times that RG began to take an interest in reading. He saw Diane and I reading and asked what we were doing. Both Diane and I are avid readers and were spending a good deal of the time reading and he couldn't figure it out as he wasn't quite two years old. I showed him what we were doing by reading aloud to him and he wanted to be taught how to do it. On a Saturday, Diane procured some *Read It Yourself* books by author Richard Scarry and we started teaching little RG to read.

He picked it up so quickly that it encouraged me to start teaching him phonics and to call my mother and ask her to pick up some flash cards with the Doltch words (simple words that readers should memorise, like what, who, where, it, she, he, up, down, etc) on them. Our son learned to read quite a few words before he was two years old, and we had a work environment that was broken up with little mini-vacations where I could read and rest between spurts of hard work.

It was during these wonderful times, however, that I had my first bit of strife with the Bond people. The publicity department had flown in the diminutive Hervé Villechaize, and they wanted me to do publicity photos with him. Hervé wasn't in *The Spy Who Loved Me* but had worked in the previous picture, *The Man with the Golden Gun*. I was very reluctant to do those kinds of publicity pictures and get categorised into the Dr. Loveless/Voltaire type of thing I'd had with Michael Dunn, as this was different. We were not working together and this kind of publicity would make it look like we were. I protested, saying that this kind of publicity would provide a carnival quality to the movie and that it wasn't appropriate. I told them that there would be plenty of opportunities for good publicity that was actually a part of the film. The publicity people were somewhat miffed at me until the following events took place that totally redeemed me.

Cubby Broccoli had built the Supertanker set on the 007 Stage, which was at that time the biggest sound stage ever built in the world. He had the publicity department invite the photo editors of every major newspaper in England and in Europe, along with some key newspapers and magazines in the US. They all descended on the lot at the same time and were treated to a tour of the Supertanker set inside that big sound stage. The photo editors were also treated to lunch in the studio and one of them was walking with Jerry Juroe, the head of Publicity for UA and Cubby Broccoli. I happened to be walking by taking RG with me, and the little guy was holding onto one of my fingers as we walked together.

As we passed Jerry and the photo editor for the *Daily Mirror*, the photo editor looked at me and my little boy and asked Jerry Juroe who I was. Jerry told him about the part that I was playing, but what this photo editor saw was a picture story in his paper. He promised Jerry that if he could have an exclusive and take a photo with me and RG, that he would start the story on the front page and continue it with a full-page picture on page three, which was known for featuring a photo of a beautiful bare-breasted 'bird', as they sometimes call young ladies in England. Jerry asked me and I said, 'Of course!'

The good thing about this was that it showed that good, clean and positive publicity can be gained from simple human interest and that you don't have to resort to gimmicks to get it. And that it was better to offer the public something that was truly interesting, unique and refreshing for a change.

All the villains die in James Bond films, never to return and fight another day. Cubby did something different from what most American-based producers do. He held weekly production meetings with all the production heads, to get their suggestions about how the film could be better or how the costs could be reduced in any area by making changes that would tell the same story more economically.

According to the stunt co-ordinator, Bob Simmons, he suggested to Cubby that perhaps they might not want to kill me off as it looked to him that Jaws was going to be very popular. He told me that Cubby's instant reaction was, 'But, Bob, we always kill the henchmen.' 'Yes,' said Bob, 'but wouldn't it have been nice if you could have brought Odd Job back?'

Cubby responded by asking Bob, 'But Jaws is dumped into a tank with a shark, what do your propose happens?

'He kills the shark,' answered Simmons, matter-of-factly.

'I don't know,' said Cubby. 'We've never brought back an actor as the same villain before.'

'Yes,' said Bob, 'but wouldn't it be nice to have that option. Why not shoot it both ways and decide later.'

Cubby made the decision to do just that. I was informed that I was going to be held over an extra week so they could shoot the alternative ending where I kill the shark and survive. Diane was at the end of her seventh month at the time and the airlines do not like women flying in their last month of pregnancy. The production staff suggested that she fly home and that I finish the movie without her being with me. Diane did not want to fly home and have the baby on her own, so she stayed.

When it came time to leave England, Cubby flew a doctor with us so if Diane were to start going into labour, the doctor was there to do whatever needed to be done. When we arrived at LAX, the doctor got in line to check in for his return flight and flew immediately back to London. I do not know what this cost Cubby, we didn't ask, but everyone flew First Class and I know that the doctor's time must have been expensive. Cubby did for Diane and I what he would have done for his own daughter or son. The man was a class act.

Jennifer Maye Kiel, a beautiful baby girl, was born just a few weeks later.

TRAVELLING ALL OVER THE WORLD

After 17 years of struggling as an actor I finally found myself being able to take Diane and my children with me all over the world while I promoted *The Spy Who Loved Me*. Many times we were able to also take my mother along to help with the children or the teenage girl who lived across the street. It was great fun!

The travelling all started when they flew Diane and I to London for the Royal premiere. Prince Philip, Queen Elizabeth's husband, Princess Anne and perhaps some others were there, and the publicity department told us how to bow and curtsy properly. The next day I was invited to attend the big press conference held for each film after the Royal premiere. Of course, Roger Moore, Barbara Bach, and Lewis Gilbert were all going to be there. As is my normal policy, I was there on time, and everyone else, except Cubby Broccoli, was fashionably late.

Because the press had already interviewed Mr Broccoli many times over the years, they immediately descended on me and I soon found out what it must be like to be the President of the United States at a press conference. The press can be extremely confrontational these days, and even 25 years ago they went after me with a vengeance.

'Mr Kiel,' one journalist began, 'have you seen all of the Bond films?' I thought for a split second. 'Yes, I believe that I've seen most, if not all of them.' 'Who do you think makes the best Bond?' asked the journalist, pen in hand. I thought, 'I'm damned if I do and damned if I don't.' Many people liked Sean Connery the best, and here I was working with Roger Moore, who had been very kind to me and whom I like very much as a friend and as an actor.

God has always given me the ability to fence with journalists in a firm but nice way that always makes them look bad if they continue to attack. He didn't let me down this time. 'I kinda go for George Lazenby myself!' popped out of my mouth like I had anticipated the question, which I hadn't. Everyone laughed, thinking I had gotten the better of that interplay. They didn't just chuckle, they roared with laughter as if to say 'Touché.'

The reporter wasn't going to be stopped by a clever or humorous answer, however. Undaunted, he proceeded, 'So you have seen all of the Sean Connery films and have worked with Roger Moore. Between them, who do you think makes the best Bond?' By then, I was thinking of what to say and I was more prepared to answer this loaded question.

'I believe that they both have their own special kind of talent. It's like asking whether you like Cary Grant or Burt Reynolds best. I like them both.'

Roger, Barbara and Lewis were beginning to arrive, thank God, but another reporter quickly began his own attack on me and, in a way, on Cubby Broccoli. 'You were just in a film, *Silver Streak*, where you wore the same kind of steel teeth. Did Mr Broccoli copy that character for this film?' I was shocked by this inane question. There wasn't any similarity between these two characters, yet this creep was trying to make hay out of Cubby allegedly stealing from another film.

'There isn't any comparison between the character I played in *Silver Streak* and Jaws,' I said with conviction. 'The guy I played in *Silver Streak* had a few gold caps on his normal teeth and he used a gun, while Jaws, on the other hand, has monstrous steel teeth and he kills people with them.'

'Yes, they are different,' said the reporter, not giving up, 'but the idea of you wearing teeth was still copied from the other film, was it not?'

I was perturbed, to say the least. 'Saying that someone copied another film because of that would be like saying someone copied a Western because in both films someone wore a cowboy hat. The films were entirely different and my character was entirely different!'

I think it was at that point that the James Bond people decided they could send me on the road with the film and that I could handle the press. And I began to realise how tough the press could be, whether you were President of the USA or an actor out promoting a film.

The day after the Royal premiere, the newspaper reviews of the film were sensational. More importantly, they were singling me out for the first time in my career as one of the most successful ingredients in this major motion picture. I was absolutely astounded by the reception given my character by the press...

June Thatcher, of the *Chattanooga News*, wrote in a big rectangular box, 'Richard Kiel creates an unforgettable character.' David Robinson of the London *Times* called Jaws 'The big success of the film.' Kathleen Carrol of the *New York Daily News* named Jaws 'The movie's most winning character.' *Time* magazine's Christopher Porterfield proclaimed Jaws 'A perfect symbol for Bond films.' Scott Cain of the *Atlanta Journal and Constitution* said, 'The most spectacular drawing card is Jaws, an indestructible bad guy.' John Barbour of *Los Angeles Magazine* called Jaws 'One of the most wonderfully loony heavies in film.' Ian Christie of the London *Daily Express* said that I was 'A splendid new heavy on the scene.' Charles Champlin, Entertainment Editor for the *Los Angeles Times*, said '[Kiel] is that unexpected item, a sympathetic bad guy.' Jeff Borden of the *Columbus Dispatch* called Jaws 'one of the best villains ever filmed in a Bond flick. He is indestructible and survives with such aplomb that he gets more cheers from the audience than 007 himself.' Marsha Steimel of the *Witchata Falls Times* wrote, 'It's Richard Kiel who gallops away with the picture.' Susan Stark of the *Detroit Free Press* wrote, '*The Spy Who Loved Me* does introduce one memorable performer, Richard Kiel – undoubtedly he'll resurface in Number II.' And finally, Bill Cosford of the *Miami Herald* wrote, 'Kiel's presence leads to the funniest moments in the film – besides providing a running joke that's bound to extend to future Bonds.'

Roger, Barbara Bach, Caroline Munro, and I went all over the world promoting *The Spy Who Loved Me*, which went on to register the biggest foreign gross of any film in United Artists' history to that date. This experience of travelling and promoting the Bond films was one of the high points of my life, as my wife and the two children got to go along too. My family and I travelled all over the world that summer, going to Sweden, Germany, Denmark, Holland, Belgium, Rome, Finland, Africa, Australia, Brazil, and Argentina.

It was difficult to maintain your sanity with the press asking the same questions over and over. 'Have you always been this big? I mean, how big were you when you were little?' or 'How tall are you? How much do you weigh? What was it like wearing those teeth? How did they put them in?'

I used my sense of humour to help me get through all those press conferences. I soon developed different humorous answers to different questions, I would say, when asked how they put the teeth in, 'They riveted them in.' When I saw them writing this down I would continue with, 'It wasn't so bad putting them in, but it was hell taking them out!'

People tend to take me seriously, and it's hard for me to tell a joke sometimes because of that. When a journalist would ask, 'What was it like growing up?' or 'Did the kids pick on you in school?', the truthful answer to that question was that I was very popular in high school because of my size. It was interesting to see how people's twisted minds want to make something negative out of everything. So I'd lead them on with, 'No, the other kids all liked me. They wanted me to be their friend. In fact, they'd give me money to be their friend. If they didn't have any money, they'd give me their lunch.'

By this time, they would catch on to the joke and begin some more serious questions. I did find, however, that it was good to catch them off guard and get them laughing a bit in order to break the ice. I remember one incident in Spain where we had flown into four cities in just one week. Madrid, Barcelona, Seville and Valencia all had literally dozens of members of the press in each instance, all waiting as the interpreter asked the usual barrage of questions.

I had talked the PR person into making up a press sheet which gave all the boring (for me) information like height, weight and shoe size, so we could get into the more interesting questions. In Spain, the interpreter hit me with a good one. 'When you're travelling,' she said, 'it must be hard for you to buy things. What is the most difficult piece of wearing apparel for you to find on the road?'

Actually, I didn't buy many clothes on the road, although I did buy a topcoat in London because it was bitter cold and I needed one. They had the typical big and tall shops there and the prices were fairly competitive. That was a boring answer though, almost as boring as answering the shoe size question.

So I thought and said, 'Hmm. What is the most difficult piece of wearing apparel for me to buy on the road?' I paused dramatically while the interpreter repeated the question in Spanish. Then I dropped both my hands down and made them into big cups with my fingers outstretched as everyone watched, wondering what in the world it was that I was about to say.

'How do you say athletic support?' I asked the interpreter. She looked at me, puzzled. The press looked at her, anxiously awaiting her interpretation. 'You know, jock strap,' I said. The interpreter put her hands over her face and started to giggle. The press were after her. 'What did he say?' they asked her in Spanish. She sputtered out the interpretation, and they all roared with laughter, making another day of the same old questions a lot easier for me.

The weekly allowance for our hotel went a long way in Spain as it was a country with reasonable prices, unlike Switzerland, Germany, Sweden and Denmark where the prices were unbelievably high. Because of the low prices we were lodged in a beautiful suite at a brand-new hotel that would qualify as a luxury hotel here in the States. The coffee table in the living room area was very large and had a plate-glass top, about a half-inch thick, that was set on wrought iron. Somehow the children (they probably were fighting) managed to knock the glass top onto the floor and it broke. The PR person for United Artist was not upset at all since we were doing a great job and hitting four cities in Spain in a week. I was concerned about what the hotel staff would think.

That night I got up to go to the bathroom and, being half asleep, I put my hand up to stabilise myself as I stood in front of the toilet. Although the beautiful wall tiles were all grouted together they must not have been properly adhered to the wall as my hand caused them to start breaking and before I knew it the whole wall of tiles came crashing down all over the toilet. Again, Jerry Juroe was unconcerned about the incident, as apparently he was used to rock star-type movie actors and husbands and wives fighting. 'Don't worry about it,' he said. 'Things happen.'

I've always wondered if he believed me and what the hotel staff must have thought, but they didn't say a word to me about it when I checked out. Maybe they were afraid to.

The Bond people found that they could send me off with one or two 'Bond girls' on the road (with my wife and children, of course) and the PR men, Jerry Juroe on *Spy* and Saul Cooper on *Moonraker*, and we would get the job done. Because I insisted on taking my family with me, the Bond girls would get to take their boyfriends, and Saul had his wife and son Andrew along with him on the *Moonraker* tour. Andrew took a lot of pictures along the way, some of which made their way into magazines and newspapers, and now he works as an on-location camera man for the studios.

No one makes a lot of money doing a Bond film except the person playing Bond and perhaps well-established stars playing the major villain roles; even then they probably do the Bond film for a lot less as it is very prestigious to be in one. As I said before, my long-time agent, Herman Zimmerman, had merged with a couple of other agents, Steve Stevens and Joshua Gray, who operated under the name Joshua Gray and Associates. When I did the first James Bond film, it was for peanuts, and when they called back wanting me to do another one, Joshua Gray handled the negotiations and he was determined that this time they were going to pay me what he thought I was worth.

When Joshua Gray told the people casting *Moonraker* how much he wanted, they said they would get back to him. Joshua received a call from Cubby Broccoli himself, who was quite upset with the price Josh was asking. He said something that irritated Josh and Josh hung up on him. Of course, I knew nothing about this or I would have been having a heart attack. Mr Broccoli called back to say that he had been cut off, and Josh explained to him that, if he were representing Cubby, he would be doing the same thing: getting what he was worth.

Josh wasn't holding them up for anything out of the ordinary, but rather a more substantial fee than I made the first time round. Cubby, being the gentleman that he was, realised that it was only fair that I share in my own success as Jaws and that I should make more when I returned.

NINE

FORCE 10 IN YUGOSLAVIA...
AND THE RETURN OF JAWS

In between the two James Bond films, *The Spy Who Loved Me* and *Moonraker*, I did three other movies. *They Went That-Away and That-Away* with Tim Conway, which was an awful lot of fun, and a spaghetti *Star Wars* film called *L'Umanoide*, which also co-starred Barbara Bach. But before doing those two films, I was interviewed and cast in one of my favourite dramatic films, *Force 10 from Navarone*. The film starred Harrison Ford, Robert Shaw, Franco Nero, Edward Fox, Carl Weathers and Barbara Bach again.

I ended up doing three films with Barbara, and we became good friends. *Force 10* was written by Alistair Maclean, who wrote *The Guns of Navarone*, and it was directed by Guy Hamilton, who had directed *Goldfinger*. The film was shot in London studios and the locations were in Yugoslavia. It was a WWII epic and the costumes were wonderful. I played a Chetnic Nazi sympathizer named Captain Drazac who pretends to be a partisan, leading the allied forces into a deadly trap. I had some great scenes with Carl Weathers playing a racist bigot and another with Barbara Bach where I literally beat her up. It was a very juicy part and fun to do, as I got to be a character very much different from the real me.

Years later, when I watched the struggle in Bosnia (Yugoslavia) and saw reports of the fighting and bombings, I remembered my good times in Rijecka and Opatija when we were there staying at the Ambassador Hotel. At that time, Yugoslavia was a semi-Communist country which allowed modified capitalism. You could own a restaurant or a lodge or even two, but you could not own a chain of them or even a hotel with more than a certain number of rooms. Hence, the Ambassador Hotel where we stayed was owned and managed by the government.

We were there with two of our children who were young enough to need high-chairs. I remember our first night in the posh dining room, having to hold our kids in our laps so they wouldn't break the china or the crystal. Dinner took about two hours to accomplish, and the hotel didn't have any high-chairs. I talked to the manager about this, explaining that we were going to be there for quite a while, and it would be good for everyone if they could secure a couple of high-chairs. It took about three or four days for this to happen because they had to have a meeting to cut the red tape so they could buy two high-chairs.

The people in Yugoslavia are quite proud of their country, and even though many of them left to work in places like Germany, they always returned home with their money and built homes or expanded the ones they had with what they earned. Although the Yugoslavians were allowed to travel out of the country, it was prohibitive for them to purchase items and bring them in, as the tariffs charged were so steep as to make it too expensive. This caused everything which was made and marketed in Yugoslavia to be very expensive and, unfortunately, inferior. I recall buying RG his first train set, which I never could get to work properly; it was no Lionel. All the clothes and shoes were drab and utilitarian, so you didn't see a lot of bright-coloured clothes. At the time, I drank Scotch whiskey, but found that the only thing affordable was the local plum brandy which gave you the runs. The duty charged to bring an automobile into the country was outrageous, so you only saw two types of cars there, the Russian luxury car, the Volga, and the Yugo. Need I say more?

While we were staying at the Ambassador Hotel in Opatija, we had a horrible experience one Sunday when we could not find our little boy who was about three and a half at the time. He had just disappeared while I was reading and Diane was cleaning up. We looked everywhere, in the closets, under the bed, and he was nowhere to be seen. Our room was on about the third or fourth floor, with an outdoor patio that overlooked a cement drainage wash, and neither one of us had the courage to look over the balcony railing until we had looked everywhere else.

Diane was pregnant by now with Bennett and I didn't want her to get any more upset than she was, so I got up and opened the sliding door out onto the balcony outside and made my way over to the railing, looking down into the wash below with great trepidation. My heart was pounding wildly, but there wasn't anything down there but an empty cement river. The pounding of my heart was interrupted by a knocking on the door. Diane opened the door to find a man standing there with little RG. The man explained to us that our curious son (his middle name is George) had crawled under the divider between our room's balcony and the next room, and continued doing this for a few rooms until he had made his way to where the man and a friend were playing cards and eating snacks on their balcony. They had called downstairs, but we had not reported him missing yet, so they went door to door until they found us.

Alcoholism was a big problem in Yugoslavia, which caused the government to pass laws that made driving with any amount of alcohol a criminal offense, with automatic jail time and loss of license. The production company hired locals as drivers, or should I say 'locos.' The Yugo of course was a piece of junk, and the English Ford Taurus-type cars that the production used were race cars to these guys. They would take us to the location driving the narrow mountain roads along the coastline as though they were in the Grand Prix. One day, a stuntman had enough of this dangerous driving and asked the driver to slow down. When that didn't work, he reached over and turned the key off in the ignition.

I soon found that the Yugoslavian people weren't the only ones having problems with alcohol. Robert Shaw had a reputation as a heavy drinker and the production company had someone with him at all times to make sure he didn't drink on the job. This seemed to make life very difficult for him and affected his acting. Oh, he still did a great job, but they had to put his dialogue all over the place in little notes pasted here and there so he could remember his lines.

A short time after I finished *Force 10 from Navarone*, Robert Shaw died on the golf course playing golf. I liked him very much. He had ten children, a young wife and a ten-month-old baby. His young wife was left without a husband or father for her children. I also had a young wife and, by that time three children, and this shocked me into reality as I was beginning to have a drinking problem myself. If Robert Shaw's untimely death wasn't shocking enough, my wife, Diane, informed me that number four was on the way.

I was a little scared as four children and a young wife are a lot of responsibility. I tried going on the wagon a number of times, but something always came up to cause me to fail. Besides, you couldn't watch a baseball or football game without seeing dozens of beer commercials, or drive down the highway without looking at billboards for Black Satin Scotch or Wolfschmidt Vodka ladies.

I even tried medical hypnosis, which had helped me quit smoking, but the alcohol problem was bigger than me and I didn't seem to have enough willpower to quit. This was difficult for me to understand. I was a pretty persistent guy when it came to other things. After all, I was the guy who took the A-Z list of agents from the Screen Actors Guild and didn't give up until I found an agent named Herman Zimmerman, the last one on the list.

THE ITALIAN EXPERIENCE

While I was filming *Force 10 from Navarone* in Yugoslavia, a director named Aldo Lado came to see me about playing the title role in a film he was putting together, to be shot in Italy, called *The Humanoid*.

We had just had a bad experience with a movie that was to be shot in Spain with a cast of big stars called *The Golden Spurs*. My agent had turned down doing another Tim Conway movie, based upon a written contract, to do this Spanish Western because of the superstar cast I would be involved with. A week before the start date, having heard nothing further from the production company, my agent called to find out that their telephone number had been disconnected. So I ended up with a contract that was worth about as much as a Confederate $100 bill.

Having learned our lesson we made sure that we were sent a ten per cent deposit on *The Humanoid* along with the contract. Aldo came through, and later on I found out that it was because of this deposit that the financier, Geoffredo Lombardo of Titanus Films, came up with the rest of the money to make the film. We also made sure that we had enough per diem and that the production company found us a reasonable apartment rather than an expensive hotel. We had learned from our experience with the Bond film and did not want to make the same mistakes again.

Well, the Italians found us a wonderful apartment called the Malia Residence just outside of Rome in a place called Balduina Square. It was by the Hilton on the Hill and was a great place, with security, an Olympic-size pool and lots of grounds with beautiful lawns and flowers. The furnishings were kind of *Playboy* modern (white leather couches, foil wallpaper with modern patterns) and it was equipped with a kitchen plus maid service twice a week. All this and it was very reasonable. In fact, it was so reasonable we rented another apartment and flew my mother and my sister Georgann's two girls, Lisa and April, over to enjoy Rome with us.

The filming schedule was five days a week, and I was furnished with a Mercedes and a driver named Sergio seven days a week. The producer, Giorgio Venturini, was a great guy. He was pretty old and suffered from palsy. I remember how difficult it was for him to drink a beer because his hands would shake so much. He was a very generous man, and the first week he asked me whether we had seen the Appian Way. I told him that we hadn't, and he said, 'Tell Sergio to take you there. Take the car, go!'

The next week he suggested Tivoli Fountains, which was quite a distance from where we were. Finally, he asked whether we had been to Florence, and when I said, 'No,' it was the same. 'Tell Sergio I said take the car and go!'

The Italians loved me because I had my wife and two children with me, and Diane was pregnant with number three. They are very family-oriented people and they appreciated the fact that I was, too. When we flew my Mom and two nieces in they were as amazed as I when Mr Venturini asked Mama Kiel if she had seen the Appian Way. And when she responded that she hadn't, he said… 'Tell Sergio to take the car and go!'

Mom and my sister's two daughters were also taken to Florence and Tivoli Fountains, and they loved it. For years, my two nieces kept in touch with Sergio through the mail as they had become good friends. Sergio was like family to us and took us to all his favourite restaurants, some of which had no signs or menu. It was like going to an Italian wedding with all the children and eating whatever they ate.

One day during filming, the director invited me to lunch and we drove to a small but very nice restaurant. The lunch was great, but we were there for at least an hour by the time they brought coffee and dessert, let alone the bill. I kept looking at my watch as we were long overdue to return to the set. Aldo noticed this, saying, 'Don't-a worry, they cannot-a start-a without-a me!'

After working a few weeks in the studio, I found out that we were going on location. They explained that they had planned on going to a desert area of Africa for a moon valley effect, but decided to go to Israel instead, where they could create the same effect by the Red Sea and use the Kennedy Memorial, which was a futuristic flying saucer-like building in Jerusalem, along with some other futuristic war memorials near Beersheba. Wow! Not only did we get the great Italian experience but we also got to go to Israel for a few weeks and see nearly everything there, as well.

We worked a five-day schedule there, too (love the Italian work ethic), and had a Mercedes station wagon and Ruben, the driver, at our disposal seven days a week. We saw Nazareth, Bethlehem, Jericho, the Sea of Galilee and even went into the water at the Dead Sea. The children were enthralled by the underwater exploration centre at the Red Sea and especially by the museum next door that had tanks of the most beautiful and exotic tropical fish you could imagine. RG and Jennifer ran from one area to another looking at all the brilliantly coloured fish. Finally, it was time for the museum to close and the children didn't want to leave. The curators were very nice, and because the children were enjoying the tropical fish so much, they gave them a couple of books to read so they would go home.

All in all, the filming in Italy and Israel are among my fondest memories in the movie business.

To be totally honest, however, my agent had warned me about always being paid in advance and that I wasn't to go to work until they gave me a bank transmittal proving that the funds had been transferred for the next week's work. He told me that it was customary for the Italian production company to not pay for the last week, and when you got home in the US it was too much trouble to try and sue and you didn't have the protection of our union, SAG, to back you up.

Sure enough, with one more week to go on my contract, the customary transmittal was not given to me on Friday for the next and final week. I told them that I wouldn't be able to go to work on Monday without it. They said that Sergio would have it when he picked me up. On Monday, Sergio arrived without the transmittal. I told him that I couldn't go to the studio without it.

He spoke to someone on the phone and at the conclusion of his conversation said he would be right back. When he returned it was with a letter from the producers to their bank asking that the transmittal be done. Of course, there is a lot of difference between a letter requesting a transmittal and a bank document showing that it had been done. I explained this to Sergio, and about an hour later he returned with the bank document showing the money had been transferred.

I have learned over the years that it is always better to make movie people do the right thing and to not let them take advantage of you. That way they respect you and don't mind seeing you again, and as in the case of Lassie, even using you again.

WHAT DID YOU EXPECT, A BOND GIRL?

I had a completion guarantee date in my contract with the Italian producers and they wanted to extend it, while at the same time the James Bond producers wanted me to come in early. The solution, of course, was that everyone had to stick to the contracts and the completion and start dates. It was agreed that any looping would be done by the Italians in Paris on my days off while shooting *Moonraker*, and they reluctantly let me go on time.

I arrived in Paris with my wife Diane and our two children, RG and Jennifer. The driver took us to the Raphael Hotel, which is near the Arc de Triomphe. It was in the evening when we checked into this fairly lavish hotel and I called to see if Bob Simmons was there. He was the stunt co-ordinator and a good friend. Bob was pleased to know that Diane and I had arrived, and he brought a script to my room as I hadn't seen one as yet.

I also hadn't signed a contract because I had been out of the country making the Italian movie and my agent felt that I could sign it when I got there. I was very pleased with the script. Jaws ended up with a girlfriend who was described as being about six feet tall. This was the first time in my career that I had a 'love interest' in a film since *Eegah*, and I was very excited about the prospect.

The next day I had my bubble burst. I met with Cubby Broccoli and Michael Wilson, his stepson, who was more and more in charge of the operation. They were happy to see me and wasted no time in telling me about some of the many things they had planned. They had no idea that Bob Simmons had already shared his script with me, but I listened patiently as they described the new storyline... that is, until they got to the part where my girlfriend was to be a 7'4" woman.

I was really taken back. First, I need to explain to you that in my early years everyone was always trying to fix me up with the tallest girl they knew. I became a member of a social group called 'The Tip Toppers' where the men had to be a certain minimum height and so did the women. I enjoyed this at first, as I dated a pretty Swedish woman who was about 6'1". One of the things the Tip Toppers prided themselves about was the number of people that married within the club. I think the other women in the club resented this attractive Swedish woman for dating me since there was a woman in the club who was about 6'5" and they felt she was more suitable for me. Well, she was not only very tall, she was also very big and looked like she would need power steering in order to dance. I dropped out of the club as I didn't like the manipulation and pressure.

The only girl that I dated in high school was about 5'3" inches tall. My wife Diane is about 5'1½" so you can see that I have always been attracted to little women. I had nothing against tall girls, though, like the Swedish blonde who was 6'1", but I didn't like the idea that I had to date only the tallest girl in town.

They say that opposites attract, and I think that there is a lot to that as I found that the really beautiful tall showgirls in Las Vegas generally date shorter men. Look at Mickey Rooney and Ava Gardner or Dudley Moore and Susan Anton. In any event, if 6'5" girls were a turn-off for me you can imagine how I felt about a 7'4" woman.

Cubby and Michael were laughing as they described how this woman would pull Jaws out of the wreckage when the cable car crashed into the tower. I wasn't amused. Sure, it was going to be a quick joke and people would have laughed, but the rest of the scenes just weren't going to work for me. It wasn't just the Romeo and Juliet music that would play when we met for the first time, it was the problem with the motivation that it would create when Jaws turns into a good guy because he needs to save his woman. A 7'4" woman who could yank him out of the wreckage didn't need Jaws' help, she could save herself.

I expressed my feelings and they didn't understand. 'What do you expect?' they asked. 'A Bond girl?' 'Yeah,' I thought. 'That would be nice. Especially one about six feet tall as described in the script that I had already read.'

They quickly arranged for me to see the opening scene that already had been shot, where Jaws jumps out of the plane and Bond rips his parachute off and Jaws lands in a circus tent. The stuntman had already done my part, and the only parts missing were my close-ups.

'Look!' Cubby said, 'we're making you into a star!' I was excited to see what they had done, but still felt very strongly that what they had in mind wouldn't work for me or the audience.

'I really appreciate what you have already done for me and what you are trying to do now,' I said. 'But that doesn't mean that I have to marry someone's daughter that I am not attracted to.' They were really frustrated at that point. I believe it was Bill Cartlidge, the production manager, who piped in with the fact that I had signed a contract and they had spent all this money and… 'But I *haven't* signed a contract,' I said.

They couldn't believe that anyone would walk away from a Bond film for what they felt was such a silly reason. 'What do you propose we do?' they asked. I knew that they wouldn't go for a six foot blonde, so I came up with what I thought would work for me and work well for the audience. 'How about a really short woman?' I suggested. 'How short?' asked Cubby with a frown on his face. 'Over five feet would work,' I said. 'Five feet?' one of them asked. 'Do you really think the audiences would believe that?' 'My wife is five foot one and a half,' I said. 'We have two children and another one on the way. They have to believe it, it works!'

They ended up casting a French actress, Blanche Ravelec, who starred in French comedies like *La Carapate*, where she played a farmer's wife with a more than ample bosom who has one boyfriend after another while her husband is away. Diane and I were sent to watch her in this movie that was playing at the time and we laughed our heads off, although we couldn't understand a word of French.

In one scene in this movie Blanche is nude with a man when her husband shows up unexpectedly. She pushes the man into a clothes closet where he discovers there's already another man inside waiting for him to leave. 'Wow!'

I thought, 'this woman is pretty cute and pretty busty.' Unfortunately they bound her breasts down for the role of 'Dolly' and added pig-tails and glasses. In spite of this, Blanche was very cute and charismatic. One day after seeing the scene in rushes, I ran into Mr Broccoli at the bar in the restaurant. All the studios in Europe have bars, and it is customary to have a drink or two with lunch.

Cubby was with a journalist and he spoke very loud to the man so I could hear, almost like he was sharing their conversation with me. 'Richard and I had quite a falling out over that scene,' he told the journalist. 'We had different ideas on how the scene should be played and it appears that Richard was right.' I couldn't have agreed more. The Romeo and Juliet theme was played when I first see Dolly and she smiles at me, and then the camera cuts to a big close-up of me grinning from ear to ear as the sun glints off my giant choppers made out of shiny chromium steel.

It was extremely effective and even a little moving, at least for me. What mattered the most was that Cubby Brocoli liked it and made a point of letting me know that in front of a journalist. It takes an awfully big man to do what he did, but that's the kind of man Cubby was.

A lot of people ask me why I always took my wife and children with me, as though I was crazy to do that.

A lot of actors leave their non-acting spouse at home or, if they do travel together on shoots, they leave the children with a nanny or in a boarding school. I believe that going on location and leaving your wife at home alone is a sure-fire recipe for a unhappy marriage, if not a divorce. There's just too much temptation when you have two lonely people thousands of miles apart – and not just for the actor, but also for the spouse at home, who is feeling neglected and possibly abused if she's handling all the children on her own.

Many actors and actresses have lost their children to drugs and suicide because they left them behind in boarding schools or with nannies. I won't go down the list of famous people this has happened to because I don't want to dredge up old hurts for them, but you would immediately recognise some very famous names if I mentioned them.

Our middle son, Bennett Jackson Kiel (named after Diane's father), who would have been named Jacqueline Martine Kiel had he been a girl, was born in Paris while we filmed *Moonraker* there. We flew over Diane's Mom and her husband James to be with Diane and help her after the baby was born. I was, of course, there for the birth and visited her at the hospital every morning on the way to the studio and every night after dinner until she was allowed to come home.

Bennett was only six and one-half pounds at birth, and was born shivering as it was winter in Paris. While he and Diane were still in the hospital, Diane's Mom took a picture of me holding the little guy in my hands with her Polaroid camera.

I had suggested to the publicity department that they should send someone out to take a picture of me and the baby, but my suggestions had fallen on deaf ears. When I looked at the Polaroid I knew that I now had the ammunition to convince them to do it. The next day at the studio I approached Saul Cooper, the publicity man, at the bar in the studio commissary with the Polaroid in hand. Saul was sitting with someone, but I was anxious to show him the picture of baby Bennett and myself, so I sat down next to them and let Saul see the Polaroid. Saul looked at it in awe and the other gentleman took it from him and exclaimed, 'If you give our paper an exclusive, we'll run this picture on page three!'

Saul wasn't any dummy and responded, 'This is just a Polaroid. I have a top photographer going to the hospital in the morning. I will give you an exclusive in England, if you wait for the good photo, but I want to put it on the wire service the day after you run it for the rest of the world.' The man agreed and the result was a photo story in the *Daily Mirror* and in newspapers throughout the world. So, as everyone in the production team found out, there are benefits to being a family man and taking your children with you on a shoot.

I remember while we were in Paris I had a call from *France Dimanche*, who wanted to send out a photographer and writer to do a feature story. I ran it by Saul Cooper, and he said that it was a newspaper much like the *National Enquirer* or the *Star* and, because it tended to do sensationalistic stories, he didn't recommend that I do it. I told him that I had experienced a good result with both the *Enquirer* and *Star* and that I had simply told them up front that my family was very important to me and I didn't want any story coming out that would hurt them. Both publications had done several positive stories on me as a family man, and the articles were of high human interest and very successful.

I was told that they didn't care if I did the interview – but they had warned me and I should be careful. I called the man who had left his number and told him that I would do the interview and let his photographer take pictures with me and my family if their editor would provide a letter giving me approval of the story prior to it being printed. He agreed, and a time was set for the interview and photo session on a day that I had off. When they arrived with the letter I, of course, read it carefully. It stated that before publishing the article they would read it to me over the phone, but there was no mention of my having to approve what they wrote. I pointed this out to them, and the writer said 'Look, we have to have our angles.'

I asked the writer to tell me who the readers of his newspaper were. He told me that they were mostly middle-aged housewives who were bored and wanted to read exciting stories about other people's lives. I said, 'Look, I'm here with my wife, my oldest son and my baby girl. We are about to have another baby right here in Paris. Now, wouldn't your middle-aged housewives be interested in hearing about this horrific giant actor who is such a sweet guy that he takes his wife and family with him everywhere he goes, even when she's pregnant and about to have a baby?'

The writer nodded his head in agreement and got on the telephone to his editor. He changed the letter and added his signature, and we took a lot of great pictures, resulting in a wonderful and huge story with a headline that read: 'Actor Richard Kiel, without his wife he is nothing!' Some men may have resented such an article, but to me it was a true statement, and the rest of the story was great.

We had some interesting times taking the entire family with us, even when we promoted the Bond films around the world. I remember 'flying down to Rio' with our family, plus Cubby and his wife Dana, to promote *The Spy Who Loved Me*. One or two of the Bond girls flew with us as usual. We flew First Class, as always, on Pan American Airlines, and thinking back on how many trips we made, with three or four of us flying First Class *before* I found out about frequent flyer miles, makes me shudder. We could have accumulated enough frequent flyer miles to take our family around the world a couple of times later on, but we didn't know about these things at the time.

The flight from Los Angeles to Rio wasn't too long, and by the time we got through customs and checked into the hotel it was almost dinner time. Diane was treated to a professional make-over by a local Brazilian make-up expert and she looked as beautiful as any South American beauty.

We didn't have dinner at the hotel as there were plans for us to attend a huge costume presentation at another big facility down the beach. The PR people arranged for a nanny to watch RG and Jennifer, and we were whisked away to the event. It was beautiful, with gorgeous costumes and amazingly beautiful women, but it went on and on and on. Diane was nursing Jennifer at the time, and Cubby had the driver take her back to the hotel while I stayed until the end of the show.

Later that evening, when I got back to the room, I asked Diane how her evening had been since she left us at the costume presentation. She looked me in the eye and with a funny little smile said, 'You really want to know?' Of course I said, 'Yes.' She began to tell me how she arrived back at the room and when she was about to send the nanny on her way, she realised that she didn't have any Brazilian money since we hadn't had time to change anything over, nor had the PR people given her any money as they had paid for the limo in advance with a good tip. She was smart enough to call down to the front desk, and the manager told her to send the nanny downstairs and they would take care of her and collect from the production company later. Diane tried to explain this to the nanny, but she wanted cash and refused to go downstairs even after speaking with the manager. Finally, the manager came up to the room with the money and the nanny left.

In the meantime, Jennifer had gone into the adjoining room and closed the door behind her. Diane had put the security lock on in that room and there was

With Linda Day George in *The Barbary Coast*

As Reece in *Silver Streak*

Jaws in *The Spy Who Loved Me*

Jaws going after James Bond

With Barbara Bach and Robert Shaw in *Force 10 From Navaronne*

With my robot dog in *The Humanoid*

As Golob in *The Humanoid*

This positive article saved my bacon with the Bond producer

The Spy Who Loved Me press cuttings

A journalist tries to wear my jacket

The Spy Who Loved Me premiere poster

Diane, the kids and I in Seville, Spain, going for a carriage ride

Caroline Munro and I pose for some publicity photos in Tivoli Amusement Park

Israel: RG on a camel

With RG and Jennifer visiting the Arc de Triomphe in Paris

Diane and the kids at the Grand Hotel in Taiwan

Mom, Diane, and my nieces Lisa and April with our children in Italy

Overlooking the Dead Sea

Our new grandson, Dawson, and his sister Sierra

My son Bennett, his wife Suzanne, and little Ben

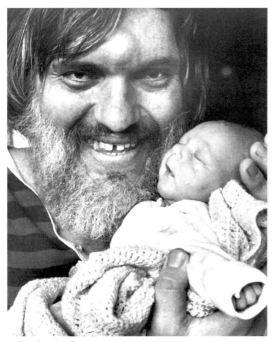

Baby Chris (and me)

Jennifer catches a fish at
Grandma's lake

Ferocious giant of James Bond movies shows his gentle side **STAR**

Richard Kiel, best known as the ferocious Jaws in the James Bond
movies, is just a gentle giant at heart. He's a family man who likes
relaxing at home near Yosemite Calif., with wife Diane and kids
R.G., 6, Bennett, 4, Jennifer, 5, and Christopher, 2.

The whole family in our backyard pool in Coarsegold, California

'Jaws' Is Hooked on Family Life

In two James Bond movies, hulking actor Richard Kiel played the villainous "Jaws," but in real life he's a 7-foot 2-inch gentle giant who loves to go fishing with his 3-year-old son Bennett. Kiel is shown here helping Bennett land a fish

Bennett and I fishing together

The whole family at our backyard pool in Covina, California

National Enquirer

Lewis Gilbert directing me in *Moonraker*

Diane's Mom, Claudie Mae, visiting Paris with Jennifer

Making the cover of *People* magazine

RG and I on the Phillipe Bouvar show in France

RG walking in Dad's shoes in our apartment in Paris

With my girlfriend Dolly, played by Blanche Ravelac

Moonraker publicity shot

With Roger Moore in *Moonraker*

With Cubby Broccoli, producer of the James Bond films, as Johnny Grant, Honorary Mayor of Hollywood, presents Cubby with his 'Official Star' on the Hollywood Boulevard walk of fame

SANS MA FEMME, JE PERDU*

L'étonnant roman d'amour du géant qui vous a étonné À LA T.V.

Il mesure 2 m 40

Elle mesure 1 m 57

Translated, the headline says 'Without my wife I am lost' I didn't mind them saying this, because it is certainly very true

I don't have a picture of my first screen kiss, but here's my first screen hug from Corinne Clery of *Moonraker* fame. Not bad, huh?

With Jackie Chan promoting *Cannonball II* in Tokyo

As Club in Clint Eastwood's *Pale Rider*

As Mr Eddie, wearing my disco duds in *So Fine*

Promoting *Think Big* in Japan with the Barbarian Brothers

Here I am as Mr Larson, bending Shooter McGavin's club

With Adam Sandler on location. I am sitting down!

With Julie Newmar in *Hysterical*

As Investigator Pewitt in *Flash and the Firecat*

My Mom, Mary Kiel, visiting the location at Kelty Meadow

Noley Thornton and I with the late Bart the bear, filming *The Giant of Thunder Mountain*

Filming at the
giant's cabin

With President Clinton and Senator Hillary Clinton

Diane and I at dinner with Bruce Weitz from *Hill Street Blues*, SF49er quarterback Joe Montana and other friends at the Caesar Awards

Our daughter Jennifer at age 8

Jennifer wins the World's Our Little Miss title in Dallas

Captain of the Yosemite cheerleaders

Jennifer and her husband Nara Sihavong and daughter Sierra

All of us on a cruise to Mexico

Our eldest son, RG, at his eighth grade graduation

Chris in Pop Warner Football

Playing Varsity Basketball

Chris in Little League

RG all grown up, with his girlfriend Lisa

Speaking at a High School in Cloudcroft,
New Mexico

SEPTEMBER 1951

BIBLE
SOCIETY Record

Me at
age 12

These are the members of the Sunday school of the Trinity Reformed
Church of El Monte, California, who through a Palm Sunday offering gave
five hundred "Good News"—illustrated copies of Luke's Gospel—and a
thousand Gospels of John to the patients in four hospitals in the Los
Angeles area on Easter Sunday

At age 12

With Ray Willey and Franklin Graham at the
Reagan Foundation tribute to Billy Graham

Meeting Billy Graham with Bill Brown, Steve Case and Ray Willey

no way to get in from the main room as the door had to be opened from the other side. There was also no way to use the key for that door by using the main entrance in the hallway, because the night security latch had been engaged by Diane. Jennifer was only eight months old and couldn't open the door from the inside, and because it became dark in the room when Jennifer closed the door, she began to cry.

Diane called the manager again, who told her that there was no way to get in the other room as the safety lock was engaged. Diane went ballistic, in a nice way, telling him that there was something that she could do since there was a glass window out in the hall with a fire hose inside and a fire axe and that if he didn't get the door unlocked very soon, she was going to use the axe to open it.

The manager told Diane to wait as he would send maintenance up to the room and they would get the door open somehow. Poor little Jennifer was screaming by this time, and Diane discovered that there was a large enough opening under the door out in the main hallway so she could put her fingers under the door, and by doing this and talking to Jennifer, she could calm her down enough so she would stop screaming. Of course, by this time, Jennifer wanted to nurse and Diane was definitely ready to nurse her.

The maintenance people arrived and told Diane that they were going to be able to send a small guy through the air-conditioning duct in the room next to the one that Jennifer was in, and for her to just hold on and please not to use the axe!

Diane said that she was out in the main hallway, putting her fingers under the door, touching Jennifer's fingers and talking to her, when a couple came out of the nearby elevator and saw her down on the floor talking to Jennifer through the crack under the door. Diane said she tried to explain that her daughter was trapped in the room etc, but the couple said something to each other in German and shrugged their shoulders and walked away.

The maintenance people finally got into the adjoining room and opened the door. Diane was able to nurse her little baby daughter, who was sound asleep when I arrived. Jennifer could be a little pistol at that time in her life, but she was a lot of fun. I remember one time on an international flight when a nice older man gave some hard candies to both her and RG. After the meal was served, the after-dinner drinks and the movie, everyone was asleep on this red-eye flight that was to arrive at our destination the next morning. I don't sleep very well on planes because even the First Class seats are not all that comfortable for me. I am so tall from the waist up that my head is way above the 'up' position of the head-rest and my shoulders hang out in the aisle so much that the flight attendants are always banging into them.

Something woke me up and I looked around to see our little Jennifer climbing all over the gentleman who had given her the hard candies before. She was going through his pockets trying to find some more. I got up and snatched her out of his lap and got some mints from the flight attendant so she would be happy.

While we were staying at the Raphael Hotel in Paris shooting *Moonraker*, and before we got an apartment on Rue Conjac Jay, we got tired of the fancy French food with all the sauce all over it. I remember one fish specialty called 'Sole Raphael' that had a sauce with capers in it. It was good even before you found out what those little black things were, but after having it twice you wanted something else. We had eaten everything on the menu at least twice and had ventured out to some of the other restaurants in the area, but the Raphael was just off the Champs Elysée and everything was pretty expensive.

One day we all decided that we had a craving for McDonald's and Diane grabbed a cab to go get some Big Macs, fries, etc. I am not a huge McDonald's fan, but after all the rich French food, it sounded good to me. I waited for Diane at the hotel lobby with Jennifer while she and RG cabbed over to get our hamburgers, fries and shakes. The two of them got out of the cab and, as the doorman at the Raphael opened the door for them, I grabbed some of the bags boldly marked with the Golden Arches logo and we trotted through the hotel lobby up to the room to enjoy. Of course, RG and Jennifer were into the bags and sipping their shakes through their straws on the way up the elevator. This was a pretty snobbish hotel, but I couldn't help but notice a few appreciative smiles among the snickers, especially from the employees who probably shared our views.

Most of the time we ate in the room at that hotel, so as to not ruin the dining experience of the regular patrons in the restaurant; our two young ones tended to be loud and break things from time to time. Our room service waiter was a very nice man from India who was quite dark-skinned, and RG affectionately called him 'Black Man'. We got to know him quite well and he liked RG and took no offence at the name RG had given him. In spite of the fact that we were there for a while, the Indian man was always a little afraid of me. Sensing this, Diane always answered the door, and he would take the silver covers off the food while keeping one eye on me to make sure that I didn't get him.

I am a prankster and practical joker. When I was 12 and about 6'2", I put a stocking over my head and knocked on the door to my house knowing that my aunt, who was visiting us, would answer the door. She just about had a heart attack and my father was mad at me for a year for scaring his sister like that.

Well, not one to learn lessons easily, like playing with guns, I borrowed the steel teeth one day after shooting was over, and when the Indian waiter came to the door, I was there to open it with my Jaws teeth in place. He shot off down the hall never to be seen again, and from that day on we had a new room service waiter.

When we took a break from filming in Paris to fly down to Rio to work on location, it was the beginning of winter in France. Our middle son Bennett had been born, and we had to get him registered at the proper place as a French-born person so we could then take those papers to the American Embassy and get him documented as a child born out of the country to two natural-born U.S. citizens. At the time these two procedures made him both a French citizen and a US citizen, and subject to the draft in France if he were to return after he reached a certain age.

Like I said before, Bennett was born shivering and it was cold enough in the apartment to require some heat, but in Paris all the landlords turned on their heat at the same time, and we hadn't reached the official date for that to happen. Because of this, we had to hold baby Bennett against our bodies at night or he couldn't sleep and he would wake up with his little gums chattering. One night, he slid off of Diane's stomach and landed on the floor. Thank God it was carpeted and the long bed that the studio had made for us was on a platform only about eight inches high.

We got him a passport with his baby picture on it in a little nightgown that had a 007 sticker on it and we flew down to Rio to continue filming *Moonraker*. Baby Bennett loved Rio because it was nice and warm and from the day that we arrived there he began to sleep without having to be held all night long. The hotel in Rio was not the same one we stayed at when we were doing the promotional tour for *The Spy Who Loved Me*, as Roger Moore or his wife Luisa had been told about this wonderful old flagship hotel on the beach that they must stay in. The production company then booked them, Diane and I, and all the other main stars into this great hotel. Or should I say 'not so great hotel', compared to the new hotel that we had stayed at before. This old hotel was hot as the air-conditioning system did not work well, and the rooms smelled musty, as it was quite old.

The production people helped us get an English-speaking nanny whose husband served as our driver, and the first thing the nanny did was open all the windows to let fresh air in. The fresh air was great, but we had a little girl who wasn't quite two years old and we were seven storeys up, and the wrought iron protective barrier that kept people from falling out of the window had bars far enough apart that a small child could squeeze through. When I saw this, I told the nanny that we couldn't leave the windows open because I was concerned for the children's safety, and I put the key to the window locks up on top of a tall dresser so our oldest son RG couldn't find it.

One day while I was at work and Diane was in our suite at the hotel with our three children, RG got sick and threw up in our bedroom overlooking the ocean. Diane got the key down and opened all the windows in that room and locked the doors so the children wouldn't be able to go in there. She was nursing Bennett when RG suddenly came out of the 'locked' room and told her that 'Jennifer is falling out of the window.' Diane put the baby down on the couch, and ran into the room to see that Jennifer had climbed through the barrier bars on the balcony and was sitting on the window ledge outside the bars and holding on to them as she surveyed the beach and the sidewalk seven storeys below.

Diane told me that she didn't yell at Jennifer or even say anything as she was afraid it might startle her and cause her to fall. She said she remembered grabbing Jennifer by her clothing and arm and pulling her head through the bars. At first Jennifer was stuck as her ears didn't want to come through. Diane thought she didn't care if Jennifer had any ears or not, she was not going to let her fall off the balcony. When she told me all this, I got the Heebie Jeebies just hearing about it, and even today it makes me shudder to even write about it.

I am not afraid of heights if I am inside an elevator or on a tram, like the one on the way to Palm Springs which rises in elevation more than any in the world, and as long as I'm in a building or elevator or a tram car, I feel safe as I trust the engineers. But to be hanging out there like Jennifer was, that's scary. I used to have to walk over the freeway on a pedestrian walkway next to the road that crossed over. The railing was only about three and one-half feet high and I'm seven foot plus, which gave me the feeling that I could fall over the side and, if the fall to the freeway didn't kill me, getting hit by one of the speeding cars in the lanes below certainly would.

When it came time to leave Rio and go back to the icy winter weather in Paris, everyone hated to go. I was told that I would not work for seven to ten days after we got back, but to check in with them daily if I went anywhere, just in case there was a change in the schedule. I had a bright idea. Why not stay in Rio, where we could now enjoy the beach since we were not filming. It was a lot less expensive to stay there than Paris, and they had a flight on the Concorde that we could book for just ten per cent over First Class that would get us back on a day's notice.

The production company agreed and we were ecstatic. There is no doubt that Paris is the prettiest city in the world in the springtime, but in the winter it's dreary, unless you enjoy slipping on frozen dog doo. The people in Paris take their dogs everywhere with them, even into restaurants and it's legal. Even cab drivers carry their dogs in the front seat with them. I remember my favourite Paris dog story. It happened when my mother-in-law Claudie Mae and her husband James came over for Bennett's birth so she could be there to help Diane with the baby.

James and I had gone to the American Hospital in Neuilly to visit with Diane and the baby while Claudie Mae had stayed at the apartment to fix dinner for everyone. We had taken a cab to the hospital and the driver had stopped across the street where he was letting us out. I was digging out the fare and a tip and James had stepped out of the back seat of the cab to light up a cigarette, and I noticed over the top of the seat that there was a huge Doberman dog laying there. The dog sat up when James got out and when he struck the match the dog snarled at him through the window, causing James to drop his cigarette.

When we got inside I told Diane this story and had her laughing so hard she almost busted her stitches from her third C-section.

The day we were to fly away on the Concorde was a sad one as we had really enjoyed our little vacation. Air France took us through customs and helped us with our children and were real nice about it when they told me that Diane and the children could go, but that I had a little problem with the police that had to be settled on Monday before I could go.

We were shocked and Diane said that she wasn't going if I couldn't go, and this made Air France a little nervous as we were four paying fares on a flight that was a surcharge over First Class. I asked what the problem was and it was explained to me that when I got the work permit in Paris to come to Rio, they had stamped a notification written in French stating that if I stayed beyond a certain date that I had to notify the police. Since I had stayed over without notifying the police, I had violated the law and it would have to be straightened out on Monday.

Diane and the children were free to go because they were all there on tourist's visas and there was no problem with them having stayed over. I asked to speak to whoever was in charge of this situation, and the Air France representative, myself, a production location manager, Diane, RG, Jennifer and the baby were all ushered into the Commandant's office.

Through an interpreter I explained that we had liked it so much in their country that we had decided to stay over and spend money, and because I didn't speak or read French, I had no idea that this notice was stamped in my passport or I would have reported to the police as required. The man said that he understood and that there would be no problem on Monday when his superior was there to get my departure approved. I asked if he couldn't call his superior officer at home, and he reluctantly agreed to do it. The Air France representative was beside herself as they were holding the flight for us and Concordes were never late!

The Commandant talked briefly on the phone to his superior at home then turned to us and smiled, and we were soon going at twice the speed of sound.

'BUT YOU'RE DEAD!'

When we came back from doing *Moonraker* in Paris and *The Humanoid* in Italy, we had been out of the country for ten straight months. While we were gone, my agent and my mother took care of our bills, and my sister and her husband and two girls lived in our house.

Sometime near the beginning of that ten-month period, the actor Ted Cassidy, who had played Lurch in the Addams Family, died.

The first morning after we came home, I was outside watering the ivy. We lived on a corner lot and I was by our neighbour's garage. The neighbour, who had been known to drink quite a bit, was pulling out of his driveway in his

Thunderbird when apparently he spotted me. He got out of the car and walked right up to me and put his finger in my face. 'But your dead!' he said, earnestly. 'I know you're dead. I saw it in the paper, and on TV!' I said, 'No, I don't think so,' as I pinched myself for his entertainment. Scratching his head, he got back in his T-Bird and drove quickly to the liquor store to replenish his supply.

Apparently, our neighbour thought the man in *The Addams Family* re-runs was me. It was a very common mistake; even some of Ted's former girlfriends would approach me sometimes like they had found a long-lost lover.

Over the years this problem manifested itself again when Fred 'Herman Munster' Gwynne died and even when Andre the Giant died. Ted and I were different heights and weights but had similar features, so I could understand the confusion there, but Fred Gwynne and Andre the Giant didn't look anything like me. I guess most people just see size. It's not fair, but I have learned to accept this fact of life, even though I don't like it.

Because of my unique size, I found it relatively easy to break into the movies and, after 17 long years of struggling, I finally made the two James Bond movies and became an overnight success. In all those 17 years I never lived in Hollywood. I only went to one small Hollywood party, and I left as soon as I saw things getting too rowdy to suit my upbringing. My social drinking was for years very modest, consisting only of the occasional beer or glass of wine.

It wasn't until the Bond films and the big success that they brought that I started having some real problems in my life. Success brought with it the ability to try fine Cognac, expensive Scotch whisky, and Dom Perignon champagne at the many James Bond press parties. In one country alone, Spain, we traveled to four cities (Madrid, Barcelona, Seville and Valencia) in just one week. In each city there was a screening and press party, complete with champagne and other drinks.

One year, my family and I spent six months flying from country to country all over the world. The James Bond producers flew all of us First Class. Now, as many of you know, this costs thousands of dollars extra over coach. In addition to a little more leg room and hip room (which, of course, I appreciate), you get a couple of freebies when you fly First Class and spend the extra thousands. The movies are free, you don't have to rent headsets, and you get free drinks. 'What would you like to drink before we take off?' 'What kind of wine would you like with your meal?' 'Would you like an after-dinner drink?'

Between these press parties and First Class flights, I found myself doing more drinking than I was used to – and, before I knew it, I was finding myself addicted to alcohol. I went from drinking the occasional beer, or glass of wine, to buying a fifth of Scotch every other day, along with wine and beer. Then it became a quart of Scotch, and finally I was also buying vodka to spike the beer and wine with it. At the end, I was also putting Scotch in my coffee in the morning.

TEN

MOVING ON

I n between the two James Bond films that I did, I made four other movies. One of those movies was with Harrison Ford and Robert Shaw. Everyone on the set respected Mr Shaw as the great actor we so enjoyed in *The Sting*, or *Jaws*, or *The Deep*. Others will always remember Robert Shaw as the killer on the train in *From Russia With Love*, but I'll always remember Robert Shaw as the father who read his son's letters to him from college to the whole crew, sharing every word with us as though we would appreciate hearing from his sons as much as he did. I also remember him as the husband whose younger wife would visit him on the set with their ten-month-old baby, and how proud he was of them.

Many in the entertainment industry will remember him as the author of several novels or the director of many plays, but I will always remember him most as Robert Shaw, the man, the husband, the father, the man who fell short on the golf course one day when his heart stopped beating as a result of too much alcohol.

I have worked with a number of actor friends over the years, like David Janssen and others, who had a problem with alcohol. Like drugs, alcohol can shorten people's lives. The human body isn't meant to operate on alcohol, drugs or cigarette smoke. I was scared to death because I knew what was in store for me if I kept smoking Pall Mall Reds and drinking like I was.

No one starts out in life to become an alcoholic or a drug addict. I mean, you don't just wake up one day and say, 'This is a beautiful morning. I think I'll become a drug addict or an alcoholic.' It just happens to people little by little.

I was watching the 700 Club on the Christian Broadcasting Network early one morning, and a man on that programme said, 'The word says when two or more of us are gathered together in his name that he (through the Holy Spirit) is there in our presence.' He also went on to say that 'when two or more of us agree touching anything (whether it be a bondage to alcohol, drugs, pornography, food, videos, cigarettes, or just plain being mean), that thing that is touched in agreement can be bound here on earth just as it is bound in Heaven.' And he invited the viewers to pray with him.

I prayed with that guy on television, and at first it seemed like nothing had happened. I mean, I didn't see any flash of light or hear bells or God's voice or anything. I didn't throw away the Scotch, beer, wine or vodka that I had in the house, but I suddenly found that I no longer desired it or was obsessed with drinking it. My friends came over and poured themselves stiff drinks and drank the beer, wine and vodka, but I had no desire or need for it anymore. After about ten months of abstinence, I finally figured out that I was no longer addicted to alcohol. This turned out to be the beginning of my spiritual growth.

Not long after being delivered from alcohol through the Lord, I was called by my agent to tell me that a man from an advertising agency would be calling me about doing a beer commercial for Schlitz Malt Liquor. He started to tell me about the commercial and he was full of enthusiasm.

'It takes place in a bar where people are sitting,' he said, 'and we hear the sound of brakes screeching and finally the sound of a horrible crash. Then you come in the bar wearing your steel teeth and with a bumper wrapped around your neck. You walk up to the bar and say 'Bull!' The bartender stammers 'B-b-b-bull?' 'Bull Malt Liquor,' you say and he gets you a draft. You start to drink it and the Schlitz Malt Liquor bull comes crashing through the wall, sees you and we do a reverse-motion trick and the bull goes back out the wall. Funny, huh?'

Yes, it was funny, extremely funny, but I had experience in bars as a bouncer and knew that bars could be very negative places. 'Does it have to take place in a bar?' I asked. 'Couldn't it be a family picnic?'

'Yes, it's in a bar,' replied the ad agency man. 'That's the only way it would work. Listen,' he went on, 'we've done demographic research on your Jaws character and you appeal to the 18 to 30-year-olds that drink beer, and they drink a lot of it in bars. We want to use your influence to get them to drink our brand.'

That was the 'kicker' and the word 'influence' jumped out at me. I am not a prude and I do not think there is anything wrong with a cold glass of beer on a hot day or a glass of wine or two with your meal. What is a problem is when you abuse alcohol like I had done, and I suddenly realised that I could lead young people down the path of destruction that I was once on by doing this 'funny' commercial to 'influence' them.

I thought about the time that one of my good friend's daughters was killed on graduation day. A young man who was not used to drinking had the typical grad day drinks and drove into their driveway, hitting the gas pedal instead of the brakes, which caused his car to roll up on the lawn, where my friend's daughter was taking pictures with a couple of her graduating girl friends. To compound the grief and misery, my friend was insured with Kaiser and, because she was taken to the nearest hospital, Kaiser did not want to pay the tens of thousand of dollars that ran up while she was in intensive care. They finally paid but that didn't bring his daughter back.

I said, 'I don't think that I want to do this!' The ad agency guy was cool and said, 'Look Richard, I shouldn't be telling you this, but we're willing to pay you $50,000 for a day's work to do this. We have arranged clearance with the Bond people and we're ready to go. Sleep on it. Talk it over with your wife, and I'll call you back tomorrow.' The guy was no fool. He knew that a man's wife could find 50,000 reasons to say 'Yes.' I did talk to Diane about it, and she said that if it bothered me, to not do it.

I didn't do the beer commercial, but a few months later I got to do a commercial for Sharp Electronics in Japan. I was their product spokesperson for the first front-loading VCR. I only made $25,000 for that, but a few months later I did a commercial for Glico Milk in Japan. We made $15,000 for that and we got to go to Hawaii and stay at the beautiful Mauna Kea Beach Hotel. I figured that this was almost as good financially as doing the beer commercial, as we had made $40,000. And I reasoned that the milk company and Sharp would not have hired me had I done the beer commercial.

Not long after we got back from Hawaii I got a part in *Hysterical* with the Hudson Brothers. It was filmed at Cannon Beach Oregon and at Depot Bay in the same state. Diane and I went up there for a while by ourselves, and then she went home to pick up two of our children and bring them back to Oregon. The other two were watched by our babysitter Krista.

One night Krista called and she was crying. We were afraid to hear what she was going to tell us, thinking that something terrible had happened to one of our children. She told us that her friend, another high school girl who had baby-sat for us, had been killed in an automobile accident on the highway. The girl was the daughter of a friend of mine and, again, the boys were not drunk but had just drunk a couple of beers. I realised again how good it was to not have to think about what brand of beer these boys had been drinking and wondering whether my 'influence' had anything to do with what happened.

Not too long after that, Pepsico called for me to do a Mug Root Beer commercial, as they had bought the California brand and wanted to introduce it nationally with a spy-type commercial featuring yours truly. It paid $100,000 and was renewed for another year for an additional $50,000. Had I done the $50,000 beer commercial, it is highly unlikely that I would have been selected by Pepsico to plug their root beer. Ironic, isn't it, that God honours right decisions that may cost you in the short term by making sure that in the long run you are rewarded for doing the right thing.

MOVING TO YOSEMITE LAKES PARK

Along the way in my early film career I had sold Lincoln Mercury cars, Toyota cars and, finally, real estate. During the real estate years, I sold property at Big Bear Lake for a broker who was very successful. When the three different subdivisions that we represented in Big Bear Lake were sold out, we moved on to other projects. One of those projects took me to a subdivision called Yosemite Lakes Park, a planned community in the foothills between Fresno and Yosemite National Park.

I really enjoyed selling property there in the subdivision. I was doing well enough to have a beautiful gold Cadillac convertible with a white top, which was usually down while I showed families this unique development. One of the local salesman on site kept horses for his children to ride, and many times when the day was over I would join them and ride one myself.

I had teamed up with another salesman, who would work my appointments when I was busy and vice versa. He was a former space engineer who had been laid off. I remember that, when we were first shown the subdivision, we were taken down to a rather large reservoir that was about a mile and one-half long. My sales partner, Don Hardy, asked the representative of the developer who was showing us around if he could leave his water ski boat parked on the reservoir so his family could use it while he was up on the project on the weekends selling lots. 'No,' the man said. 'The reservoir is a back-up water supply for Yosemite Lakes Park subdivision and you can't run a gasoline engine boat on it. Rowboats, canoes, sailboats and boats with electric motors are all fine, but not water ski boats.'

Years later, Diane and I bought an existing home in the subdivision and together we tilled the soil with a machine, and Diane and I leveled and rolled the ground so we could plant grass and trees. We had a man and his father put in an automatic sprinkler system and we planted a combination of Deodar Cedars and Coastal Redwoods in the front yard and a lot of fruit trees in the back. We planted alternating swathes of purple-red and white verbena along the front circular driveway and alternating white and purple-red oleanders down each side of the property line. In the back yard we had all kinds of ornamental flowers like pansies, petunias, and other colourful varieties planted around the trees in circles. I installed a hammock between a couple of trees so I could enjoy my handiwork and read novels. The sprinklers would fire one set at time until the entire property was sprinkled or dripped, and it was gorgeous.

Another gentleman who was a retired race car driver named Bill Vukovich had a similar property to ours, except his home was on a corner. The real estate sales people would drive people by his home and ours and point out who lived there. I remember that well as I would be on my hands and knees putting gopher bombs down holes when they would drive by and point. But Bill Vukovich and I weren't the only people with beautiful yards – there were a couple of dozen other properties scattered around the subdivision where folks had beautiful trees and gardens.

There were only about 300 homes built at that time in a subdivision with over 2200 building lots, so our homes encouraged many people to buy. It was a beautiful place, with a Robert Trent Jones nine-hole golf course kept a verdant green with large water hazards which were kept brim full with water. The clubhouse was laid out so as to be surrounded by beautiful lakes which could be seen from both the lounge and restaurant. An Olympic-size swimming pool and a couple of tennis courts were also located at the community clubhouse.

We thought we had found heaven until the next year when we had over a dozen days in May that went over 100 degrees. Notices were mailed from the water company that told everyone that the storage tanks were being depleted of water and we were going to have to conserve. Then there was a fire in the subdivision that used up some of the stored water, and another notice was sent out saying that a couple dozen property owners were using way too much water and that the subdivision had a pumping capacity of 285 gallons per minute which was being pumped 24 hours a day, and that just 300 homes were using more than that. Everyone was asked to water just every other day. Even lot numbers could water on even days and odd number lots on odd days. They also directed that no outside watering at all should be done on the weekend, which meant that whether you were even or odd you couldn't water for three days. And, in 100 degrees plus, that meant that all the beautiful young plants we had planted were going to die!

A meeting was held at the community clubhouse, which was attended by the Vice-President of the development company that still owned the water company, a couple of representatives from the State Health Department and the Public Utilities Commission. I had asked other residents about the back-up water supply at the reservoir, and they answered, 'What reservoir?' I said the one where we're supposed to be able to sail boats and canoes. 'Oh, that one!' they answered. 'The developer fenced off those entrances a couple of years ago and we can no longer go down there.'

I went to the meeting and listened to a presentation that was literally blaming the race car driver and myself, along with a couple of dozen others, for the problem. I remembered that when we sold property in the subdivision there was supposed to be a completed water system paid for by the developer, which was under the multi-million dollar completion bond held by the County. I thought, 'If there's supposed to be a water system here capable of supplying 2200 homes, how could they be running short of water with just a few hundred homes built?' It didn't make sense.

The man representing the developer told of how we had used so many million gallons of water during the last 90 days. They knew this because each property had a water meter so they could add it up.

I noticed that the man next to me had a calculator and I asked him to multiply 285 (the gallons per minute) times 1440 (the number of minutes in a day) times 90 (the 90-day period). He did and the number exceeded what we had just been told by over a million gallons. I piped up and asked if they had pumped the 285 gallons per minute 24 hours a day for the past 90 days, and the man said 'Yes.' I asked, 'What happened to the extra million gallons?'

He was perplexed and I explained my calculations. The man from the State Health Department and the men from the Public Utilities Commission pulled out their calculators, and of course they came up with the same numbers I did. I then asked how a water system that was supposed to be capable of supplying water to over 2200 lots could be running short of water when only a few hundred homes had been built. The developer's man said, 'If you want to form a committee and investigate our books, you are more than welcome to.'

I did form a committee, and we found that the developer hadn't completed the water system as promised. We also found that all but $100,000 of the many millions in bonds had been released, and that the county still held the $100,000 in cash. I became president of the homeowners' association, and we took on the developer and the County through a lawsuit in an effort to make things right for myself and all the people that had bought lots there, some of whom had bought from me.

In the meantime, the developer scurried to make things right (at least temporarily) and they put in another one and one-half million gallons in storage tanks and drilled a number of new wells. The only problem was that they were charging the utility with the cost of all this expansion, which was supposed to have been done and paid for, and our water rates were doubling and doubling again.

The developer-owned utility company quit pumping water into our golf course and clubhouse lakes, instead using it for drinking water and domestic use. The lakes were drying up and the whole place was taking on the look of turning into a mudhole. In fact, during that summer, the lake bottom at the clubhouse was so dry it developed cracks.

I decided that in order for me to be effective I would have to let my lawns, fruit trees and flowers die! I turned off the sprinklers and the drip lines as I didn't want them to be able to use my use of water as an excuse to attack me and win. To add insult to injury, we found that not only had the reservoir property been deeded over to a creditor, but that the vice-president of the development company and a former president of the homeowner's association had gone to work for the creditor and had developed a plan to build 1000 condominium units on 40 acres on the banks of the reservoir that was supposed to have been our back-up water supply. We found that booster tanks that were along the roads going up the hills had no pumps installed or even electricity available. Pipes went into the ground that were not connected to anything.

During my two or three-year term as president of the homeowner's association, there were some people who apparently felt that I was getting in the way of the money they could make in the construction or sale of the 1000 condominium units. Two times these people tried to frame me with false charges of criminal assault upon them, which I was totally innocent of as a sheriff's investigation and polygraph lie detector test proved. At a public meeting I invited the person making the charges to take the test that I had passed. That person refused. People made subtle threats to me and my family in the middle of the night, and there was even a plot uncovered where someone was trying to hire a person to burn my house down.

A number of other people were involved with me in bringing out the truth about our water system and the potential negative effect of 1000 condos, and many people suffered a great deal because we were willing to stand up for what was right. A lot of propaganda was distributed in an effort to make those good people appear to be evil. It didn't work, and the State Health Department stopped the condominium project on the basis that it was going to be built upon a water supply that had already been promised to our subdivision.

This took place shortly after I wrote a letter to President Reagan about what was going on, and he wrote back promising to have someone from the EPA look into the situation (*see frontispiece*). The letter to me resulted in headlines in our local newspaper. The Public Utility Commission forced the developer-owned utility company to resume providing irrigation water to the golf course and clubhouse lakes.

It took a few years, but the homeowner's association ended up getting a settlement of a few hundred thousand dollars from the developer and the County. This gave us money to drill more new wells and to hook up the booster pumps. We also gained control of the utility company, access for fishing and boating at the reservoir and first right to a substantial amount of water impounded there each year.

I learned a great deal about politics from this experience. No matter how well you do, you won't make everyone happy. In fact, if you make two-thirds of your constituents happy, you're doing great! That means that the other one-third probably either hate you or at least dislike you. You have to be thick-skinned to be a politician, and if you are going to try and do the right thing you have to realise that many people will disagree with you and not always in a pleasant way. People tend to be selfish and want what they want from you even if it's at the expense of others.

FIRST SCREEN KISS

It was sometime after the two Bond films that my agent called to say that I had a part in *Simon & Simon*, a new private investigator show starring Gerald McRaney and Parker Jameson. I was amazed when I read the script that not only did the character talk and have a girlfriend, but he kisses his girlfriend on screen in the episode. I had received my first screen hug from Corrine Clery in the Italian movie *The Humanoid*, but no kiss.

It wasn't an easy thing kissing a girl for the first time on the screen. Some stars do it all the time and probably really get into it and end up falling in love with their co-stars, but when you are a happily married guy with a young and pretty wife it isn't so easy. Do you keep the kiss quick and demure or do you resort to acting and make it sloppy like you see some of the other actors doing? The girl they cast as my girlfriend was real cute, and I just decided to pretend I was kissing my wife. I realised when it was over that she wasn't my wife and that she probably was somebody on the show's girlfriend or at least good friend. It was kind of embarrassing to say the least.

The other problem was that my back had gone out for some strange reason, and I was seeing Gerald McRaney's chiropractor. In the scene where I kiss my girlfriend they wanted me to pick her up, as she was only about 5'2". If it looked like kissing a girl was a painful experience, it was because my back was hurting when I picked her up.

My wife, Diane, was a little amused, I suppose, when I told her not to worry. 'If it's taken me 20 years in my career to get to kiss a girl on the screen, by the time I get to do anything more than that I would be too old.' Unfortunately, I was right. Here we are 20 years after that and I haven't even repeated the kissing part.

A lot of fans liked that episode, however, and if any producers are reading this then you better hurry up and cast me as a lover before it's too late.

ELEVEN

WITH BURT REYNOLDS, JACKIE CHAN, CLINT EASTWOOD... AND ALL BY MYSELF

I n *The Cannonball Run II*, I wondered why they cast this Chinese guy as my co-driver. I thought that maybe the studio was trying to balance racial quotas or something. Warner Bros sent me to Tokyo to promote the film and Jackie Chan joined me there. I soon found out why they had hired him: Jackie Chan was as popular as the Beatles or Elvis Presley in Japan. Of course, today he is popular all over the world, but at that time, unless you were a martial arts movie buff, you didn't know who he was. Japanese teenyboppers knew who he was, however, and they were coming out by the thousands to see him, even at 7.00 am in the morning when we were doing a live news show.

Like myself, Jackie had a sense of humour and he was my best audience, cracking up when the little Japanese newscaster asked me if I had any trouble with the beds and the size of the room at the hotel. I answered her very seriously, 'No problem. I just stick my feet out the window!' The Japanese newsmen and the newswoman all had mouths agape as they believed every word of my joke, and Jackie was beside himself laughing.

Like all Burt Reynold's films (where he's the main star), this film was a lot of fun to work on. Everyone had a motor home or their own trailer and everyone had a golf cart to get around in. I really appreciated that as walking has never been one of my favourite things to do, especially in the 110° Tucson summer sun.

I was asked by someone whether I had seen the first *Cannonball* film as I was in number II. I thought that I better take a look at a video so I wouldn't appear ignorant if asked about it. I was shocked! There wasn't that much difference between the film that I saw on video and the one that I was doing. There's nothing wrong with sequels; in fact, some people say that *The Godfather II* was as good as the original. But, if you are going to make a sequel, it should be different in storyline from the original. In spite of the similarity, the film had some very funny moments.

I had an ulcer on the ball of my foot at that time (it healed up after a subsequent surgery) and it got infected during the filming. I checked myself into the hospital, and they determined that the infection was a serious one called 'pseudomonas' and I had to be treated with antibiotics administered through an IV. When you see me dressed in my racing uniform, you have no idea that I have a heparin block in my arm under the jacket and in between takes I had to administer antibiotics through my own IV.

That's why I let Jackie Chan take care of the motorcycle riff-raff without my help in the scene at the Japanese fruit stand. He was happy to do it and it was kind of funny to see me watch him perform while I ate a watermelon. Today, it makes even more sense to people watching the video, as Jackie Chan needs no help from me to take care of a half-dozen hoodlums. At the time, however, having a needle in my veins was the reason.

MAKING IT BIG IN THE ORIENT

After the first James Bond film, I was asked to do a film in Taiwan. The film, *The Phoenix*, was terrible, but we got to go to Taipei and stay at the famous Grand Hotel that was built by Madame Chaing Kai Chek. The hotel was great but the movie-making was the most primitive I have ever experienced. The studio had dirt floors, there was no heat except portable heaters, and it was freezing cold. Instead of the camera dolly being made out of aluminum and pulled by a guy who followed your movements, it was instead made out of wood with rubber tyres and was pushed by a burly guy, and you had to follow him and walk and talk at the same time. We did enjoy the Mongolian barbecue in downtown Taipei, and Diane enjoyed staying in the luxurious Grand Hotel while I toiled on dirt floors in the freezing cold studio.

I made another film a few years later in Taiwan called *Mob Busters* and it was a lot more sophisticated, although it was still a B or C-film, by our standards. It was made near a port city there and we stayed at a Holiday Inn, making the experience more nearly American.

Finally, I made another film in Hong Kong, which when it came out was the biggest grossing film of all time there. It was called *Aces Go Places III*, and starred Sam Hoy, who was one of several Hoy brothers who were famous in Hong Kong. Sam was a good-looking young man and was also a singer whom the ladies loved. The film was pleasant to work on, except that the Hong Kong style of shooting was to go all day and night sometimes, and I had to explain to them that I wasn't capable of doing that.

We have stayed at the famous Peninsula Hotel a number of times. One of the Peninsula's trademarks was that they furnished Rolls-Royce cars to pick you up and deliver you to the airport (for a price, of course). They are all the same jade-green colour with the hotel insignia on the side. This time we stayed at the Royal Garden Hotel where we saw the Chinese New Year's fireworks display explode in the sky from our hotel window.

We also paid for and brought back towels, bathrobe and ash-trays with the Royal Garden's 'RG' emblem for our son of the same name. The only thing left today with the hotel insignia is an ash tray as we do not smoke and neither does RG. The best part about working in Hong Kong is getting to taste real Chinese food and, for me, being able to take advantage of the Hong Kong tailor shops. I bought suits, sport coats, and custom-made shirts for a song compared to what they cost here. Any Hong Kong producers reading this, I could use some new clothes, so make me an offer.

'SO FINE' IN NYC

I was sent a script from Mike Lobell and Andrew Bergman called *So Fine*. Bergman, Billy Crystal's brother, had written the script and would be directing the film. I read the script, in which I would co-star with Ryan O'Neal and Jack Warden along with Mariangela Melato (of *Swept Away* fame), who would play my wife. In this movie I played a no-class but very rich gangster whose wife ends up having an affair with the Ryan O'Neal character. Although Mr Eddy, the guy I played, is so rich he has a large painting of himself hanging over the fireplace, he still talks in short, staccato phrases like 'sleepy-peepy' and 'hungry.'

An interview was arranged and I met with Bergman and Lobell at a hotel. When they answered the door I said, 'Hungry!' This, along with my size, cracked them up and I was hired on the spot.

Doing *So Fine* meant living in New York City for a few months, and that was great. We took all the children with us and an apartment was arranged by the production personnel. The apartment was located at East 80th between 2nd and 3rd Avenue, as I recall, and we checked RG into a private Christian school called All Souls. It was wintertime and RG came home from school the first day all excited, saying, 'Mom, Dad, you ought to see this school. It's really neat! The playground's on the roof and there's snow up there.'

We got to go to a number of Broadway shows: *Evita*, *They're Playing Our Song*, *42nd Street* and *A Chorus Line*. We took the kids to the Metropolitan Opera to see *Hansel and Gretel*, and went backstage to see the gingerbread house.

Living in New York is great, especially if someone else is paying for it and you have the budget to go everywhere in cabs. The take-out food is fantastic, especially the Chinese and pizza. Why? Because there are so many Chinese and pizza places that deliver and it's so competitive that everything is good and it's delivered hot. They even deliver your groceries from the little markets which can be good. I saw the movie *Death Wish* with Charles Bronson, where his wife is killed by people delivering groceries, so I was a little paranoid.

We had a part-time nanny and housekeeper named Josie to help Diane with the kids while she went shopping, etc. She was from Haiti and very honest and hard-working. One afternoon when I came home and had a cold soft drink on the couch I didn't realise that my weekly per diem money had dropped out of my pants pocket. We were going to a play that night and I had gone into the bedroom to change clothes when I heard a loud knocking on the door. When I opened the door I found Josie standing there holding a wad of money. She was frantic to give the money to me and we found out later that in Haiti stealing is really frowned upon. They cut off a finger the first time and the second time they may cut off your hand. Worse than that, the family and friends of the thief quit talking to him or her and this is almost worse than the amputation.

They have a chain of cookie stores in NYC called David's that makes the best cookies I have ever tasted. One day I was walking by David's and it was snowing outside and the smell of those cookies baking was overwhelming. I bought 18 of them as there were six of us at that time and I figured that would be three each. By the time I walked the three blocks in the snow I had eaten all but five of them since they were hot and so scrumptious.

The sit-down restaurants are terrific in New York City. Diane and I both like fish and there was a little restaurant called the Butterfish Hole just around the corner, and the fish they served was caught off Long Island and brought in fresh daily. Mmmmmm.

The Italian food was second to none. I particularly liked a family-style Italian restaurant called Carmine's. The first time I went there it was with some friends and we all started to order an entrée each. The entrées seemed pretty pricey until the waitress explained that one entrée was enough for four people. Not convinced, we ordered two entrées for four people and it was way more than enough; the meatballs were about the size of tennis balls.

So Fine is one of my funniest movies and I especially enjoyed doing the scenes at the opera. If you haven't seen it, check it out.

PALE RIDER

Burt Reynolds did *The Rookie* with Clint Eastwood and there was another very large actor in it. According to Clint, Burt asked him why he didn't use me in the film. Clint said that he would consider using me in the future and I got cast in *Pale Rider*.

Clint was the director and executive producer and saw to it that my family had a nice condominium in Sun Valley, Idaho to live in while we were shooting. When we had friends come up and they went out to the location, Clint would come over and introduce himself, as though anyone didn't know him. I thought this was a very nice gesture on his part as most movie stars are often too busy to go out of their way to be gracious.

Sun Valley, Idaho is a beautiful town for skiing in the winter and a beautiful place to visit in the fall, which was when we were there. Ketchum, which is a little town down the road from Sun Valley, is very quaint and well-preserved. The buildings there all fit into the style and theme of another time, and the main road goes around the town leaving it quiet and peaceful. Our family really enjoyed our time there.

The gold mine in the movie was located at a working gold mine, which we were told was quite productive. They did not employ hydraulic water blasters as seen in the film, but they did haul a double trailer of ore out of there about every hour on the hour. The mine was at an elevation of about 10,000 feet, making the early morning calls bitter cold. I bought a bunch of a new kind of hand-warmer, consisting of a packet of chemicals which you broke to activate and then they heated up, keeping your hands warm; I'd put one in each pocket.

Among other things the part called for me to ride a horse into a scene, get off and threaten the townspeople and get back on and ride off. I employed the service of a local horseman to tune me up and make me look like I was experienced with horses. The horseman told me that the main thing in getting on and off the horse was to make it look easy and natural like you did it all the time. He said that when you got off the horse you did not look down as this made you look like a novice, but rather to dismount without taking your eyes off of your adversary, thus making yourself look cool.

Unfortunately, the horse that they picked out for the filming was a small pony that was chosen to make me look bigger. The only problem with that was that the little horse was very uncomfortable with such a big and heavy person on its back and it let me know this by constantly whinnying and moving its body. We rode into the scene, and my horse was shuffling all around because of its discomfort with me. I tried to be cool and get off without looking down, as I had been instructed by my horse mentor to do. I was looking the townspeople in the eye as I got off and didn't realise that the horse had moved over to the edge of the small canyon, and as I stepped out of the stirrups and planted my foot on the ground that wasn't there, I found myself plummeting down the canyon. Fortunately, I wasn't hurt, simply shaken but not stirred.

After that fiasco, they tried tying the horse to a bush so he wouldn't move, but the horse simply pulled the bush out of the ground and moved around anyway. They then tried hobbling the horse with steel hobbles that hooked his front legs together, making it very difficult for him to move around. Well, he moved around anyway doing a funny little shuffle with both front legs moving together. Finally, they had a man stationed there who laid on the ground and held the horse's reins tight so he couldn't move and I wouldn't fall down the canyon again.

Clint reworked the script, and although he whacks me in the family jewels in that scene with a sledgehammer, he also recommends ice for my pain. Later on, when the young girl visits the mine and is about to be raped, he turns me into a somewhat good guy, as in the new scene I am opposed to the girl being raped and move to stop it.

Clint is as much of a businessman as he is a director and has a reputation for bringing films in on budget and on schedule. As a result of this everyone doesn't have a motor home and a golf cart, but he treats everyone well. Warner Bros gave Clint a Bluebird Bus motor home for his own use as a gift in consideration of his always being on budget or under.

There were some very good actors in the film and I enjoyed working with such professionals. Everyone who was cast seemed perfect in their role, and the film had a very realistic quality because of that. All in all, it was a very pleasant and rewarding experience working on *Pale Rider* and with Clint. I hope to do another film with him in the future.

GIVING BIRTH TO MY OWN MOVIE

A movie producer, Tim Penland, who had made a nicely-done film starring Roy Rogers called *McIntosh and TJ*, was talking to me about starring in a movie that he wanted to make. During our first interview he talked about making a movie about circus freaks, and he must have noticed me grimacing as he changed the concept to a movie called *The Harder They Hit*.

This eventually changed to a movie about a winner-take-all bareknuckled fighter in a Roman arena-type concept. Penland tried to get a number of writers to work on various concepts he gave them – without success, as they kept bringing in scripts they had already written that were good, but not anything like what Tim had in mind. Finally Penland came up with a story idea of his own about a giant and some little boys. He tried to get someone to write it for him but no one seemed to write exactly what he had in mind. I decided to have a crack at it and wrote a 25-page treatment about a giant and a little girl who had a couple of brothers. He liked it a lot and had a writer friend of his polish it a little for a consultant's fee.

A couple of years went by and it seemed that Tim Penland had put the story aside so I decided to buy it back from him so I could pursue it on my own. He put a price on it of $15,000 cash and, with the help of several friends and investors, I bought it back from him. Another aspiring writer friend, Tony Lozito, had a computer and the two of us developed my story into a shooting script. Another good friend, Neil Brown, helped me package the film, and together we pursued investors.

For anyone trying to put together a movie deal, I must tell you that the average movie deal takes about five to ten years to get financed, and that's if you have a quality screenwriter, a known director and big stars. We finally found a man named John Herklotz who was willing to put up half the money if we could find someone with the other half, and we set out to find that someone. While on a search that took us to Costa Rica, Mr Herklotz decided to do the whole thing. My friend Tony and I got paid for our script after repaying the people who helped buy Penland out, and I was delegated the job of co-executive producer, along with the money man, and we set out to produce what was to be my first film. The movie was called *The Giant of Thunder Mountain* and earned a couple of four-star reviews and the Film Advisory Board's Family Film Award of Merit.

The most exciting thing about producing a movie is to watch the sets that you helped design, the costumes that you envisioned and the actors you helped to cast all come to life on the screen.

I had found a company in Montana that put together log homes and cabins that would custom build a log cabin for our giant, which had much taller ceilings and very rough-hewn logs that were two or three times as big as normal. The whole cabin was pre-cut and came in a kit on a truck with two men and a crane and a box of nails. Filming was supposed to begin on a Monday at this cabin, which had to be built in a remote area of the National Forest called Kelty Meadow. The Forest Service, while co-operative, made us put up a bond and promise that we wouldn't hurt the forest or the meadow. Consequently, the cabin had to be built on a pad of sand, and aluminum tracks had to be put down for the trucks to bring in the supplies so we wouldn't hurt the grass.

The materials for the cabin were supposed to arrive about a week before shooting, but there was a delay and everything arrived late Thursday afternoon. I had hired about a half dozen interns from several different Christian colleges where they had theatre arts and television production programmes. Plans were being made for alternative sets and locations to film at instead of the cabin while the two men and our construction people, along with the interns, raced to get everything up and in place. On Monday morning I arrived at Kelty Meadow to find a completely furnished cabin with smoke coming out of the chimney, chickens in the vegetable garden, and logs piled up next to it for firewood. It was almost like having your first baby. Wow!

The only negative part about making the movie was the fact that, originally, my little girl Jennifer was supposed to play the part of the little girl in the movie, Amy. I had two directors read her and they both said she was capable. By the time we raised the money, Jennifer was no longer a little girl and I had to make a decision based upon what was best for the movie. Jennifer understood perfectly and even helped us pick out the perfect little girl. One day when Jennifer was visiting the set, watching Noely Thornton doing a great job, I noticed that she was mouthing the words silently that she had memorised and it brought a tear to my eye.

Everything went very well during the production of *The Giant of Thunder Mountain*. One of the things that happens more often than not in the movie business is that films go over budget, usually way over budget. Because of this, many investors require a completion bond backed by a reputable insurance company like Fireman's Fund. The investor, John Herklotz, was no exception and a completion bond was in place.

With a completion bond company guaranteeing that you will complete the production for the budgeted amount, you have to be very careful as they monitor your spending almost daily, and if it even looks, in their opinion, like you're going to go over budget, they have the right to fire the producers, director, or whoever they want to and bring in their own people to complete the film.

Although this may give the investor a completed film, it may not have the same quality, as the completion bond company isn't as caring about those things as they are about getting the job done.

As an actor, I knew that most actors are hoping the film will go over schedule so they can work more days or weeks and make more money. They don't care if that means the film goes over budget since that is not their concern. This is also true for the director, production manager, first assistant director, second assistant director etc. If the film goes over schedule and over budget, they all make more money.

Now, almost all movie budgets have what they call a 'contingency fund'. After you 'guesstimate' to the best of your ability how much a film is going to cost, you add in this amount, which is a percentage of your estimated budget. The contingency isn't always enough as films go over schedule because of artistic differences, etc, and big-time producers are prepared to step in with additional investors and more money if they have to. Consequently, a small first-time producer has to plan and budget very carefully so the film doesn't get taken away from him.

I had a different idea. What if we took the contingency amount and made it a potential bonus fund to be split among the key actors, producers, director, production manager and assistant directors when the picture is completed? A director or actor making $10,000 a week could earn five per cent, for example, of a $500,000 contingency fund on a $5,000,000 film if it comes in on schedule and without going over budget and using up any of the fund. Five per cent of $500,000 is $25,000, which is more than the $10,000 the actor or director would make if the film went over schedule an additional week. So the incentive is greater for all these key people to get it done on time, make more money and have more time to enjoy the extra money.

My plan worked almost to a fault. Everyone involved was working so hard towards keeping the film on budget that some decisions were made that took away somewhat from its quality. I had planned to go to a little town on the Pacific Coast called Garberville, where the fog rolls in from the ocean and the sun shines through the extremely tall coastal redwood trees, creating shafts of light that shine down on the four-foot tall ferns that cover the ground between the trees, making for a very ethereal scene, especially with the giant and the little girl walking through all this. It was decided, without my previous knowledge, that this could be done with smoke-emitters in the forest at hand, saving the cost of a move to the coast and Garberville. The smoke-emitters didn't work since the smoke didn't look like fog and the entire scene was left out of the finished product, because it looked more like there was a forest fire somewhere.

Another shot that I wanted consisted of filming the children going through a covered bridge over the Merced River in Yosemite and through a little village of authentic buildings that had been moved there. The covered bridge was built in Abraham Lincoln's time, and I envisioned having someone on its shingled roof sprinkling Fuller's Earth through the cracks so the tiny shafts of glittering light would be seen as the children come through the bridge, and then we would pan up with our crane to expose the larger scene and the roaring Merced River. Later in the film, the posse would ride over the covered bridge at night, torches in hand, and, with the whole scene punctuated by the almost deafening sound of clattering horse's hoofs on the wooden floor of the bridge, create a very dramatic moment.

We were experiencing some difficulty with the new governor of Yosemite, who had just been appointed. He was worried about something happening to the covered bridge with the posse all coming through at once. I believe that with the help of some Senators, Congressmen and even the President, if necessary, that we could have filmed in Yosemite and used that bridge. We may have had to show two or four horses going through at a time and interspersing that with shots of horses' hoofs, but I believe we could have pulled it off. Because of the potential bonuses, however, it seemed more prudent to substitute a small bridge on private property that, again, was near the location. End result? We not only came in on schedule, we came in ahead of schedule, and not only was none of the contingency used, approximately $200,000 were saved as well.

As co-executive producer, I benefited from the bonus myself, so I can't complain financially, but as co-writer and star of the film, I believe we could have still done the scenes as originally intended. And, although we wouldn't have saved the extra $200,000, everyone would have earned the same bonuses, with the difference being the extra quality of production. My bonus plan would be viable if people were made to stick to the original production values. A lesson to use later.

The Giant of Thunder Mountain was still a very good film. In fact, by family film standards it was exceptional, and as I stated earlier it earned two four-star reviews and a family film award of excellence.

The other area of potential savings, which would have changed the quality again, I *did* find out about. The film had a scene where a bear kills the giant's parents, and later in the film, the giant and the bear have it out in what is without a doubt the best fight scene with a bear that's ever been shot on film. To accomplish this, I intended to use Bart the Bear that was in the movie *The Bear*. Bart was love-trained and could do a large number of tricks upon command. Using Bart was going to be expensive, however. In *The Bear*, it is said that Bart made over a million dollars for himself and his group of trainers. I had seen Bart with his owner and trainer, Doug Sues, on the cover of *National Geographic*. Bart was floating down a river on his back and Doug was sitting on him like a raft.

I sent Doug a copy of the screenplay, and he really liked it because he was a family man himself, and also because it portrayed Bart as a real bear and not a Disney-type caricature. Real bears are something to be afraid of, and as much as Bart truly loved Doug, he still was like a 1,800-pound loveable Doberman that had claws six inches long and a muscular structure capable of decapitating a person with a single swoop. Anyway, Doug liked the script so much he was agreeable to bringing in Bart to play the role we had in mind for about $100,000, and we were also going to use some of his other animals and trainers. I had learned from making the Bond films that a stuntman doesn't have to be my size as long as he looks like me and moves the same way. Doug assured me that he could do the stunt fight with Bart, and we figured that we could dress him in smaller duplicates of my clothes and that I would just be involved in the close-ups.

With everyone trying to save money in order to make their bonuses, I was approached about using a much cheaper bear that didn't have an owner-trainer who would do the stunt fight with him. I was assured that a stuntman we'd hired for the film would do the same stunts and that we could save about

$75,000. Other people working on the film told me that this bear they were talking about was mean and unpredictable and that someone could get hurt. I talked with the stuntman and asked him how he intended to go about the fight. He said that he would just do it and see what happens.

The biggest expense on a film production is the enormous cost of having everyone there on location and any kind of delays are very costly. I had visions of this stuntman trying to do this, getting hurt and still having to bring Bart in from Montana while everyone waited around. I told the line producers and the stuntman that I would rather send the stuntman to the bear, have him try to do the fight, and for them to get it on videotape so we could see whether it would really work. Well, it never happened and they all decided to use Bart. If you ever get a chance to see this film and the stunt fight with the bear, I know that you will agree that the decision was a good one.

In addition to having a plan to bring the film in on budget and on time, our little company had devised a marketing plan to help make sure that it was a success. Being a wholesome family movie, we thought that America's church-going families would especially enjoy it and would take their children to see it if they knew in advance that it was suitable and had none of the elements of language, sex and gratuitous violence they didn't like. We had made a contract with Tim Penland, who had promoted three films for Warner Bros through the churches.

One film in particular, *Chariots of Fire*, was not a religious film per se, but rather a well-made wholesome film with good acting and a good story. The film did not do so well until Tim and his partner devised a plan to get the churches behind it. Penland and his partner screened *Chariots of Fire* for the churches and came up with a ticket plan that would provide savings and benefits for the church groups that helped to get the movie seen by their congregations. The plan worked beautifully, and people all across the country began filling theatres to see this great film, which won an Academy Award for best picture that year.

I knew that we had made a very good film but, like *Chariots of Fire*, you have to reach the right audience in order to get the word of mouth out about it. Our contract would have had Tim Penland doing his thing with the churches, and our little company doing something similar with youth groups like the Boy Scouts and Girl Scouts, Campfire Girls and Boys, Woodcraft Rangers etc.

Like the contingency bonus programme, there were many facets of a programme like this that would have to be worked out and perfected, so a test programme in three marketing areas was envisioned to fine-tune this marketing approach before applying it nationally. We put together a budget that we felt would accomplish this in addition to the budget for the film.

Although the investor who backed the movie never interfered with its production during the filming, things changed after the film was made. The actual joint venture contract wasn't presented to me until we were well into the filming stage, and since it was prepared by an attorney that was supposed to be working for both the investor and myself, I wasn't too concerned about signing it.

There was a clause that gave the investor the right to break deadlock in his favour in the event that we disagreed upon the day-to-day decisions. There was another clause that said that certain decisions and actions would require unanimous consent between us. These actions were specific to selling the film, encumbering the film by borrowing money against it or licensing it. Licensing means making deals for domestic and foreign distribution, and video and cable arrangements. We had hired Sam Oetinger, a man who had headed up the sales for a family film distribution company that had been very successful in releasing a large number of family films in the American market.

The man that financed the movie didn't get along with Tim Penland and it was decided that he should be paid off, and the amount to take him out of the picture and still use the information he had provided was $15,000. We did the three marketing tests in the Fresno California, Colorado Springs Colorado, and Norfolk, Virginia markets. In Fresno we used the church marketing programme, screening the film for pastors and their families and providing their youth groups with a fund-raising discount ticket programme for Monday through Thursday nights. We did four times as much business in Fresno as Colorado Springs, which didn't employ the church marketing programme. This was in about the same number of theatres and with approximately the same advertising budget. The results in Fresno as compared to Norfolk Virginia, which also did not use the church marketing programme, were almost eight times better.

The main factor that made the difference was determined by me to be the church screenings and the Mon-Thurs discount ticket fund-raising programme. I felt that the proof of this was the fact that we had theatres in Fresno where we screened the film for pastors and their families averaging about $1600 per weekday and doing over $2000 on a Tuesday, which is highly unusual.

We took the film to NATO Showest, which is a big convention of theatre owners that go to see what the studios have to offer and a place where deals are made. This particular year it was in Las Vegas. Our company ran two-page spreads in the trade magazines about the film, and we bought time on the in-house video channel in the hotel that showed all the new films that were available. We had a booth and had co-star Jack Elam and myself there to sign beautiful brochures for the theatre owners' children. As a result of all of these things, we were a big hit at the convention and had so many people in line to get signed brochures that we were asked by the fire marshall to speed things up.

Out of a clear blue sky the investor decided that he wanted a certain company to distribute *The Giant of Thunder Mountain*. I disagreed, as that particular company was known for low-budget horror and foreign specialty films. While Diane and I were at the Cannes Film Festival in France, promoting the film, the investor had our attorney execute a contract for distribution with the horror film company and another new and unproven company for the foreign distribution. I was flabbergasted. The distribution agreement called for the investor to put up all of the money for prints and advertising and to pay for all other expenses, which meant that these distribution companies had little or nothing at risk. The contract with the domestic distributor allowed them to drop the distribution of the film yet still be paid for any sub-distribution agreements they negotiated, such as video, cable and free television rights.

I didn't think that this company was the right one to distribute the film, nor did I believe that the agreement was a good one, and I had an attorney go to court and try and stop the investor from going through with this contract – as the joint venture agreement, as I read it, required unanimous consent or arbitration. Our attorney had confirmed that opinion by getting the same one from a leading school of law that provides opinions for a fee. Unfortunately, the judge ruled in favour of the money and determined that the person putting up the money should be able to make the decisions. There was nothing I could do.

In the Fresno test market where we did the church screenings and utilised the discount ticket fund-raising programme, *The Giant of Thunder Mountain* came in right between two Disney films, *White Fang* and *Shipwrecked*. Two sequels were made to *White Fang*, and I had two sequels drafted in my head for *The Giant of Thunder Mountain*. But, with the company that specialised in low-budget horror films distributing a wholesome family film, the results were appalling. They did a church-marketing approach that, instead of screening the film, consisted of a letter sent to churches stating that they should recommend it (apparently sight unseen). There was no discount ticket fund-raising programme and, consequently, instead of $1200 to $2000 weekday grosses they were more like $0 to $100.

I could have been really hard-nosed about the joint venture contract when it was presented to me in the midst of filming, as I really had the investor by the tender parts at that point. I didn't take advantage of the situation and I should have. I learned this the hard way as my dream and its two potential sequels went down the drain with the stroke of a pen.

For the next five years, I tried to rejuvenate our small company and put together several family film packages complete with scripts, detailed budgets, cast commitments, location contracts and even set construction bids. Unfortunately, without a proven record of success, I could never quite get the financing that we needed. We seemed close several times. Once, we had all of the officers of the corporation waiting in a hotel in Burbank while we waited for an investor to open an escrow so we could sign the papers. After nothing happened for almost a full week we decided to pack up and go home. Another time we were instructed to open a special checking account in a Nevada bank so we could receive funds, and we had letters promising that those funds would come at a certain date which came and went with nothing happening. I couldn't keep the production office open any longer and I reluctantly closed it.

OVER THE HILL IN A VAN

Right in the middle of the litigation regarding the movie, I got invited to a Christian Businessmen's breakfast meeting higher up the mountain from where I live in Oakhurst, California. They started early, at 7.00 am, so I set out from my house in my new extended Ford van at about 6.30.

It was dark and rainy that morning, so I had my lights on and my windshield wipers going as I headed down Yosemite Springs Parkway, the main thoroughfare in our subdivision. As I rounded a blind corner, a car suddenly appeared before me that looked like it was stopped on the road. I swerved to the left to avoid it, which I managed to do except for hitting the tail light.

As I got around the car and into the lane on the other side of the road, I saw a small foreign pick-up truck heading right at me. I tried to stay as close as I could to the car I was going around, and the small truck tried to stay as far as it could on the shoulder on the other side of the road, but we just couldn't quite make a three-laner of what is a two-lane road. The left front fender and wheel of my van crashed against the left front fender and wheel of the small truck and literally spun it around, while my van continued careening down the hill because of its weight and momentum. The force of the impact tore my brake lines off, blew out my left front tyre and bent my bumper against the wheel, sending me slowly over to the left. I couldn't steer and I had no brakes to stop or even slow down with.

It seemed like an eternity, and my life flashed before me as I rode out the event. The van went off the road and over an embankment, bouncing onto a big flat rock, sending the van back up in the air and then down again. I was bouncing up and down with it thinking that this was probably the end, and I wished that I had been able to live long enough to see grandchildren, when the front end of the van hit a large tree, stopping it dead in its tracks.

I was up in the air, with my head up near the overhead videotape player and television set, when the van slammed to a stop, ramming my forehead against the wooden frame that held the television set and breaking it into pieces. My knees had hit all the knobs and switches on the dash and I was holding onto the steering wheel so hard that it was twisted into a strange elliptical shape. I do not remember being unconscious at any point, but I do remember the horrible sound of metal being crushed and glass breaking, which seemed to happen twice during the initial collision and the final impact.

I was never afraid to die, I just didn't want to go yet. I unbuckled my shoulder harness and tried to open the driver's side door, but it was jammed shut. I then tried to open the passenger door, only someone opened it for me and helped me clamber out. You could smell gasoline, as at least one of the dual fuel tanks had ruptured from the impact, and we got as far away from the van as we could before stopping to rest on a big flat rock.

It wasn't long before an ambulance arrived and two small women attempted to lift me onto a little stretcher and carry me up the wet rocks on the hillside and up to the street. I protested as I was afraid they would slip and fall on the wet rocks, injuring all of us. My oldest son arrived at that point, and I heard him yelling back at a policeman who was yelling at him that he couldn't go down there. He did anyway, and the policeman was kind of okay with it when he found out that I was his dad. With RG's help, I managed to walk up the hill myself, and they had me sit down in the ambulance.

I had no idea what I looked like, but later RG told me that a head wound that I had sustained during the crash was gushing blood and it was all over me and my shirt and pants. The ambulance attendants tried to persuade me to let them take me to the hospital, but I told them that my son would drive me. They warned me that I was probably injured a lot more than I realised and that I should go to the hospital and have an MRI done. RG took me to St Agnes Hospital in Fresno, and they suggested that I see a plastic surgeon. I knew the name of one whom I had previously consulted about removing the cyst on my forehead, which had grown bigger over the years. He now had an office right behind the hospital, so they called him and my son drove me around back to his office where the plastic surgeon was waiting for me.

My forehead was split from eyebrow to hairline and right through the middle of the cyst. At first, Dr. Shanklin thought that he would take care of the cyst later but, as he proceeded with the surgery, he realised that he had to do it then. One of the side benefits of my accident was that I turned out better-looking afterwards due to the removal of the cyst. Kind of like in *The Longest Yard* when Burt Reynolds resets my broken nose and tells me it looks better.

The accident did affect me adversely, however, as my auto-balance and auto-matic reflexes are no longer automatic. Besides my auto-balance mechanisms being affected, which makes it impossible for me to do simple things like standing still in place, it also affected my auto-gait mechanism where we swing alternate legs and arms when we walk. I have to do all these things consciously now, and it's very difficult.

GETTING 'HAPPY' WITH ADAM SANDLER

I have been able to do shows like *Happy Gilmore* where people take these things into consideration and work with me. In *Happy Gilmore* they let me lean on things in scenes and made a dolly to push me on when I was supposed to be running with a crowd alongside of me. I was just moving my arms like I was running while being pushed on the dolly with the crowd running alongside. They overcranked the camera, creating a slow-motion effect, and put in the football-type running sounds and made me look great.

Happy Gilmore was one of my most successful roles, second to Jaws in the James Bond movies, and it showed how people can work with an actor's hand-icaps and still have a successful movie. I still hope to be in movies in the future. I may have to play judges that 'sit' on the bench. That's all right, I'll be able to wear my glasses and be more like myself for a change. A producer from Canada recently approached me about playing this kind of a role in a film that he's going to be shooting near Saskatchewan. I look forward to it.

Lately, I have been helping my court reporter wife, Diane, pay the bills and help our children through college by doing autograph shows, commercials and cameos in films where they will work with me. I enjoy doing the autograph shows, as it puts me in touch with fans all over the country and even other parts of the world. I get to hear from them what they've enjoyed seeing me do, and sometimes they cause me to remember pleasant experiences that I had long forgotten. My fans have given me copies of photos from movies that I haven't seen for years and videos of shows that had been long forgotten or not totally remembered.

A year ago, I got to do a cameo in a movie in India which starred Jason Connery. I had been to Egypt but not to India and I wanted to do the film, if for no other reason than to see the country. Travelling to places all around the world is educational and makes one aware of the fact that there is more to this world than the little community we live in, pushing the boundaries of our minds past just the experiences within our own families.

WRITING THE BIG ONE

In the late 1970s I got reacquainted with Arch Hall Sr, the man who produced *Eegah*. He was living on Lido Island with his little dog, Pooh Bear, in a modest but nice home. He had changed a lot from the producer of low-budget exploitation films to a man who had traveled and learned a great deal about life. Diane and I found him to be most pleasant and a nice man to visit and talk with. He and I eventually co-wrote a screenplay called *The South Shall Rise Again*. Arch had written some original songs for this movie idea that were very poignant and moving. Kenny Rogers agreed to record a few of them, which he did, and I fleshed out Arch's story idea into a full-fledged screenplay which Arch helped me with.

During these times, Arch told me about a couple of projects that he had worked on that were near and dear to his heart. One was about Pocahontas and the other was about a man in history named Cassius Clay. I was fascinated with the Cassius Clay story. Arch had learned about the man from his sister, who was working at Berea College in Berea Kentucky, and had done a labour of love, no-money documentary about the man.

I was intrigued by the fact that Cassius Clay had helped found the first inter-racial college in America – in Berea, Kentucky – and that he had actually run for the Presidential nomination of the Republican Party and had been Mary Todd Lincoln's first choice as a husband. All this, and the fact the boxer Muhammad Ali originally had the same name, perked my interest. I thought it was a story that needed to be told and I shared the Cassius Clay story with a lot of friends and even people at major studios.

Nobody seemed to catch the vision that I saw. I suppose it was because I married a girl from rural Georgia who wrote a term paper on Lincoln and who did not have a racist bone in her body that made me astonished to learn that 93 per cent of the people in the South never owned a slave and that those white, working people also suffered because of slavery. Why? Because they had to compete with this almost-free slave labour and consequently they couldn't make any money.

Books have been written about Cassius Clay, but they seemed to be written from a bias that didn't coincide with the facts that were known about the man. A good friend of mine decided he was going to write a book about Cash, but when nothing happened for years in that regard, I decided to continue my earlier research and see if I couldn't unearth the secrets of the real Cassius Clay, the man behind the name given to the legendary Muhammad Ali and his father.

Trips to Kentucky, visits to museums, looking at microfilm of newspaper articles and copies of actual letters and speeches given by this man, caused me to dig into the history of Lincoln, Mary Todd, his wife, the Clay family and the politics of that entire era. What I found wasn't just enlightening, it was astonishing. I had grown up with all the negative stories about slavery as represented by the miniseries *Roots*. What I discovered was that there was a lot more to the story than just that one side of it. There was a lot more to Lincoln than I had ever read in the history books. Indeed, there was a whole untold history that needed to be told in order to dispel some of the one-sided tales that have caused so much bitterness, anger and even hate between the races and the North and the South.

Action, romance, duels, courtroom drama, politics, greed, hate, murder, attempted murder, divorce, lust, affairs and much more made up the story of the real Cassius Clay and I found it the most exciting project that I had ever worked on. I wrote three screenplays to tell the man's life story and finally a 542-page novel that compresses his whole exciting story into one great read. While I am writing this I am also working on finding an agent and a publisher who can catch the vision that I see and why it's so important for this story to be told.

A half-million Americans died so that slaves could be free, be able to marry and be educated. None of these things were allowed before men like Cassius Clay and Abraham Lincoln put their lives on the line. Other men passed laws in the 1860s that created an equal playing field for people of all colours and creeds. It was just the beginning of a struggle that didn't see full results until Lyndon Johnson saw to it that these same laws were enforced a hundred years later.

Readers will enjoy learning that the Tsar of Russia, Alexander II, was a Christian man who freed over 23,000,000 slaves. And how he came to the Union's rescue during the Civil War and why, as a result of that, we bought Alaska for two cents an acre. They will also be surprised to read the resolution passed by the United States Senate, calling for a day of prayer and fasting and asking God's forgiveness for the sins of the nation in hopes that he would honour these prayers, end the Civil War and reunite the country once more. So much for the new age theories put forward about the separation of church and state.

Richard "JAWS" Kiel
40356 Oak Park Way, Ste. T
Oakhurst, CA 93644
(209) 683-3922

September 12, 1997

William Jefferson Clinton
President, United States
1600 Pennsylvania Ave.
Washington, DC 20500

Dear Mr. President,

As a Christian man, I have been touched by your desire to issue an apology with respect to our country's role in allowing slavery to exist for so many years. As a writer, I have been doing considerable research in regards to the Civil War era and slavery and I have just completed a screenplay about Cassius Clay, the white hero of the slaves and poor people and the man Mohammed Ali's father was named after.

In the process of doing my research, I discovered that the United States Senate, with the concurrence of President Lincoln, did pass a resolution to set aside a day where everyone was to take a day off *"to pray, fast, and in humiliation, to confess our sins as a nation"* (see enclosed Presidential Proclamation).

I know that your desire for an apology regarding slavery is based upon wanting to cause a healing effect within our nation (and between its still-divided races).

It is clear to me that this resolution issued by President Lincoln in 1863 was, in fact, a public apology by the nation, at that time, for the sins of slavery. Its purpose was to seek God's *"pardon of our national sins, and restoration of our now-divided country to its former happy condition of unity and peace."*

You would do the country a great service by bringing this little-known historical document to light and by reminding the American people of the continuing need for us to look at any racial bias or other prejudices that we may still have as a people and as a nation, and to pray to God for forgiveness (II Chronicles 7:14).

No one can successfully argue against the profound words of this proclamation as it was issued by the United States Senate and put forward by President Lincoln.

Continuing to pray for you and your family.

Sincerely,

Richard "Jaws" Kiel
P.S. I would be happy to send you an advance copy of my screenplay, if, you would like to read it. An "Academy Award" winning writer is doing a final edit and polish on it and it will be ready right after the first of the year.

National Day of Prayer

By his excellency, Abraham Lincoln, President of the U.S.A.

WHEREAS, The Senate of the United States, devoutly recognizing the Supreme authority and just government of Almighty God in all the affairs of men and nations, has, by a resolution, requested the President to designate and set apart a day for National prayer and humiliation.

And Whereas, it is the duty of nations, as well as of men, to owe their dependence upon the overruling power of God, to confess their sins and transgressions, in humble sorrow, yet with assured hope that genuine repentance will lead to mercy and pardon, and to recognize the sublime truth announced in the Holy Scriptures and proven by all history, that *those nations only are blessed whose God is the Lord.*

And, inasmuch as we know that by His Divine law, nations, like individuals, are subjected to punishments and chastisements in this world, may we not justly fear that the awful calamity of civil war, which now desolates the land, may be a punishment inflicted upon us for our presumptuous sins, to the needful end of our national reformation as a whole people?

We have been the recipients of the choicest bounties of Heaven. We have been preserved these many years in peace and prosperity. We have grown in numbers, wealth, and power as no other nation has ever grown.

BUT WE HAVE FORGOTTEN GOD.

We have forgotten the gracious hand which preserved us in peace, and multiplied and enriched and strengthened us; And have vainly imagined in the deceitfulness of our hearts, that all these blessings were produced by some superior wisdom of our own. Intoxicated with unbroken success, we have become too self-sufficient to feel the necessity of redeeming and preserving grace, too proud to pray to the God that made us!

IT BEHOOVES US, THEN, TO HUMBLE OURSELVES BEFORE THE OFFENDED POWER, TO CONFESS OUR NATIONAL SINS, AND TO PRAY TO THE GOD THAT MADE US!

Now, therefore, in compliance with the request, and fully concurring in the views of the Senate, I do, by this my proclamation, designate and set apart Thursday, the 30th day of April, 1863, as a day of National Humiliation, Fasting, and Prayer. And I do hereby request all the people to abstain on that day from their ordinary secular pursuits, and to unite, at their several places of public worship and their respective homes, in keeping the day holy to the Lord, and devoted to the humble discharge of the religious duties proper to the solemn occasion.

All this being done in sincerity and truth, let us then humbly in the hope authorized by Divine teachings, that the united cry of the Nation will be heard on high, and answered with blessings, no less the pardon of our national sins, and restoration of our now divided and suffering country to its former happy condition of unity and peace.

In witness whereof, I have hereto set my hand, and caused the Seal of the United States to be affixed.

Done at the city of Washington the 30th day of March, in the year of our Lord 1863.

Signed by
Abraham Lincoln
President of the U.S.A.

THE WHITE HOUSE

WASHINGTON

March 15, 1999

Mr. Richard Kiel
Suite T
40356 Oak Park Way
Oakhurst, California 93644

Dear Richard:

Thank you very much for your message of support and for the
material you enclosed.

As we prepare to meet the challenges of the 21st century, it
is important to me that I know the thoughts and experiences of
people who care about the future of America and our world. I am
confident that, working together, we can protect our shared
values and meet our common challenges.

I'm glad you took the time to write, and I welcome your
involvement.

Sincerely,

Bill Clinton

TWELVE

WHAT *REALLY* MATTERS...

When asked what she wanted to be when she grew up, our little daughter Jennifer would say, 'A movie star or an Olympic gymnast.' I tried to get her to set her sights a little more realistically by suggesting that she say 'actress' instead of 'movie star.' She replied, 'But, Daddy, you were just an actor and you weren't doing that well until you became a movie star!' Unfortunately, she was right, but I sure worried that she would be disappointed if she didn't become either one. I wasn't sure that I wanted her to be an actress, anyway, with all the casting couches in Hollywood.

We helped her pursue her dream of becoming an Olympic gymnast by taking turns driving her from her school in Coarsegold to Clovis Academy of Gymnastics every day. She would sleep on the way there, and I or Diane would pick her up about nine at night and, after having a hamburger, we would drive home with her sleeping until we got there. At home she would do her homework, going to bed sometimes near midnight, get up the next day and start the routine all over again.

Jennifer was also taking dance lessons at two dance academies and she was very good at dance and gymnastics. Then she got involved in pageants, first winning the national Miss American Pre-teen crown and then the World's Our Little Miss crown, which required having a talent. Along the way she tried dancing, singing, and a gymnastic/dance routine that combined both her dance and gymnastic skills. In gymnastics she was All-Around California State Champion in her age division or level. All these things were very exciting to watch, especially for her mother who would grab my arm so hard when Jennifer was teetering on the balance beam that it would be sore for days.

In high school, Jennifer became captain of her cheer squad and was known as 'Flipper' because of her tumbling skills. In her senior year she won a cheer-leading competition in the individual dance area and also won a *Friday Night Live* talent competition, which awarded a $1000 scholarship. In her senior year, she was also homecoming queen, which made me feel very proud, and she and Diane packaged up some videos and sent them off to Hawaii in hopes that she might get a scholarship for cheerleading. She *did* get that scholarship, and it consisted of a full tuition waiver at Hawaii Pacific University.

In her freshman year at Hawaii Pacific the dance coach saw her tremendous talent for picking up dance steps and asked her cheer coach if she would have any objections if Jennifer switched to dance. The cheer coach gave her approval, and Jennifer received full tuition scholarships for dance the next three years. Jennifer is married now and has two children. She is going to be a schoolteacher instead of a movie star. In the meantime, she is enjoying being a full-time, stay-at-home mother.

BEING A FAMILY MAN

Having three sons has been a real treat for Diane and I. It says in the Bible that, to a father, sons are like arrows in his quiver; I take that to mean that sons are a form of protection from adversaries. In another way I found that going to see my sons play Little League, Pop Warner Football, wrestle, debate, be an advocate in a mock trial, play basketball in high school, was something that took me away from the humdrum hassles of the world.

All three of my sons are what you would call jocks. I think it comes from having a father who is 7'2" and 340 pounds. Size doesn't seem to intimidate them. Bennett, for instance, was wrestling in the eighth grade and, being slight of build like my dad, he wasn't very imposing or intimidating to the other wrestlers. One day, when Diane and I were at the school to watch him in a tournament and he was about to wrestle, we overheard the mother of his opponent say to her more bulky son, 'Look at him, he's a piece of cake!' Bennett, who had also overheard this remark, complained to us, and we told him, 'You know that you're no piece of cake, just do the best you can.' Bennett pinned the other boy in about three seconds flat, which caused the boy to practically break into tears as he had been set up by his mother to be in a must-win situation.

Our approach to sports was that it was always a game where you did the best you could, but more importantly you were there to have fun and to always be a good sport. This is also true in debating or mock trial. One side wins and the other side loses and you, therefore, can't always win. Part of the lessons in life that are learned through sports is that you don't always win and that you have to be a gracious loser as well as an enthusiastic winner. This is true in all aspects of life as there is always someone who has a bigger boat or yacht, a bigger airplane, a better camera, a bigger and more beautiful house or even a more beautiful wife. We have to learn to be happy with what we have and what God has given us, and sometimes sports teaches us those lessons.

Bennett didn't always pin his opponent or even win all of his matches. RG, who was very good at mock trial, didn't always win in mock court, and in college he found that in the finals, where he and his debating team went all the way to Baltimore Maryland, it was good to come in second or even third. Chris was the one that had the hardest time learning that you didn't always win. He was not a good loser and this meant that he was constantly challenging the umpire's decisions in baseball, and the referee's decisions in basketball, consequently being thrown out of a lot of games. Chris is very competitive; being the youngest of three sons he had to be. He's not easily intimidated having a father as big as me, and two older brothers, and he learned to hold his own.

None of my sons is really tall, as their mother Diane is just 5'1½". Chris is the tallest, being almost 5'11", but, being a very good basketball player, he wishes he had been 6'3" instead. But as my mother often says, 'If wishes were horses, beggars would ride.'

If Chris's knees hadn't bothered him so much from crouching down in his catcher's stance, he could have been a professional baseball player as he was a very good hitter and, with a great arm, he could throw runners out that were trying to steal second or third. The whole family had so much fun watching him play Pop Warner Football, as he would sack the quarterback five times in one game in his position as inside line backer and then as a running back he would always be good for three, five, or 30 yards.

One time the young boys on Chris's Pop Warner team saw the varsity players at our high school execute a trick play that they decided to use the next time they played. The way it worked was that the coach would call out to a player to come off the field just as the team was coming out of their huddle, as though there were too many players on the field. The player would look like he was running off the field, but stop short of going out of bounds and being careful to stay behind the line of scrimmage. Of course, you had to tell the referees in advance that you were about to execute a trick play. Naturally, the player chosen to pull this off was our son Chris. The coach yelled 'Chris!' and he ran almost to the sideline and, when the ball was snapped, he ran straight down the field along the sideline where he caught the pass thrown to him by the quarterback, leaving the other team scratching their heads. Although his team lost the game, they sure had a lot of fun playing it.

Between junior high and high school, Chris played on a summer league basketball team. He ended up being high scorer in the league and really got turned on to basketball. So in high school Chris decided to drop out of football and concentrate on basketball, which had become his first love.

I had seen a set of instructional video tapes done by the late Pistol Pete Marovich and I bought them for Chris. He practiced the techniques faithfully and even bought a pair of special shoes which helped him to develop his jumping ability by training his muscles. All this paid off for him, as the coach would point to him as an example for the varsity players to emulate when Chris was on the freshmen team and taking a free throw or doing a three-point jump shot.

Chris did end up playing varsity basketball in his sophomore year, and one of my fondest memories regarding him was at a game where we were behind by about seven points with just a little over a minute left to play. Our team had stolen the ball twice and made two-pointers, each time bringing the game to within three points. The other team missed their shot and time out was called with only a couple of seconds on the clock. The team was told to get the ball into Chris, as he had good three-point technique and was cool under pressure. He got the ball and went up for a three-point jump shot but was fouled on the way up, sending the ball off and away from the basket.

Now, Chris had three free throw opportunities to tie the game and send it into overtime. He made the first attempt with the ball swishing through the net without touching the hoop. The other team calls timeout to break Chris's rhythm and he had to wait until the timeout was over. He made the second shot and they called timeout again. When the timeout was up, Chris stepped to the line and started to prepare for his shot. One of the players on the other team motioned to the officials that his shoe was untied and the officials called an equipment timeout. Finally, Chris shot the third freethrow, and it swished through the net, tying the game, which our team went on to win.

Chris never grew tall enough to get a college scholarship or play in the NBA; today, 5'11" is really short in basketball. To Mom and Dad, though, it didn't matter as we will always remember that game.

All of our sons have been very special and unique in their own way. Bennett got into archery and began doing target practice using a compound bow. Eventually he became a hunter and, at the age of 12, got the first and biggest Barbarosa Ram at a hunt in Riverside, California. Ben also became an excellent chef, capable of making the best shark with mango fruit salsa, spring greens salad with roasted pine nuts, gorgonzola cheese, raspberry vinagarette dressing, and finally, the most scrumptious double-baked cheese-cake you've ever tasted. Bennett is now married to a wonderful girl named Suzanne and has a 'Little Ben' Kiel of his own.

Although RG delighted us in his abilities in mock trial and debating, we were pleased when we learned that he decided to become a doctor instead of being a lawyer. He is getting straight A's in college and is on the Deans list. He is among a select few whose grades are in the top two per cent in the nation.

By the way, RG was in *The Spy Who Loved Me*. He was the little boy on the beach in Sardinia who is the first to point at the Lotus car as it comes out of the water. Bennett was in *The Giant of Thunder Mountain*. He played one of the boys in the clubhouse who dares Amy's two brothers to go up the mountain and spy on the giant as their initiation into the club.

Chris is living in Hawaii and is enjoying surfing, playing the guitar and going to college. He was in a school play in the eighth grade and I thought he was a natural actor. I tried to encourage him by telling him so, but he responded with, 'I hate it! Why does that teacher always pick me to do these things?' Now that he is in college, though, he is taking drama as an elective. Hmmm...

I've really enjoyed being a father of four. It was tough at times, travelling in our van with four stairsteps all yelling: 'When are we going to get there? Are we there yet? I'm hungry! I'm thirsty! I have to go to the bathroom! He hit me! She hit me first! Well, he was looking at me! She took my seat! He had that seat the last time! Are we there yet?'

It was even more interesting when all four were teenagers, but we did it and they survived somehow. So far, we have a son-in-law and a daughter-in-law and we love them both. Now that Diane has her own career as a court reporter, I can collect my SAG pension and Social Security and spend my time writing and enjoying myself at autograph conventions. Oh, I like to do the occasional part to keep my union insurance active and to keep me alive in the hearts of audiences, but holding my grandchildren when we have them and especially holding my wife when we are home alone – that's my biggest thrill.

I've had my successes along with my failures and my disappointments but that's only because I tried. Henry Ford said, 'Nothing ventured, nothing gained!' Live, love, venture. That's been my life and I've enjoyed almost every minute of it. It's tough when the dog dies, or your favourite cat gets run over, but that's part of life. It's even harder when a friend or relative dies. I know where most of my friends, relatives and loved ones are going and I know where I'm going to end up.

That's important! It's great to make it big in the movies and to be able to enjoy the short time that we all have here. Finding real happiness is even more important. Many people never find it. Movie and TV stars and famous rock singers have sought it and, even though they seemingly had everything, real happiness seemed to elude them. An old man once told me, 'Richard, there are three things that we need in life to be happy. To love, be loved and have a feeling of accomplishment.' He kind of winked and said, 'Two out of three ain't bad.' That's what life is all about!

WHAT *IS* LIFE ALL ABOUT ANYWAY?

This last section is about my faith as a Christian, how it started and how it grew, from my early simple belief to the witnessing that I did later in my life, and finally about my taking part in supernatural miracles and healings. If your mind is totally closed to this sort of thing, then you might want to just skip this chapter and call it a read. If, however, you are curious, yet somewhat dubious, then I invite you to continue on, as I was much like you at one time. I warn you, though, if you *do* continue on, it could change your life.

Like a lot of people, I received the free gift of salvation at the tender age of nine. My family lived in the South San Gabriel area, just east of Los Angeles, and my parents attended Walnut Grove Baptist Church. My father had refused to go to church for many years, and my mother continued to pray all that time that one day my Dad would agree to go. The Holy Spirit must have touched him as a result of all my Mom's prayers, because one Sunday morning he said, 'Why don't we start going to church?' – just like it was his own idea.

Not long after we all started going to church as a family, a youth evangelist named Uncle Wynn Johnson came to do a youth revival. Uncle Wynn wrote children's books and told us how Jesus died on the cross to pay for our sins, and he used John 3:16 to show us how God so loved the world that all we had to do was believe upon His Son as God's only begotten, to put our trust in Him and turn over our lives to Him, and we could be saved. Many young people, including myself, professed our belief in Jesus that night in Uncle Wynn Johnson's meeting, and we were also encouraged by him to go out into the surrounding neighbourhood to invite others to the church.

I remember going to many houses and inviting quite a number of people to come to church. Uncle Wynn had prizes that he promised to the person who got the most new people to actually show up. First prize was one of his children's books. I won second prize which was a pencil that would write in three colours. I was pretty disappointed, as I really wanted the book. In fact, I had prayed to get more people to visit our church for the first time so I would get the book. My Mom and Dad were very proud of me and explained to me that the girl who won probably prayed even more than I did, and no doubt knocked on even more doors and invited more people. They simply bought me the book and I was happy.

I share this with you as many of you know me as the actor who played Jaws, who came out of Hollywood, and you know that I had a problem with alcohol and you probably think that I found Jesus and got saved and delivered from alcohol all at the same time.

On the contrary, I grew up as a young enthusiastic 'church person.' My family had moved from South San Gabriel to North El Monte, California and we found this nice little neighbourhood church that happened to be Dutch Reformed. These were great people with names like Van Beek, Van Damm and Vanderslice. The things that I remember most about my early church experiences were the wonderful hymns that we would sing like, 'What a friend we have in Jesus, Oh what needless pain we bear, all because we do not carry everything to God in prayer.' Or, 'He Lives.' Or, 'I serve a risen saviour, he's in the world today, I know that he is living, no matter what men say. You ask me how I know he lives, he lives within my heart.' Or, 'Blessed Assurance, Jesus is mine, oh what a foretaste of glory divine.'

I remember something else about both these churches and that was that a lot of the men smoked at that time because it was the thing to do, and cigarettes were advertised heavily on television. In fact, almost all the big stars smoked in the movies. My father was one of the many men who would walk a half-block away from the church and light up as soon as they were dismissed because they couldn't break away from the bondage of their addiction to tobacco and nicotine. If only they would have known that their 'friend Jesus' who lived 'in their heart' could give them a 'foretaste of glory divine' and God's almighty power by delivering them from these kinds of addictions, if they would only ask. 'Oh what needless pain they bore.'

These churches had a terrific handle on evangelism. They taught great sermons on grace and redemption, but they just weren't plugged into the reality of the relationship that we all now had as adopted sons and daughters of God or the power of the Holy Spirit.

When I was 12 years old, I can remember hearing a beautiful sermon on Ist Corinthians 13, the 'Love Chapter', which is very important because without love our lives have no meaning. I do not remember, however, any mention of what is found in Ist Corinthians 12, or 14. These particular chapters turned out to be important in my life and that's why I have recommended you read them later. At the age of 16 I also made a further commitment and open dedication of my life to the Lord at a youth camp near Crystal Lake in the San Bernardino Mountains.

During the many years after I became an adult, I seldom attended church. I would watch church programmes on TV and would occasionally try and read the Bible. Unfortunately, it seemed like a lot of gobbledegook to me and I would soon give up. I had no doubt that I had received the 'free gift of salvation,' though, and I figured that was all that really mattered.

A Baptist minister I ran into one day in a restaurant asked me if I had been baptised and I had to admit that I hadn't. Although I felt down deep in my heart that it wasn't absolutely necessary for my salvation – as Jesus said, 'John the Baptist baptises with water, but I baptise with the Holy Spirit' – I felt that it was a good expression of my faith, and I got baptised at his church at the age of 27.

I tried reading the Bible again and found that it had more meaning to me. I prayed for wisdom and randomly opened the Bible to a page where I read, 'The beginning of wisdom is the fear (or respect) of the Lord.'

Recapping my spiritual life, I had accepted Jesus as God's only begotten Son at age nine, made an open commitment to turn my life over to him at 16 and was baptized at 27. Yet, with all this behind me, I still abused and became addicted to alcohol.

Alcoholics and drug addicts don't all live in alleyways, or on the street. Some are doctors, lawyers, and businessmen. Others, as I found out, were actors or salesmen. Some are even Christians (I John 1:8, 9 & 10 and I John 2:1 & 2 or Romans 23, 24 & 25). Yes, even Christians find themselves falling short or missing the mark in life, especially those who are not in a church fellowship. It could be for a lot of reasons; for most of us, though, it's just from doing nothing. After all, Jesus said, 'Confess me before men, and I'll confess you before my father in Heaven. Deny me before men, and I'll deny you before my father in Heaven.' Jesus also said, 'I give you a new commandment, that you love one another even as I love you. By this you will prove to the world that you are my disciples.' Finally, Jesus said, 'Go into all the world, and preach the gospel to every creature, baptising them in the name of the Father, the Son, and the Holy Spirit.' How many of us fail to fulfil this great commission by doing nothing?

Many of us are not willing to love those in the world that need Jesus so desperately, let alone our neighbours and fellow workers. We fail to love them enough to make sure that they are saved, to lay hands on them and pray for them when they need healing, to take authority in the name of Jesus and bind the demons of alcoholism and drug addiction.

As a Christian, I knew at least that abusing alcohol was wrong. Not only wrong for me, but wrong for my family. The Bible says that Satan is out to kill and destroy not only unbelievers but believers, as well. What went wrong? The same thing that happens to not just a few Christians or a lot of Christians, but to *all* Christians. I fell short.

Not every Christian has problems with alcohol or drug addiction, but all of us fall short or miss the mark in some way. Maybe you *don't* drink, swear, smoke or chew, let alone use drugs, and you don't run with those who do. My dog didn't smoke, drink alcohol, chew, swear or use drugs, but that still didn't make him a Christian, did it? The real question is whether you realise that you are a sinner and are willing to literally turn your life over to Jesus and put your total trust in him so that you can be 'born again.'

You may already be a Christian, just like I was at age nine, 16 and 27, and just yell too much at your wife or kids, or simply call someone a jerk when they cut you off on the freeway. Jesus says that when we do that, we can be guilty of Hell's fire! You may find yourself thinking the wrong kind of thoughts when you are at the beach and watching a girl's (or mens's) volleyball game. Jesus said that adultery is a terrible sin, but when we lust in our hearts for another man or woman, it's the same as committing the act in the eyes of God. That's why the Bible tells us that we are all sinners and that there is none that is worthy. All of us can be better imitators of Jesus. All of us can be better Christians, a brighter light in the darkness, or a saltier salt in the world. Many of us fall short in this regard by simply doing nothing.

The Lord let me bring myself down with alcohol to allow the Holy Spirit to lift me back up and teach me something that I hadn't learned in church, although I should have. He wanted to use me, just like he wanted to use Saul of Tarsus, just like he wants to use you to reach people that only Saul (or Paul) or I could reach in my business or you can reach through your contacts.

My pastor Cody Gunderson (he's a former drug addict and dealer) says that the church is like a hospital for Christians. A place where we can all get better and be better Christians. It makes sense when you consider that when we get saved, no one puts a funnel in the top of our head and pours all the wisdom and teaching contained in the Bible directly into our brain.

My pastor now looks like the 'Ivory Snow Baby' grown up. He is so squeaky clean that he exemplifies a 'new creature in Christ.'

We have to grow in the word. I had to grow. Even though I was 7'2" and 350 pounds, I still was a spiritual baby. I didn't even know that I was adopted at age nine by God and, as an adopted son, I didn't have to live in a spirit of fear of alcohol or anything else, because the word says that as an adopted son or daughter of God, we can cry out 'Abba' to God, our perfect Father, just like Jesus did the night before the crucifixion. 'Abba' translated directly from the Aramaic is like 'Daddy' or 'Poppa' is in English, as opposed to the more formal 'Father.'

I didn't know that. I didn't know that Jesus says several times in the New Testament that when we read his word and do it (obey his word), that we are his brothers and sisters. When we accept Jesus as God's only begotten son, we actually do become a part of the family of God as we are 'adopted' and are literally joint heirs with Jesus Christ.

When I began to reluctantly share my testimony of how Jesus broke the bondage of my alcoholism with others, more miracles began to happen in my life. One of my very favourite aunts had a stroke that left her hopelessly in a coma, a vegetable, written off by the medical profession and even her husband, a retired judge. When my cousin, his wife, my wife, my mother and I prayed for my aunt, she immediately came out of her coma after ten long months. Her first words that day in response to whether she would like a television in her room were 'That would be sensational.' It took her a couple of minutes to get those words out, but that wasn't bad for someone who had been written off as a 'vegetable' with no hope of ever responding to anything, let alone talking. She asked to have her dog brought to the hospital window so she could see him, and she soon went home to live a fruitful life for six or seven more years.

It wasn't until I moved to the foothills just south of Yosemite National Park that I began to understand all this. I had been having some serious problems with an ulcer on the ball of my foot that wouldn't heal up. It all started with a surgery that I had on the foot where the doctor apparently had inadvertently left some bone fragments in the foot when he sewed it up. For years, I experienced problems with a large ulcer as a result of this. The ulcerated area, because it was on the bottom of my foot, was very prone to infections, and I had several bouts with very serious infections such as pseudomonas. I couldn't even take a shower without wrapping my foot in plastic and tying the plastic off with a large rubber band so the bath water couldn't get into the ulcer. In spite of these precautions, I would still get infections in the foot from time to time. In fact, during the filming of *The Cannonball Run II*, my foot got infected and, after being hospitalised, I had to finish the movie with an IV connection (Heparin lock) under my racing suit, which I would hook up to a bottle of powerful antibiotics between scenes.

Living in the foothills turned out to be wonderful. There is a big beautiful lake named Bass Lake nearby, and my family got invited to the home of a dentist who had access to one of the docks on the lake. Down at the dock our whole family was swimming, all, of course, but me. It was an extremely hot day, and I was the only one sitting as everyone else was enjoying the cool refreshing water. A man asked me why I wasn't in the water, and I explained to him how I couldn't take a chance on getting an infection from the lake water because I had an ulcer on the ball of my foot.

He and his wife got out of the water and started to talk to me. His name was J B Watson and his wife's name was Betty. JB asked me whether he and his wife could pray for me and what kind of problem I was having with my foot. I was there with a whole bunch of people from the church and I said, 'Sure, why not?'

I really didn't think it would do any good, as I had been to all kinds of doctors who didn't seem to be able to get my foot to heal up, and it was very frustrating for me. JB and Betty started to pray to the Lord for a healing in my foot, then they began to rebuke Satan and the spirit of infirmity affecting my foot. They spoke to and commanded that spirit to go from my foot in the name of Jesus and then they started talking funny, speaking in tongues.

When they saw the look on my face, they realised that I was shocked by all of this, and JB said, 'You aren't familiar with any of this, are you?' I said, 'No.' And they told me to look in the Bible when I got home for Ist Corinthians, Chapters 12 and 14. I urge you to read Ist Corinthians Chapters 12 and 14, too, because I know that what I found there was a revelation to me. I read Chapter 12, where it talked about how we can receive different spiritual gifts such as miracles, healing, evangelism, exhortation, tongues, prophesy, and discernment of spirits etc. The chapters talked about how we each could receive different gifts. It may be the gift of evangelism, which certainly Billy Graham has. It may be the gift of encouragement or 'exhortation,' as it is called in the Bible.

When I reached Chapter 13, the words became more familiar and I could remember a sermon at Trinity Reformed Church about this chapter. But when I started reading Chapter 14, I realised that I was on unfamiliar ground. Paul was saying that he wished that we all spoke in tongues like he did, but that he would rather we desired to prophesy so there would be someone to interpret what was said in tongues, so it could be edifying to both the saved and the unsaved. Chapter 14 contains very important instructions about how we should not speak in tongues in church unless there is someone to interpret, and then only two or three utterances. Finally, I Corinthians 14:39, which basically tells us not to forbid to speak in tongues. Although the Lord has not seen fit for me to speak in tongues in church, I believe that it is biblical and can be real.

Whew! All this stuff was blowing my mind. Keep in mind that I had already been delivered from alcohol and my aunt had come out of a ten-month coma after the sincere prayer of love by my family. In spite of these miracles that had happened already in my life, I still didn't know the Biblical principles and scriptures upon which they were based.

Soon after that experience with my foot, I was to receive the shock of a lifetime. Our Pastor at Yosemite Lakes Community Church announced one Sunday morning that we were going to be visited the following week by a 'healing evangelist.' He explained that this healing evangelist, Colonel Lewis, was formerly a television producer and the husband of Loretta Young. He said that he was coming all the way from Ojai California, and that he was coming out of love as he was receiving nothing from our church. This was understandable as our church at that time consisted of about 50 people that met every Sunday in the planned community's clubhouse and, as long as we left before the bar opened at 12 o'clock, we could use the facility.

I really wanted to be there that weekend and learn more about what had been somewhat of a mystery to me, and I made a mental note that I didn't want to miss that service. I even discussed it with my wife Diane, and she wanted to attend, too. The weekend that this event was scheduled, we were also supposed to visit my mother at her desert home, which is located between the freeway to Las Vegas and the one to Needles, about 20 miles to the east of Barstow, California. Mom's place was about six to seven hours away and we would stay at her place overnight when we would go there. Like all mothers, Mom hated to see us go on Saturday night, as we usually would not go home until late Sunday afternoon. Dinner that Saturday evening ran unusually late and there was dessert that kept us even later. By the time we got home Saturday night, it was actually about two o'clock Sunday morning and, quite frankly, we were not thinking about being at a 9.30 am church service.

About 7.00 am I was awakened by an audible voice calling my name: 'Richard.' Naturally, I thought it was my wife Diane, but it turned out that she was asleep and did not appreciate my waking her up so early after such a long, late drive home the night before. I started to go back to sleep and, just as I closed my eyes, the same soft voice called my name again. I was wide awake now and I went out into the kitchen to read the Bible until I felt it was an appropriate time to wake up the family and go to church.

At 8.45, I awakened Diane and told her what had happened earlier and that I thought that the Lord wanted us to go to this special healing service. She could not find a brush and my middle son Bennett could not find his shoes, but we decided that we were supposed to go and headed off with Bennett wearing his sister's pink tennis shoes. Suffice it to say that this former television producer's testimony as to how he got involved with a healing ministry spoke directly to my heart. When Colonel Lewis talked about hearing an audible voice telling him to tell a woman to accept her healing, I could identify with that because of what happened earlier that morning.

Through that testimony and those of other believers, I began to learn of the healings that took place after Jesus went to be with his father. I learned that the disciples actually raised people from the dead after Jesus had returned to the Father and left us with the Holy Spirit to dwell in us always. I learned scriptures like James 5:14, 15, 16, 17, 18, and 19 as I read books by Charles and Francis Hunter on how to heal the sick. My daughter received a healing in accordance with James 5:14, which says that if you are sick, that you should go find the elders of the church and have them pray for you and anoint you with oil, as the prayers of the faithful shall heal the sick.

Jennifer was determined to become an Olympic gymnast and was working out every weekday evening at Clovis Academy. One day she twisted her elbow so much that the X-Rays showed a hairline fracture. It was so painful that she was going to go early the next morning to the orthopaedic surgeon to have it put into a cast, which would have put her totally out of competition for the rest of that year. On the way to the orthopaedic surgeon, Diane stopped to see some elders and they prayed for Jennifer. When she got to the orthopaedic surgeon, he couldn't get her elbow to hurt no matter how hard he tried, and after looking at the X-ray he said he could not find a fracture or anything wrong with Jennifer.

Later that same year, Jennifer sprained her wrist so bad that every little bump that we hit on the way to the elder's house brought tears to her eyes. After they prayed with her, anointed her with oil and rebuked the spirit of pain, she walked around their apartment on her hands. That year Jennifer was the California State Champion All-Around Gymnast in her particular class. It's not the 'oil' but rather the obedience to God's word of those of us who will have it applied to us and those obedient enough to be willing to do the applying.

Those 'elders' were simply people that had experienced God's power in their own lives. Ray was bedridden with several serious medical problems. He wore a full, heavy metal back-brace and could only get out of bed for an hour or two at a time. His wife Margaret saw that a healing evangelist was coming to Fresno and tried to talk Ray into attending the service. Ray didn't believe in such things and refused to go at first, but with Margaret's urging and with nothing to lose, he went to a Charles and Francis Hunter healing service where he was healed of several things. Ray then attended a Morris Cerullo healing service where his back was healed by the Lord. He was totally healed and there is a picture of him throwing away his back-brace. Ray was an apartment manager when I met him. He could install water heaters when he needed to.

Charles and Francis Hunter prayed over Ray and Margaret's hands that they, too, would receive this healing gift from the Holy Spirit, and it was through the gifts that the Holy Spirit gave them and their faith that my daughter and many, many others received their healings. Ray and Margaret have received the very special gift of healing and have prayed for many of our friends who also received healing. Ray and Margaret take no credit for this because they put their faith in Jesus, the Father, and the Holy Spirit.

In my experience with Ray and Margaret praying for people the healings occur 75 to 90 per cent of the time. In fact, I have witnessed dozens of healings where God has used them to help people receive healing. Ray and Margaret have prayed over me and anointed my hands, asking the Holy Spirit to pass on to me the gift of healing through our Lord Jesus. I do not seem to have received this gift of healing yet; at least it doesn't operate on a consistent basis like it does with them.

Ray and Margaret do not have a formal ministry and they ask no money from anyone that they pray with. They do speak in tongues and they do command these illnesses and diseases to go from people in the name of Jesus.

I know that some people have trouble with all this, and I think we have to be careful in these areas, but if we apply that standard that Jesus gave us to discern whether it is being done in his name out of love or for personal gain and glory, it is easy to determine that Ray and Margaret are encouraging people in the Lord out of love and obedience to the word and are *for* Jesus and not against him. Jesus said in John 15:7, 8 & 9: 'If you abide in me and my word abides in you, ask anything and it shall be given unto you for it glorifies the Father and you shall bear much fruit and so prove to be my disciple.'

Because I have experienced God's miracle power and can believe, I, too, have on occasion prayed for people who have received a healing through the power of the Holy Spirit. I didn't set out to be one to actually pray for healings in people, but as I encouraged them with my testimony of supernatural miracles in my family, I found them coming to me expecting me to pray with them. In some situations there were so many people that needed prayer that I felt funny not participating so I joined in.

The first experience that I had of seeing God's power through the Holy Spirit heal someone that I had laid hands on, anointed with oil, and prayed with, was a woman who played the piano professionally in an orchestra. She had been injured in a serious accident which crushed one of her hands to the point where she could no longer play. That night she acted upon her faith and believed in her healing and got up on the platform and played a concerto on the church's grand piano.

Another evening, after giving my testimony of deliverance and the other miracles that I had seen or even been a part of, I had a woman come up and get in line for prayer and say that she was tormented by multiple voices. When I asked her whether she had received Jesus Christ as her personal saviour, she literally went berserk and started making some very strange noises. I summoned all the mature Christians who had offered to help pray for people, and we cast out her demons through the power of the Holy Spirit, and she received Jesus as her saviour. That night, when I left to have dinner with the pastor and his wife, I saw her talking with some ladies in the church about various church activities, and she was perfectly normal.

Now I know how the 70 felt when they returned from casting out demons in Jesus' name. It's exciting! But as Jesus told them, 'You should be rejoicing because your name is written in the book of life!'

A few years ago, I was in Gainsville Florida, sharing my testimony at a church and a Florida Sheriff's Youth Ranch. While I was there, I was invited to visit a large teaching hospital and say hello to a lot of kids who were there for some pretty serious reasons. Although I was told that I really wasn't supposed to pray with people, I felt compelled to lead families in prayer as some of their children were going into surgery that very day.

I always asked the parents' permission first and, believe me, no family members had any objection. I was also told that no pictures were to be taken with any children. This soon changed when doctors, nurses and interns brought out a Polaroid camera to take pictures with me. I found myself getting requests to have my picture taken with children up and down the halls of the hospital along with requests for prayer with families. Before I knew it, the Director of Volunteer Services, Sandra Wigglesworth, was hauling me all over the hospital to take pictures with people and to pray with everyone who wanted prayer. Sandra had never heard of her famous relative (Smith Wigglesworth, an English plumber who had the God-given gift of healing) but was so moved by the tearful gratitude and relief that she could see on the faces of those that prayed with me, that she forgot about all the hospital rules for a few hours that day.

I'll never forget this one particular couple that she took me to on another floor. The husband had been waiting for a heart transplant for several months, to no avail. You could tell that his wife loved him very much, especially when we prayed together, as the tears of trust and peace were flowing like fountains of water down her cheeks when we finished. Their faith made them believe when everything seemed to be in so much doubt. The man soon received his heart transplant, and I later received a letter from his wife telling me this and that they were about to leave Gainsville to go home and live a normal life.

I say their faith because when I pray with people for a healing in their type of circumstances, healings occur much less than half the time. Manifestations of healing happen perhaps 15 per cent of the time. I think that in my case we are talking about two or more believers agreeing and coming together, touching something and seeing God honour that faith and obedience rather than the 'gift of healings' that my friends Ray and Margaret have.

All the healings, however, are temporary, anyway. The bad news is that we, like Lazarus, Matthew, Mark, Luke and John, will die in this flesh. Ray and Margaret will die. That woman who had the demons cast out of her will die. One day my daughter will die in her flesh.

The good news is that if our names are written in the Book of Life, we will all be raised up at the second coming to be with our Lord in eternity.

Blessed assurance, Jesus is mine! Remember, it all started with me getting saved at that little church in San Gabriel at age nine. I had received the free gift of salvation because I went to a youth revival where the evangelist was a writer of children's books. That writer of children's books was used as a vessel to deliver that simple salvation message contained in John 3:16 – 'For God so loved the world that he gave his only begotten son, whosoever that believeth on him, should not perish, but have everlasting life.' Little did I know that one day I would be standing in his place delivering the same message.

I got the free gift of salvation that day when Uncle Wynn Johnson invited me to ask Jesus into my heart, but I needed to grow in his word and through fellowship with other Christians, especially mature ones. There are many other benefits to learn about as we study the Bible.

I have also learned that when you give freely out of your heart to others, not caring if you get something back, that you are truly blessed and that you get back much more than you gave.

There are so many blessings that we receive from being obedient and those are found in that great owners' manual called the Bible.

'Oh what a foretaste of glory divine' we can receive by being obedient to his word.

The bottom line, however, is whether *our* name is written in the Book of Life?

Do you know for a *certainty* that you have been born again, and have been adopted into God's family?

Do you know for *sure* that you are an adopted Son or Daughter of God?

Are you *positive* that you are a joint heir with Jesus in God's Kingdom?

Do you feel *free* to call out to God, as Abba or Daddy, just as his only begotten Son, Jesus, did, the night before the crucifixion?

Do you have Jesus as your advocate before the Father or to act as your '*big brother*' when you find yourself in trouble?

Do you know for *sure* that if you died today, or if you were killed in an accident tonight, that you would spend eternity with Jesus in heaven?

If you can't say yes to all these questions then you need to confess your sins, and turn your life over to Jesus and enjoy all the benefits of being a part of the family of God, knowing that when this brief time on Earth is over, you will enjoy a perfect life in a perfect place forever and ever.

How do you do that? It's easy! Just say out loud:

Jesus, I'm a sinner, please forgive me. Come into my heart Lord Jesus and change my life.

I know that you are God's only begotten Son and that you are the only perfect person that has walked this earth.

Help me to be more like you Jesus.

I want to be adopted into the family of God.
I want you to be my perfect Brother.
I want to have eternal life.
Lord, I want to have your Holy Spirit living in me.
I want to turn my life over to you Jesus and to learn to be more like you.

I want to be born again.
I pray this prayer in your name Lord Jesus.
Thank you Jesus for changing my life and making it eternal.
Thank you Jesus for making me a part of your family.
Amen (so be it). Hallelujah (praise the Lord).

Welcome, my Brother, or Sister, to the family of God.

If you prayed this prayer I would like to hear from you and you can contact me at my e-mail address: kielfanclub@sierratel.com

Or, you can write to me at PO BOX 1719 Coarsegold CA 93614.

Thank you for letting me share my life with you.

EPILOGUE

As I sit across from my lovely wife Diane in the French restaurant of the Green Park Hotel on Half Moon Street, in London's busy Mayfair district, I can't help but be soothed by the charm of this quaint old building built in the 1730s. The hotel, recently acquired by Hilton, is undergoing a transformation, yet it still retains the beauty of its magnificent lobby and old mahogany bar, with step-down railings that take you into the dining area with its ornate draperies and decorated ceilings. We haven't been here a week, but we already have our favourite spot by the window looking across the narrow street at Fleming's Mayfair Hotel, with its lovely flowers and ivy-covered, wrought iron trellises overhanging its windows and main entrance.

We enjoyed a wonderful meeting with some of our James Bond friends earlier today, and it was nice to see producers Michael Wilson and Barbara Broccoli again after all those years since I first became Jaws. We compared pictures of children and felt very proud to show off pictures of our three grandchildren. Michael and Barbara asked if there was anything they could do for us while we were in London, and I jokingly replied, 'You could get us tickets to *The Lion King*.' We had tried to do that over the internet without success. The next day their secretary delivered two complimentary tickets for *The Lion King* to our hotel.

I am in the UK to do a three-day convention in Northampton called Autographica 2001. We have already completed the convention, where we saw Caroline Munro and Valerie Leon, two of the Bond girls in *The Spy Who Loved Me*, along with many other actors, astronauts and cosmonauts. The convention was a great success for us financially as well, as fans were buying autographed pictures off my table as fast as I could put them out. We finished the show on Sunday and checked into the Green Park in London on Monday, and I did a television interview for Carlton Television on Tuesday morning.

Diane and I have already been to see *Les Miserables* and not only was the show brilliant, to use the current London buzz word, but the architecture of the old Palace Theatre with its many balconies was just about as impressive as you could imagine.

Friday we are going to Geoffrey Moore's restaurant Hush to meet with one of the writers of *007 Magazine*, and we just found out that Luisa Moore will be there as well as Roger's oldest son Geoffrey, the owner. We have heard great things about the scrumptious gourmet food there and are looking forward to seeing Luisa after all these years.

It has been over 20 years since I did my last Bond film, *Moonraker*, yet the benefits keep coming as though it was filmed yesterday. I have become accustomed to the notoriety brought on by playing the character Jaws, but had not experienced the English version of Jaws' great success until now. I am 62 years old, and even though I certainly look different today, the people walking by the restaurant window seem to spot me immediately. Diane and I can't help but laugh as we watch many of them do a double-take as they go by and then wander back to take another look.

The Bond phenomenon is incredible. It brought me many other roles in my career that I never would have been asked to play if I hadn't been in two of the famous 007 films. Because of Bond, I did at least a half-dozen commercials that helped with my children's orthodontics and their college.

It's funny that I had to come back to London, one of mine and Diane's favourite places, to get to tell my story of how I became an actor and finally got to play Jaws in two James Bond movies, something that no other actor has been privileged to do: play the same 007 villain twice. I believe that playing Jaws twice may have given me an unfair advantage when the BBC took a poll last year and the public voted Jaws as their favourite James Bond villain. Jaws edged out both Odd Job and Blofeld and it makes me very proud to know that audiences liked Jaws 20 years ago and still do today.

This certainly is a tribute to the late Cubby Broccoli who envisioned the character in his mind. To Roger Moore whose heart was big enough to allow Jaws to share his spotlight. To Lewis Gilbert who let Jaws have a winning personality and to Lewis's grandson who liked Jaws and asked why he had to be a bad guy. And finally, it's a tribute to Bob Simmons, the stunt co-ordinator who suggested to Cubby Broccoli that he film an alternative ending where Jaws lives and comes back to fight another day, this time on the side of Bond.

INDEX